The Rhetoric of Genocide

Lexington Studies in Political Communication
Series Editor: Robert E. Denton, Jr.,Virginia
Polytechnic Institute and State University

This series encourages focused work examining the role and function of communication in the realm of politics including campaigns and elections, media, and political institutions.

Recent Titles in the Series

The Rhetoric of Genocide: Death as a Text, By Ben Voth
Almost Madam President: Why Hillary Clinton "Won" in 2008, By Nichola D. Gutgold
Communicator-in-Chief: How Barack Obama Used New Media Technology to Win the White House, Edited by John Allen Hendricks and Robert E. Denton, Jr.
Centrist Rhetoric: The Production of Political Transcendence in the Clinton Presidency, By Antonio de Velasco
Us against Them: The Political Culture of Talk Radio, By Randy Bobbitt
Studies of Identity in the 2008 Presidential Campaign, Edited by Robert E. Denton, Jr.
*Internet Policy in China: A Field Study of Internet Cafés,*By Helen Sun
*Campaign Finance Reform: The Political Shell Game,*By Melissa M. Smith, Glenda C. Williams, Larry Powell, and Gary A. Copeland
The Perfect Response: Studies of the Rhetorical Personality, By Gary C. Woodward
A Communication Universe: Manifestations of Meaning, Stagings of Significance, By Igor E. Klyukanov
Presidential Campaign Rhetoric in an Age of Confessional Politics, By Brian T. Kaylor
Manipulating Images: World War II Mobilization of Women through Magazine Advertising, By Tawnya J. Adkins Covert
The Politics of Style and the Style of Politics, Edited by Barry Brummett
Communication Realities in a "Post-Racial" Society: What the U.S. Public Really Thinks about Barack Obama, By Mark P. Orbe
Politics and the Twitter Revolution: How Tweets Influence the Relationship between Political Leaders and the Public, By John H. Parmelee and Shannon L. Bichard
The Rhetoric of Soft Power: Public Diplomacy in Global Contexts, By Craig Hayden
Coming to Terms: The Collected Works of Jane Blankenship, Edited by Janette K. Muir
Reelpolitik Ideologies in American Political Film, By Beverly Merrill Kelley
Media Bias in Presidential Election Coverage 1948–2008: Evaluation via Formal Measurement, By David W. D'Alessio
Gender and the American Presidency: Nine Presidential Women and the Barriers They Faced, By Theodore F. Sheckels, Nichola D. Gutgold, and Diana Bartelli Carlin
The George W. Bush Presidency: A Rhetorical Perspective, Edited by Robert E. Denton, Jr.
New Media, Old Regimes: Case Studies in Comparative Communication Law and Policy, By Lyombe S. Eko
Culture, Social Class, and Race in Public Relations: Perspectives and Applications, Edited by Damion Waymer
Purpose, Practice, and Pedagogy in Rhetorical Criticism, Edited by Jim A. Kuypers
Dark Money, Super PACs, and the 2012 Election, By Melissa M. Smith and Larry Powell

The Rhetoric of Genocide

Death as a Text

Ben Voth

LEXINGTON BOOKS
Lanham • Boulder • New York • London

Published by Lexington Books
An imprint of The Rowman & Littlefield Publishing Group, Inc.
4501 Forbes Boulevard, Suite 200, Lanham, Maryland 20706
www.rowman.com

16 Carlisle Street, London W1D 3BT, United Kingdom

British Library Cataloguing in Publication Information Available

Library of Congress Cataloging-in-Publication Data
Voth, Ben, 1967–
Rhetoric as genocide : death as a text/ Ben Voth.
pages cm.--(Lexington studies in political communication)
Includes bibliographical references.
ISBN 978-0-7391-8205-5 (cloth : alk. paper) -- ISBN 978-0-7391-8206-2 (electronic)
ISBN 978-07391-9532-1 (pbk : alk. paper)

1. Genocide. I. Title.
HV6322.7V68 2014
304.6'63014--dc23
2014013445

Printed in the United States of America

Contents

Contents

Acknowledgments

I thank my family for their support in writing this book. My wife Kelli is a tireless editor and proponent of my writing. She raises the quality of my efforts every day. My three daughters, Rebecca, Sarah, and Anna, motivate and inspire me continually with their zest for life and practical optimism. I am especially thankful for a variety of intellectual inspirations that arose from some great American institutions. The survivors and Ellen Blalock from the United States Holocaust Memorial Museum in Washington DC were the primary motivation to this book and the manner in which they serve as witnesses to one of the most devastating genocides of all time principally motivated my further thought and research on this topic. Jackie Johnson who directs the archives at Miami University regarding Freedom Summer 1964 was a great colleague and support to my work in Ohio. The Bush Library and Bush Institute provided great resources and content helping me understand how policy and idealism merge toward solutions of some of the world's worst problems. SMU provided great support from my division of Communication Studies and the Meadows School of the Arts to allow me to research and complete this work. It is not possible to thank all the undergraduate students, graduate students, and debaters at Miami University and Southern Methodist University who every day of my great life as a professor inspired me to see how the world that is, can be transformed into the world that should be. Teaching is such a joy because the future unfolds before our eyes, and this book was an outpouring of watching how student lives are changing the twenty-first century into a world without genocide.

Introduction

This book is the culmination of many years spent considering, studying, writing and teaching about the problem of genocide. Most central to its emergence was a teaching experience at the *United States Holocaust Memorial Museum* (USHMM) in Washington D.C. during the summers of 2006 and 2007. Those pivotal weeks spent with the Holocaust survivors anchoring that institution forever changed my perspective on the power of communication and what its highest purposes can be. Those seminal moments equipping survivors to better have their voice in telling their own stories about such a profound tragedy provided the moral clarity, inspiration, and intellectual framework for this book. In many respects, the events leading to and following that service at the museum are an important analogy for understanding this book.

Prior to my work at the USHMM, I had not had occasion to visit the museum. It was a young passionate student by the name of Terri Donofrio who first asked me what my advice was about accepting an internship position in the Survivors Bureau of USHMM. She was graduating in the fall, and unsure about what to do next. I thought it was worth a try. It was not long before I heard she was hired as a paid assistant.

Terri quickly became convinced that the survivors needed to have public speaking workshops that mirrored ongoing work with their writing of Holocaust memories. Terri was an exceptional student of rhetoric and excelled in both speech and debate competitions while in college. Communication courses convinced her that being able to express oneself in public was critical. She contacted me back in Ohio about how to design a public speaking program for the survivors. We corresponded regularly about the project and I presumed that based upon my recommendations she would find a local instructor of communication and public speaking in the D.C. area and imple-

1

ment the program. When she contacted me to say that her grant had been approved and the project would proceed, I was happy for her. I was not prepared for her conclusion to the call. She wanted me to fly out and do the training of the Holocaust survivors.

That was a life changing moment for me. Though I loved rhetoric and believed that every person should have their voice, I was in awe of the prospects of working with survivors and trying to shape their voices toward greater use and confidence. How could one evaluate their oral testimonies? Yet, that was inherent in this project designed by Terri. I remember vividly saying "yes" to her request on the phone. We collaborated intensely with the director of survivor affairs Ellen Blalock to design a four-part program built around lectures and performance/practices.

When I arrived on-site in late May of 2006, I remember attending a social event on a Sunday evening honoring the volunteer work of the survivors at the Museum. I had no responsibilities for the evening apart from socializing with the survivors that I would begin working with on Monday morning. I recall a small and slight female survivor grabbing me by the arm that evening:

"Dr. Voth, Dr. Voth, I am so glad you are here."

"I am delighted to be here as well," I responded—surprised at her urgency.

"I have such a hard time telling my story," she continued.

"I can hardly imagine. I know it must be difficult," I offered—beginning to realize the depth of the task I was about to embark upon.

"Every time I try to tell my story, I break down crying. I cannot stop thinking of the children I wanted to have . . . but I was sterilized by Dr. Mengele."

With those words, my confidence plunged as I pondered the history of Josef Mengele and the infamous medical experimentation he was so well known for in history. I tried to grasp a conversation with someone personally victimized and now decades later shadowed by the event. I was staggered. I tried to recover:

"You know. I would like to hear your story. I imagine many people would like to hear your story. But I want you to know, that these workshops are not mandatory. They are not required. Given the trauma, I am curious to know why you might even want to try to do this?"

I vividly remember her straightening her spine, leveling her eyes toward mine and saying with stern conviction:

"There are people out there saying that the Holocaust didn't happen. And before I die, I want them to know. The Holocaust happened! And it happened to ME!"

She punctuated her last two sentences with a finger pointed toward me but then landing on her chest when she said "ME."

Emotions soared within me to see an individual fighting back against cruel cultural graffiti written against her soul. It was heroic and inspiring.

"Well. I guess those are the feelings you will need to hold onto as we go through these workshops."

Her remarks steeled my resolve that night. If she could rise up against her haunting trauma so cruelly inscribed, then I would manage my own apprehensions about academic pretense prevailing against the sincere memories of survivors. For most people, the hearing of a Holocaust survivor is a treasured memory of a lifetime. I would hear almost three dozen survivors tell their stories week after week and I felt my soul being seared in the furnaces of human emotions on this question of genocide. After two summers of work at the museum with the survivors, my fundamental perspective about the museum changed. I originally thought of the museum as an epideictic commemoration of one of humanity's most savage acts— a sobering memorial to a terrible tragedy. I now view it as an ongoing heroic story of human voices rising out of the ashes of genocide.

It was in the summer of 2007 that I finally noticed a subtle but compelling feature of the museum's flow and architecture. In the midst of an edifice designed to look like Auschwitz sits a small desk staffed by survivors. The survivors are queried by visitors and some will even pull up their sleeves to show the numbers inscribed by Nazis on their bodies. Thinking about the survivors' willingness to re-live and abide within this memorial of tragedy in an effort to prevent similar tragedies from happening again, lead me to the conclusion that the museum has a much more positive message than I originally understood. The survivors are heroes within the defeated scene of the Holocaust. I hope this book will capture that sense of optimism. Many of the specific exercises and discussions there motivated chapters in this work.

One of the more salient aspects of this successful survivor project is the manner by which it was achieved. This was a project envisioned and created by a student. Her original optimism like so many student efforts before it and since then almost made me giggle as a professor. Is this possible? Students continually challenge me to throw off the blinders of cynicism that cause knowledge to hide the status quo behind a wall as if we know the world cannot change for the better. Terri's vision like so many other young people did change the world on the important question of genocide.

When the speaker's workshop began, barely ten survivors were willing and comfortable with going outside the museum to tell their story to the public. By the end of 2007, more than twenty-five survivors were prepared to do so. Terri more than doubled the number of survivors that could work so broadly with the public at a time when survivor voices are growing ever more scarce. Each survivor at the DC museum that speaks in public reaches an average of ten thousand listeners a year in talks that take place around the nation. Military bases, police trainees, state department employees, churches,

synagogues, schools, and a variety of community groups are all reached by
oral testimonies given by survivors. Many tens of thousands of people more
could be reached by these stories because of a vision held by a young student.
The project was a reminder to me about why teaching is so important and
inspiring. I hope this book will make teaching in this area more possible and
compelling.

Terri's work became a model and inspiration for further work in this area.
One of my master's students in Ohio (Allison Fisher Bodkin) went to a
doctoral program in Illinois and started a public speaking program for rape
survivors. The program had a similar concept and premise. Being able to
speak in public about a past trauma was empowering. It was an important
step in recovering an identity deformed by a cruel intentional act of hate.
Ultimately, the program became self-sustaining.

Another student, Aaron Noland, became a communication instructor at
James Madison University and reached out in an academic program to the
"lost boys" of Sudan. His heart for the victims of genocide was evident and
enacted for his students in a way that goes beyond the statistics and the
politics. Seeing my students act out this serial idealism motivates me every
day and gradually convicted me to write this book. There are dozens of
students that I could name from Kansas, to Ohio, to Texas that factored into
inspiring this book and I hope they understand this if they come to read this
work.

As highlighted by these examples, this book is unique in emphasizing the
role of communication in the subject of genocide. There are several dimensions to this: 1) genocide is a symbolic act that involves defining groups out
of existence, 2) genocide is perpetrated through the abuse of symbols by
communication manipulators known as genocidaires, 3) communication is
stifled in the prelude to genocide, and 4) communication is a profound pre-
ventative, remedy, and remediation for genocide. The centrality of communication and the deeper philosophical commitment to the human processes of
rhetoric animate the content of this book and make it different.

This book is built upon strong foundations discernible in at least three
other seminal books on genocide: 1) Samantha Power's *A Problem from
Hell*, 2) Totten's work *Century of Genocide*, and 3) Goldhagen's *Worse than
War*.[1] These excellent books are the starting point for this analysis that seeks
to take those political, journalistic, and documentary approaches to the question of genocide and apply a communication framework toward a unique
paradigm that views genocide as a problem that can be potentially mitigated
and resolved in the twenty-first century. That rather strident idealistic goal is
not a function of naiveté but the peculiar successes of idealism that I have
seen in students. Positive outcomes I could not anticipate were not only
possible, but immediately possible. I am convinced that much of the problem

of contemporary genocide is rooted in our own persistent cynicism in academic circles that the matter is interminable—essentially human nature.

This ambitious goal of the book leads to the second primary motivation for the book: James Farmer Jr. Without giving away later content covered in this book, Farmer was an individual who graduated from college and responded to his father's question of what he wanted to do with his life by saying, "Destroy segregation!"[2] Only a young idealistic student coming out of college would say such an audacious thing in late 1930s America. It is not unfair to suggest, that Farmer did, in fact, accomplish that life goal of destroying segregation in America. That profound conclusion, which I have not arrived at lightly, leads me to believe that Farmer's life is an analogy for every young life infected with a hope of changing the world from what it is, to what it should be. Genocide expert and global political figure, Samantha Power is prone to such a view. *Prospect* magazine detailed this life moment for Power:

> Idealism is a word that comes up time and time again in discussions about Power. In 2004, she sat next to the journalist Mark Bowden, author of *Black Hawk Down*, at a dinner in Boston. "At some point that evening, she leaned over to ask me what was my ambition in life," remembers Bowden. "I assumed she meant professional ambition, so I said, "I want to write good books." Then I asked her [what her ambition was]. Power said, "I want to change the world."[3]

I hear this same sentiment again and again on college campuses. I believe that not just here in the United States, but around the world there is a deepening conviction that genocide can and should be banished from the world. It is not cancer. It is not a mysterious virus. It is not a natural disaster. Genocide is a rather specific and intentional act that is very nearly the deadliest of all practices among the human family. Human beings make genocide happen. Human beings can make it stop.

For many years, when I taught classes in Ohio, every class began at a location called the Freedom Summer memorial. It did not matter whether I was teaching the introduction to public speaking or the graduate course on rhetorical theory. We began our first class there to be sure we knew "Why?" we were studying communication and rhetoric. As passionately as I could, I wanted to muster an argument on the first day that would leave an indelible impression on my students that what they might learn that semester could matter powerfully. Whether in an ability to speak for themselves or on behalf of others, the ability to communicate, to speak, to influence others was a deeply moral cause.

Students would sit at the memorial and listen to Martin Luther King Jr.'s "I Have a Dream" speech. We would talk about why it was a great speech. I would then talk about three young men: Mickey Schwerner, James Chaney, and Andy Goodman. I explained that in the summer of 1964, inspired by rhetoric like that of MLK, these men trained in Oxford, Ohio, to go into Mississippi to change the world from what it was to what it should be. Their ambitions were short lived because they were murdered in Mississippi by radicals committed to segregation in that state. Their deaths would constitute a profound catalyst for the process of desegregation that would be accomplished along the lines of Farmer's original vision and expectation. At this opening lecture I would often present the words written on the tombstone of James Chaney who was a Mississippi native:

> There are those who are alive yet will never live
> There are those who are dead yet will live forever
> Great deeds inspire and encourage the living.[4]

I ask students to think about how young people just like themselves, used rhetoric to change the world. I explain that changing the world is not always as apparently dramatic as it seems now in the memorial at Oxford, Ohio. But every person should learn how to argue, advocate, speak, and communicate.

Ultimately, upon my arrival in Texas, my sense of the civil rights movement came to a certain full circle when my studies introduced me to James Farmer Jr. Coming out of anonymity for me in Denzel Washington's excellent film, "The Great Debaters," I came to recognize that Marshall, Texas, produced, through education on a college campus, the arguable architect of the American civil rights movement. In his biography, *Lay Bare the Heart*, Farmer discussed how a visit to Oxford, Ohio, inspired him to see civil rights as an actionable and reasonable cause.[5] In reading that biography my sense of the civil rights movement rooted in Farmer's vision became clear. His biography and the apparent results of his efforts lead me to believe that the bold claims of young people to "destroy segregation!" and "change the world," are not only realistic, but the only reasonable course that anyone can hold about our future.

This book unpacks that idealism and lays bare the idealistic heart of James Farmer and those survivors at the United States Holocaust Memorial Museum. The world can change. The world must change. By communication, rhetoric, and argument, it will change. We know this from a careful and honest study of the human past. This book is a communication-based guide as to how this can be accomplished.

NOTES

1. Power, Samantha. 2002. *A Problem from Hell: America and the Age of Genocide*. New York: Harper Perennial; Goldhagen, Daniel. 2009. *Worse than War: Genocide, Eliminationism, and the Ongoing Assault on Humanity*. New York: Public Affairs; and Totten, Samuel and William Parsons 2012. *Century of Genocide: Critical Essays and Eyewitness Accounts*, 4th edition. New York & London: Routledge.

2. Gubert, Betty. 2004. "James Farmer." *African American Lives*. Editors: Henry Louis Gates and Brooks Higginbotham. Oxford University Press. March 23. p. 287.

3. Broadwell, Paula. 2013. *Prospect Magazine*. July 17. Accessed September 24, 2013. http://www.prospectmagazine.co.uk/magazine/the-doctrine-of-power-paula-broadwell-samantha-power/#.UkH4oRY9roM.

4. Inscription on the tombstone of James Earl Chaney in Meridian, Mississippi.

5. Farmer, J. 1985. *Lay Bare the Heart: An Autobiography of the Civil Rights Movement*. Texas Christian University Press: Fort Worth.

Chapter One

The Role of Rhetoric and Communication in Genocide

What hurts the victim most is not the physical cruelty of the oppressor but the silence of the bystander.—Elie Wiesel[1]

These words by a noted Holocaust survivor establish central communication premises for the resolution of the world's most serious problems. Human hatred shaped by words bear the fruit of painful actions: rape, murder, violence, and genocide. These painful actions are not inevitable and are entirely preventable. Unlike so much disease or disaster that may kill by accident, these crimes are designed by the human mind and expressed in communication to make those things that should not happen—happen. Because communication is such an important part of these terrible actions, it is morally imperative to introduce a communication framework to the study of these problems.

Our present literature on genocide is comprehensive and impressive. We have vivid understanding of how the past century witnessed the deaths of more than one hundred million human beings in the diabolical premeditated action of genocide.[2] Our studies offer a variety of synonyms to describe the process: ethnoviolence, eliminationism, and democide.[3] Each of these crystallizes a motive as to how human beings choose to kill one another. Perhaps because of the vivid and overwhelming nature of these descriptions so well documented by our technology and historical tenacity, audiences reading and observing these explanations are left with a sense of moral hollowness. If humans can do these things such as the Holocaust, Rwanda, and Cambodia, is there any hope of stopping such crimes? This book moves in a unique and ambitious direction by recognizing how the problem of genocide is being reduced and clarifying the means for furthering these trends to a point where such tragedies are largely unknown by the end of the twenty-first century.

Wiesel's observation offers some key ingredients as to why communication is the critical pedagogical tool for slowing, stopping, and reversing the violence humans have chosen for one another. Initially, the important pretext to systemic violence is the absence of communication: silence. Whether it's the Holocaust or individual acts of abuse, perpetrators need a sense of collective silence to commit their protracted and extensive crimes. In the recent scandal engulfing Penn State, an extensive pattern of silence allowed Jerry Sandusky to continue in his abuse against children.[4] Sarah Ganim rose to the challenge of exposing Sandusky's abuse while she was a young journalist in her twenties. She refused to allow her youthfulness and relative inexperience as a journalist to prevent her from toppling a profound injustice founded in the football program of Penn State. Silence is an important and necessary ingredient toward enabling unethical actions and the social passivity necessary for those worst actions of genocide to be cultivated by the political communication of an elite. Communication study inherently empowers individuals to resist this pattern of silence at every step in the process. Whether a Bonhoffer[5] or a Mandela,[6] a King or a Farmer,[7] or a Ganim,[8] individuals can rise in the power of the human voice, to the exigence of social oppression and resist, slow, and stop the problem of ethnic violence.

This reveals a second implication of Wiesel's observation. The opposite of silence is to give voice. When we are not silent, when we are communicating, we are taking an action to reduce the risk of genocide and other forms of human abuse. In studies of genocide and systemic violence, it is easy to feel that nothing can be done. Communication of our awareness about a problem is an action that resists the further advance of the crisis. Communication theorist Kenneth Burke excellently described a peculiar philosophical character to human habits surrounding communication. The ethical distinction he offered was one of action and motion. In Burke's view, motion is that tendency of human beings to engage in unthinking behavior.[9] This is a morally failed human behavior. We are going "through the motions" in our lives. In contrast, human beings are capable of a higher moral behavior: action. Action is deliberate, intentional, and rational behavior. The careful study of communication with a purpose of revealing the possibility of action is known as *rhetoric*. Carefully related and connected to communication study, rhetorical study seeks to define how the individual can move from a world of passive motion and into a world of intentional action.[10]

Rhetorical study is an ancient form of communication study traceable at least to the ancient Greeks. One of its chief purveyors and practitioners, Aristotle, defined rhetoric this way: the faculty of observing in any given situation all available means of persuasion. Aristotle's definition of rhetoric delineates four key concepts to the study of rhetoric:

1. Rhetoric is a *faculty* of the mind. Human beings have a mental muscle that they exert in the study of communication that enables moral action. That mental faculty can both interpret a world of messages and create messages in response. A strong rhetorical faculty is necessary to becoming a moral agent within the world. This awareness was central to Aristotle's teaching function in Greek society. He prepared human beings for their moral roles as citizens through the study of rhetoric. [11]

2. Rhetoric can be learned through *observation*. The study of rhetoric need not be complicated. We can observe a world of symbols around us and derive how human beings are influencing one another. We may even find ourselves discovering categories of communication as Aristotle did. In any case, careful observation of the communication around us will develop our mental faculties and make us better at leaving a world of motion and entering the world of action that changes the world from what it is to what it should be. We can overcome the inherent barriers rooted in cultural difference by immersing ourselves in a committed program of observation.

3. Rhetorical understanding is derived from a clear recognition of a specific *situation*. Great rhetoric arises in the most challenging situations. Our ability to explain this depends primarily upon an accurate reading of the situation. We are naturally driven to the symbols chosen by a speaker—whether for a Gettysburg address, the sermon on the mount, or sharing a "dream"—powerful symbols are offered by authors who intimately understand the situation into which they are communicating. King's dream was compelling because it was so well suited to the time and place that it was delivered into in the summer of 1963. The careful student of rhetoric who seeks that critical moment where change is possible, must understand the situation.

   The notion of situation can be enhanced by recognizing a related and more compelling synonym: exigence. Exigence is how a situation makes communication necessary. [12] We feel we cannot remain silent. We must say something. The sense of "must" is exigence. Great speakers are aware of an exigence that is found within a situation and they craft messages that well suit that occasion. At Gettysburg, Lincoln sensed in the staggering toll of death in the scene, that a succinct but profound summary of the nation's essence was deserved and necessary.

4. Rhetoric has many means. Aristotle sought to catalog all the means of persuasion in early Greek society and yet there are many means he could not know today. There is an inexhaustible amount of means in communication that we seek to observe and understand. Human creativity is so boundless that we must continually observe and expect to be surprised.

We must continually re-learn communication. To believe that we will completely master and not encounter new means is to misunderstand the ethical potential of rhetoric. Human communication can bring forth new means not previously anticipated to change previously intractable situations for the better. Civil rights advocate Martin Luther King acknowledged the centrality of communication in resolving the enduring problem of human hatred:

> Men often hate each other because they fear each other;
> they fear each other because they don't know each other;
> they don't know each other because they cannot communicate. [13]

The rhetorical approach is ancient and well tested. Teachers of rhetoric have, for centuries, elaborated two sides of a communication coin that prove invaluable to individuals and society. [14] Those two sides are the ability to send messages and the ability to understand messages. The study of rhetoric increases the ability of persons to create a message and to make sense of a message. These mutually related aspects of a communication coin, can be a social cornerstone for preventing the worst of human inspired crimes, so often rooted in misunderstanding. There are many reasons why rhetorical studies are an intimate and necessary starting point for repealing the death as text that defined the twentieth century and enacting the rich communication world of the twenty-first century that is so much safer for humanity. Death is not always accidental. In many instances, the death of a human being is better thought of as a communicative act—one which ought to concern us. In the chapters ahead, we will focus our attention on the most acute practice of death as a text: genocide.

First, our explanations of genocide have tended to rely upon the realm of the political to describe the reality of this dreadful social crime. [15] The political effectively documents the role of governments and institutional power in the rise of groups like the Nazis or the Khmer Rouge. Those political aspects of genocide are important and relevant but leave us unable to understand some of the more intimate uncertainties of how this crime arises. How were Hitler and Pol Pot able to be so persuasive? Why did the public receive their arguments so readily? Questions like these are vital to understanding how the process of genocide is intimately tied to communication.

Secondly, the progression and activity of genocide is intensely symbolic. Public killings are often performed in these activities not for mere utilitarian outcomes such as removing an undesirable person from society, but to communicate a message to broader society. Essentially, killings can be seen as a performance and a symbolic order suggested by the powerful toward a broader public. [16] The straightforward message is one that seeks silence from the public: this killing is what will happen to you if you do not cooperate. Forming a more intimate communication based understanding of this crime will suit individuals to the proper tools and actions for resisting this insidious message.

Thirdly, an emphasis on explanations regarding power, politics, and institutions establishes a basis for cycling the problem of genocide. As a victim rises from victimhood to power, it is difficult to resist the motive of revenge. The cycle of violence in Rwanda is illustrative of the difficult problem of forming political and institutional solutions to the problem. The rhetorical approach with its emphasis on the power of the individual voice aims to instill solutions more widespread than an international court or a carefully trained army of soldiers. The communication approach, seeks through educational techniques, to teach every individual that their voice matters and constitutes a ready bulwark against the first step toward systemic violence: silence.

Defining terms is an important step to any intellectual task. The most obvious and central term of analysis is genocide. Samantha Power's book on genocide properly traces the history and development of the term to Raphael Lemkin who researched the concept of genocide in the aftermath of the Holocaust. He carefully traced the activities back to early twentieth century activities such as the Armenian genocide in Turkey. [17] This is a classic definition of genocide found in international law and most academic discussions of the question:

> Genocide means any of the following acts committed with intent to destroy, in whole or in part, a national, ethnical, racial or religious group, as such: (a) Killing members of the group; (b) Causing serious bodily or mental harm to members of the group; (c) Deliberately inflicting on the group conditions of life calculated to bring about its physical destruction in whole or in part; (d) Imposing measures intended to prevent births within the group; (e) Forcibly transferring children of the group to another group. [18]

There are several challenging aspects of this specific criterion-driven explanation of genocide. Initially, the matter of intention is central. More than mass killing or even accidental deaths, a genocide must demonstrate an *intention* to destroy a group. This has of course proven difficult in the prosecution of genocide. In most cases, the perpetrators hide or evade the characterization of these deadly results as intended. This practical problem gives immediate exigency for this communication approach. Intention is a long-standing concept in the study of communication because scholars of communication deduce intentions from speakers based upon words and symbols used by the speaker.

The definition of genocide suggests destruction of groups based on various criteria—primarily cultural. National, ethnic, racial, and religious are all offered. This relatively narrow list has given rise to further elaborations like those offered by Goldhagen. His view of eliminationism expands the concept of mass killing to include political exterminations. The effort to kill political opponents in a complete way might cross various categories of ethnic, religious and racial composition. It might also leave many in those categories untouched if they held political beliefs consonant with the perpetrators of the violence. This makes Goldhagen's expansion of the term practical and useful and yet further grounds the processes of violence in a communication context wherein a political movement is trying to win a political argument in the deadliest of ways. Goldhagen's definition of eliminationism is characterized by a set of tools used by the Sovereign:

- Forced transformation, such as forced religious conversion: destroying a group's essential and defining political, social, or cultural identities
- Extreme repression: reducing, with violence or its threat, a group's ability to inflict real or imagined harm upon others
- Expulsion, often called deportation: removing people more thoroughly, by driving them beyond a country's borders, or from one region of a country to another, or by forcing them into concentration camps
- Prevention of reproduction: diminishing a group's normal biological reproduction by preventing its members from becoming pregnant or giving birth, or by systematically raping the women so they bear children not "purely" of their group
- Extermination: the most final eliminationist act, as it is not interim or piecemeal[19]

Democide, eliminationism, and genocide (figure 1.1) are intimately related terms of the State's power to kill the innocent. At its broadest periphery, the sovereign may kill in its neglect of social contracts that lead to mass death in the events of natural disaster. In such cases, benign governments are prepared and open for aid in such events, but the closed society is neither prepared nor willing to receive aid—so thousands more die. In its most morally intense center, the sovereign establishes concentration camps and systems for delivering the innocent into places of mass killing like Auschwitz. In the broad middle is an uncivil war against prospective civilian enemies where the sovereign tries to kill perceived political rivals—often by the tens of thousands. Goldhagen's expansion of the genocide concept to larger political projects of threat, diminution, and expulsion are highly relevant and useful to this discussion. Though eliminationism broadens the ethical conversation beyond targeted killing, it adds another penumbra to the bullseye target of public killings. It remains a centered discussion on political orders that kill for purposes of silencing a broader social conversation. Fixating on the exact nature of a boundary to the point of denying the necessary social call against evil must be avoided. The contribution of broader agendas feeding genocide amplifies the discussion of how to stop genocide by making ourselves aware

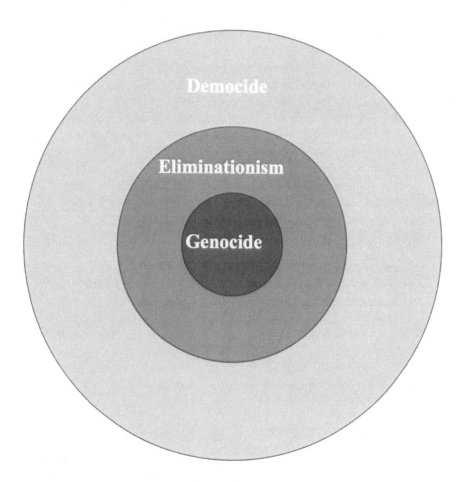

Figure 1.1. Rhetorical Relationsips among Sovereign State Nations of the Kill

of its broader predicates. We cannot wait until the subjects are standing in the gas chambers or waiting in the killing fields. We must see the bullying of the sovereign as it moves the victim in that direction. Those directions are signaled in the forms of rhetoric and communication and it is in the power of intellectual communities to attend to these signals and defeat them prior to genocide.

This definition remains central to twenty-first century discussions and applications of the question of genocide. International Criminal Courts like the ICC seek to derive judgments answering the question of whether a genocide has been committed. Policymakers like the Clinton administration in the mid 1990s faced awkward considerations of whether international events met the standards of genocide.[20] Here again the communicative and argumentative processes of definitions are integral to the consideration of genocide.

This table provides a compilation of scholarly efforts to define the process of "death as a text" wherein the central concept of genocide is often expanded to include state purposes beyond ethnic and religious cleansing. Lemkin, Rummel, and Goldhagen provide useful specific definitions for helping us understand how these mass symbolic killings are authored by sovereigns against society. Table 1.1 describes how these three definitional concepts can be viewed in relationship.

Our knowledge thus far on the important question of genocide points to the emergence of a communication pedagogy addressed to this question of stopping genocide. Both students and teachers can play active roles in diminishing the social practice of genocide. For teachers, there are several actions envisioned by this book:

1. Teachers should direct communication study in the classroom toward topics related to genocide so that students can leave the realm of silence created by ignorance of these questions. Students can study speeches, political campaigns, actions of resistance, and many other discrete aspects of communication in relation to the large social prob-

Table 1.1. Definitions for Mass Killings

Term	Author	Agent	Victims	Definition
Genocide	Lemkin	Genocidaire	Primarily ethnic groups	". . . any of the following acts committed with intent to destroy, in whole or in part, a national, ethnical, racial or religious group, as such . . ."
Democide	Rummel	State	Civilian subjects	"The murder of any person or people by a government, including genocide, politicide, and mass murder."
Elimination-ism	Gold-hagen	State	Political enemies of the State	Even if eliminationism's many forms are better known by their particular and spectacularly horrible consequences, such as genocide, the desire to eliminate peoples or groups should be understood to be the overarching category and the core act, and should therefore be the focus of our study.

Source: Power, 2002; Rummel, 2004; and Goldhagen, 2009.

lem of genocide. Hate speech is a well-understood area of study in many communication courses.[21] Most every course of conventional communication study can touch on the dimensions of propaganda, hate speech, argumentation, crisis rhetoric, political communication, organizational communication, and interpersonal communication that were necessary for the massive social crime of genocide to emerge successfully in the past, present, and future of humanity.

2. Teachers should adopt a positive intellectual approach that empowers students to change the world from "what it is" to "what it should be." In many respects the most serious barrier to further solutions is a lack of human imagination. The relationship of teacher and student is the foundational basis for stirring imagination for one generation to resist and overcome current problems. Teachers should take care with their knowledge. Knowledge is power. Power can corrupt. Does our teaching approach and deploy the power of knowledge in a creative way or a destructive way? Teaching in a way to reify our own prowess or stature while diminishing the possibilities of how students may change present understandings is counterproductive both inside and outside the classroom. Of course immediate solutions are not known but our teaching approach should leave open the possibility of dramatic social change. I tell students on the first day: I am cynical about one thing—cynicism.

3. Teachers should create learning outcomes and student results that show lasting impact. Students can become aware of the problem of genocide and demonstrate this on conventional student products such as tests and essays. They can also go beyond these conventional forms and produce a variety of communication driven outcomes that will have lasting effects of empowerment. Outcomes I have used include: 1) speeches, 2) performances, and 3) online videos. One of the most common outcomes I use is for students to produce YouTube videos about some genocide related question. Many of these outcomes are still online and informing the public. In a few cases, tens of thousands of people have viewed their communication messages. Students should produce educational products that take advantage of the vast digital tools we have today in communication study.

Reciprocally, there are several important communication outcomes envisioned for students:

1. Students should end their silence on the question of genocide. Students regularly ask on topics like these and so many others: What can I do? I have a vital and useful first step you can take. You can end your silence about this important question and begin communicating about

the problem of genocide. Of course you do not know everything about this and you may even make mistakes analyzing and trying to understand the complex problem. That cannot prevent your pursuit of that most important solution suggested by Wiesel: ending our silence on this question. Your study and communication that results constitutes an action against genocide. This has always proven to be the most important step in preventing and stopping such atrocities.

2. Students should remain sensitive to the problem of silence within society throughout their lives. Each student lives and interacts within a unique set of communities. Those communities will need you to step up at the right time to speak and end the silence that is allowing some wrong to continue. These problems are not always as serious as genocide but many times they have an initial relationship to a cynical cultural spiral of crime that conditions us to believe that it is okay to mistreat a group of people. This sensitivity can go beyond the classroom and should be lodged permanently in the mind of the student in the form of a constant question: Is it time for me to speak up?

3. Students should pursue the healthy habits of the mind that encourage critical thinking and consideration of multiple points of view. In studying genocide, you will see that the certitude of an elite cadre lead to fundamental misunderstandings about valuing human life. We can become infatuated with our own sense of knowledge to a point of dangerous supremacy. Seeking out various points of view and developing the patience to listen to others when you disagree is part of developing human character necessary to stop the processes of genocide.

4. Students should maintain their idealism. For many students this idealism is natural and sometimes initially confusing. You want to help. You want to make things better, but you are not sure how to go about it. You worry you might be naive. Your idealism is the first and most important ingredient to change and it is something that many of your more educated and mature leaders have a hard time mustering. Idealistic determination inspired and maintained the great social movements of the world. Do not view learning as a compromise to your idealism or an inherent setback. Discovering the depth and scope of a problem need not squelch your ambitions.

In the chapters ahead, I will outline a communication-based approach to the problem of genocide. Such approaches are needed in the communication discipline demonstrate the utility of our work to practical world problems.[22] The missing pieces of academic description will be described so a more comprehensive and ultimately effective pedagogy for resisting genocide can be brought to bear globally. Key concepts to be covered in the next few chapters include: discursive complexity, the genocidaire, and the cell phone versus the AK-47. These theoretical chapters will be followed by methodological approaches that can reduce the problem of genocide. Despite the grim topic of this book, it is my firm belief that genocide is a problem that is being reduced and will be increasingly reduced to a point where it is largely unknown by the end of the twenty-first century. That process of ending genocide begins with a simple moral premise of ending our silence on the question of genocide.

NOTES

1. Wiesel, Elie. 1986. Foreword. *The Courage to Care.* Eds. Carol Rittmer and Sondra Myers. New York: New York University Press.

2. Bassiouni, M. Cherif. 1998. "The Normative Framework of International Humanitarian Law: Overlaps, Gaps and Ambiguities," *Transnational Law & Contemporary Problems,* 8.; Power, Samantha. 2002. *A problem from Hell: America and the Age of Genocide.* New York: Harper Perennial.; Voth, Ben and Aaron Noland. 2007. "Argumentation and the International Problem of Genocide," *Contemporary Argumentation and Debate,* 28: 38-46.

3. Goldhagen, Daniel. 2009. *Worse Than War: Genocide, Eliminationism, and the Ongoing Assault on Humanity.* New York: Public Affairs.; Rudolph Rummel. 2002. *Power Kills: Democracy as a method of non-violent action.* Transaction Publishers: New Brunswick, New Jersey.; and Totten, Samuel. and Parsons, William. 2009. *Century of Genocide: Critical Essays and Eyewitness Accounts.* New York & London: Routledge.

4. Matt, Semino. 2012. "Jerry Sandusky and the pain of silence." *Huffingston Post.* June 13. Accessed September 22, 2013. http://www.huffingtonpost.com/matt-semino/jerry-sandu sky-trial_b_1594397.html.

5. Metaxas, Eric. 2011. *Bonhoeffer: Pastor, Martyr, Prophet, Spy.* Thomas Nelson: Nashville, TN.

6. Dixon, Maria. 2011. "With Faith in the Works of Words: The Beginnings of Reconciliation in South Africa, 1985-1995 (review)" Rhetoric & Public Affairs, 14 (3). 562–65.

7. Severo, Richard. 1999. James Farmer, Civil Rights Giant In the 50's and 60's, Is Dead at 79, *New York Times.* July 10. Archives. Accessed August 2, 2013. http://www.nytimes.com/ 1999/07/10/us/james-farmer-civil-rights-giant-in-the-50-s-and-60-s-is-dead-at-79.html?page wanted=all&src=pm.

8. DeLuca, Matthew. 2012. "Reporter Sara Ganim, who won a pulitzer prize for breaking Sandusky story." *The Daily Beast.* April 17. Accessed September 22, 2013. http:// www.thedailybeast.com/articles/2012/04/17/reporter-sara-ganim-who-won-a-pulitzer-for-breaking-sandusky-story.html.

9. Burke, Kenneth. 1969. *A Grammar of Motives.* Berkeley: University of California Press.

10. Comas, James. 2012. "The question of defining Rhetoric." January 1. Accessed September 22, 2013. http://capone.mtsu.edu/jcomas/rhetoric/defining.html

11. Aristotle. 1991. *On Rhetoric: A Theory of Civic Discourse.* Translated by George A. Kennedy. New York: Oxford University Press.

12. Bitzer, Lloyd F. 1968. "The Rhetorical Situation." *Rhetoric: Concepts, Definitions, Boundaries.* William A. Covino ed. Boston: Allyn and Bacon: 1995.

13. King, Martin Luther, Jr. 1958. *Stride Toward Freedom: the Montgomery Story.* New York: Harper Collins.

14. Comas, James. 2012. "The question of defining Rhetoric." January 1. Accessed September 22, 2013. http://capone.mtsu.edu/jcomas/rhetoric/defining.html

15. Goldhagen, Daniel. 2009. *Worse Than War: Genocide, Eliminationlism, and the Ongoing Assault on Humanity.* New York: Public Affairs.; Rummel, Rudolph. 2002. *Power Kills: Democracy as a Method of Non-violent Action.* Transaction Publishers: New York.; and Totten, Samuel and William Parsons 2009. *Century of Genocide: Critical Essays and Eyewitness Accounts* New York & London: Routledge.; Bassiouni, M. Cherif. 1998. "The Normative

Framework of International Humanitarian Law: Overlaps, Gaps and Ambiguities," *Transnational Law & Contemporary Problems*, 8.

16. Voth, Ben and Aaron Noland. 2007. "Argumentation and the International Problem of Genocide," *Contemporary Argumentation and Debate*, 28: 38–46.

17. Power, Samantha. 2002. *A problem from Hell: America and the Age of Genocide*. New York: Harper Perennial.

18. *Convention on the Prevention and Punishment of the Crime of Genocide* (1948). Article II

19. Goldhagen, Daniel. 2009. *Worse Than War: Genocide, Eliminationism, and the Ongoing Assault on Humanity*. New York: Public Affairs. 17–18.

20. Burkhalter, Holly J. (Winter, 1994/1995). "The Question of Genocide: The Clinton Administration and Rwanda," *World Policy Journal* 11, 4. 44–54.

21. Whillock, Rita Kirk and David Slayden, eds. 1995. *Hate Speech*. Newbury Park, CA: Sage. (Tulane).

22. Kidd, Nancy and Trevor Parry-Giles. 2013. "Another View on Communication Scholarship." *Inside Higher Ed* August 13. Accessed August 15, 2013. http://www.insidehighered.com/views/2013/08/13/essay-defends-state-communications-scholarship#ixzz2eLqUIrBE; Wilson, Ernest J. 2013. "Communication Scholars Need to Communicate," *Inside Higher Ed*. July 29. Accessed August 15. , http://www.insidehighered.com/views/2013/07/29/essay-state-communications-scholarship#ixzz2eLqcyeyp.

Chapter Two

State Killings as Public Argument

KILLING AS ARGUMENT: AN INTRODUCTION

Human history is filled with instances of dramatic killings designed to not only remove individuals from society but to perform a public act of intimidation between the sovereign state and its human subjects. In a communication analysis of killing as argument, this chapter examines how mass killings such as genocide constitute a social symbolic form that may be subject to symbolic disruption. As noted previously, Holocaust survivor Elie Wiesel explains "what hurts the victim most is not the physical cruelty of the oppressor but the silence of the bystander."[1] Such insight suggests that the murder of the innocent is an intensely symbolic act and intimately associated with deep intrinsic human needs, such as justice. This communication analysis uses an approach to study emphasized by noted French theorist Michel Foucault: a genealogy.[2] A genealogy establishes historical patterns of epistemological logic that make cultural understanding stable. As a genealogy, this chapter begins with an examination of the murders performed in Mississippi in 1964 of Michael Schwerner, James Chaney, and Andrew Goodman by state sovereigns who viewed civil rights advocates as usurpers of State power. Noted civil rights activist Robert Moses observed in his eulogy for fellow activists: "The tragedy here is the work of people who believed in an idea enough to kill for it. The problem of Mississippi is the problem of the nation and of the world. A way has to be found to change this desire to kill."[3] Schwerner, Chaney and Goodman were principal advocates for voter registration and freedom schools in the South designed to increase the autonomy and presence of African-Americans in Mississippi. The murder of these activists by White Citizen's Councils and the Mississippi Sovereignty Commission was met with stony silence by the local community, who refused to convict

21

anyone of the murders. Twenty-five years later the Mississippi secretary of state, Richard Molpus, broke the silence at a memorial service for the families.[4] The peculiarities of symbolic violence intermingled with concerted social silence make this incident a model for understanding State arguments of death as a text. Projecting the Freedom Summer struggle associated with this activism toward our twenty-first century dilemmas surrounding contemporary genocide, this analysis suggests how the events of 1964 provide a template of argumentative resistance for interpreting violence among the 193 sovereign states in the modern global public sphere. By viewing the international order as a reified defense of state power, it is possible to imagine transcendent human activism connecting human beings across state boundaries and drawing a critical perspective against the symbolic order of state violence designed to intimidate the proponents of human freedom and the "community of the beloved."[5]

Drawing upon my personal experiences teaching rhetoric to Holocaust survivors at the United States Holocaust Memorial Museum in Washington DC, I am working to establish useful pedagogical templates for teaching how genocide can be overcome in contemporary contexts. Weaving together theoretical communication work such as Michel Foucault's notion of biopower[6] along with contemporary reviews of genocide as offered by experts such as Samantha Power[7] and Totten and Parsons,[8] we can see the role of potential "specific intellectuals" in ending the silence that "hurts the victim most" and limits the space created in that silence for the reign of injustice. This genealogy organizes key terminologies such as "terror," "sovereignty," "international law," "genocide," and "genocidaire." Several of these details will be examined further in future chapters. As a site of resistance, the struggle for justice in the American South during 1964 raises deeper questions about the provinciality of freedom and human dignity and its possibilities as a shared global argumentation frame.

A STARTING POINT IN THE GENEALOGY

In the summer of 1964, the United States and its associated public sphere were shocked by the deaths of James Chaney, Andrew Goodman, and Mickey Schwerner.[9] These three young men advocated for civil rights among black communities in the State of Mississippi. Through processes of youth education and voter registration, these advocates sought to establish a productive pattern of resistance that would hopefully overcome the segregationist policies of the State of Mississippi. The killing of these advocates who risked their lives to *change the world from what it was to what it should be* (rhetoric), was meant by those committing the murders as more than a practical end to the advocacy of Chaney, Goodman, and Schwerner. The State of

Mississippi sought to communicate "death as a text" to the broader community of advocates that might seek to disrupt the sovereignty of their segregationist community, which had for many decades, utilized dramatic murders such as lynchings to signify their domination and the expected subordination of black human beings living in the state of Mississippi. This genealogy of those communicated and argued murders constitutes a rhetorical means of connecting human killings across state lines and formulating a broader global understanding of human resistance to state sovereignty as it may or may not exist in places such as the states of Sudan, Syria, North Korea, and Iran.[10] Human beings have an intrinsic dignity that transcends the value of states' rights.

MISSISSIPPI'S SOVEREIGNTY

Under the rhetorical guise of "states' rights," the governing authorities of Mississippi argued that the presence of civil rights workers such as Chaney, Goodman, and Schwerner constituted threats to the organic integrity of the State Body of Mississippi. The comprehensibility of genocide is rooted in an intellectual sense of the state body transcending the local individual civic body. The threats to that larger political idea of the state galvanize all manner of vigilantism and public killings necessary to prove loyalty and value to the meaning of the State. The sense of connection among the civil rights activists was described by leaders such as John Lewis as the "community of the beloved."[11] But this sense did not transcend the sovereignty of the state of Mississippi as argued and understood by governing authorities including informal citizen councils, the governor, and related state officials.

The killings were accompanied by a resilient silence of the State of Mississippi. Governing authorities for the state refused to prosecute anyone for the murders of these three advocates. In essence, the State of Mississippi held that no crime had been committed and that their deaths constituted a message and argument that these killings were organic and productive functions of the State of Mississippi. Mississippi had in 1956 established the Mississippi State Sovereignty Commission in the aftermath of *Brown v. Board of education.*[12] The commission's purpose: to "do and perform any and all acts deemed necessary and proper to protect the sovereignty of the state of Mississippi, and her sister states . . ." from perceived "encroachment thereon by the Federal Government or any branch, department or agency thereof."[13]

One indication of the totalizing power from the state of Mississippi was the refusal of the local coroner to conduct an autopsy of negro, James Chaney. An unofficial examination of Chaney's body allowed by authorities described his condition this way:

> I could barely believe the destruction to these frail young bones. In my twenty-five years as a pathologist and medical examiner, I have never seen bones so severely shattered, except in tremendously high speed accidents or airplane crashes. It was obvious to any first year medical student that this boy had been beaten to a pulp . . . I felt like screaming at these impassive observers still silently standing across the table. But I knew that no rage of mine could tear their curtain of silence. [14]

The supreme annihilation of Chaney's body was more than accidental and constituted a persuasive message from the state penned by the bigots who confronted him in the summer of 1964. It was an extraordinary rage that took the killers to lengths well beyond murder to disfigurement—desperately trying to erase the dignity and embodiment of justice that James Chaney represented in his life.

The State of Mississippi was never alone in its political sense of external threats. Prior civil rights history demonstrated that threats existed and they were not limited to or even principally expressed by workers like Chaney, Goodman, and Schwerner. Before the events of Freedom Summer, activists were taking powerful steps toward integration. The Federal interventions into the Sovereignty of Mississippi were apparent in the integration of James Meredith at Ole Miss in 1960. The attendance of a Negro at the major Mississippi university lead to the deployment of forty thousand federal troops into the state of Mississippi. Local law enforcement officers were narrowly prevented from firing on federal troops as they accomplished by force the argument that Negroes should be able to access the state educational system represented by Ole Miss. [15] Justice arrived for Meredith at Ole Miss at the point of a gun. The Federal intervention against the unjust state of Mississippi obstructed one of the most heated implementations of segregation in the South.

BREAKING THE SILENCE

In the summer of 1964, the profound power and pain of silence, as previously noted by Wiesel, was apparent in the state of Mississippi's refusal to investigate and prosecute the murders of Chaney, Goodman, and Schwerner. The silence stood as a monument to the community commitment to segregation and the refusal of justice for victims of these state killings. The silence was aimed squarely at the "community of the beloved" that cared for these three men and the many human beings victimized by segregation. Given the longevity of this painful silence, it is profound what transpired in 1989.

Twenty-five years after these murders, the families of the victims had gathered again at a local church in Mississippi to remember their losses and reflect on this painful silence. They were joined by the secretary of state for

Mississippi, Richard Molpus. Molpus gave a brief but profound speech. Addressing the families he expressed regret and said on behalf of the state of Mississippi, "I am sorry." Years later, Molpus further explained in 2004:

> When we have heard murderers brag about their killings but pretend those words were never spoken, when we know about evidence to help bring justice, but refuse to step forward and tell authorities what they need to know . . . that's what makes us in 2004 guilty. Pretending this didn't happen makes us complicit. We must provide the help prosecutors need to bring closure to this case.[16]

In so doing, Molpus disrupted twenty-five years of stony silence from the state that had been intended to repudiate the advocacy and dignity of Chaney, Goodman, and Schwerner. The 1989 speech made more than an immediate emotional impact. The speech precipitated the formation of a social action group known as the *Philadelphia Coalition*. That group began to argue for justice in the criminal case of Chaney, Goodman, and Schwerner.

Ultimately, the arguments of this group would culminate in a trial for Edgar Ray Killen. The state of Mississippi initiated a legal case nearly forty years after the original killings. The actions of the State came as a result of diligent public arguments by the *Philadelphia Coalition*. The social movement sparked by Molpus' speech apologizing for the crime progressed to a prosecution of Edgar Ray Killen. Though many other individuals were understood to be involved with the crimes, Killen was an unrepentant minister who seemed to boast about the crimes long after they were committed. Ultimately, the State of Mississippi had to settle for manslaughter charges for Killen who was now advanced in age and in rather poor health. The peculiar case of trying someone for a crime committed forty years prior posed a serious challenge to prosecutors and the larger legal system.[17]

STATES' RIGHTS AND THE GLOBAL SPHERE

The example of civil rights in Mississippi poses an important analogy for the present practice of global politics. Approximately 193 states preside in sovereign rule over the individual lives of more than six billion individual human beings. In the majority of global locales, incidents like the one that happened to Chaney, Goodman, and Schwerner are commonplace. The murder of Iranian protesters on the streets of Tehran in 2009 is illustrative. Dozens of additional scenarios can be found in places such as Zimbabwe, Burma, Syria, North Korea, Egypt, Sudan, Libya, or Mexico. Massive individual human rights violations take place in all 193 states. In a strong percentage of cases, the violence is sanctioned by the state, while social remedies of justice are actively stymied by the state to instill the cold chill of intimidation on human populations. The gaze of the state upon human bodies is a rather cold and calculated view that recognizes that almost any level of violence practiced by the state against civilian subjects cannot be interrupted due to a rhetorical system dedicated to the preservation of state sovereignty.

The global public sphere's preference for state sovereignty is apparent in the dramatic reduction in the practice of war since World War II. Measures of international state-to-state violence show a precipitous decline of combatants fighting fellow combatants in the regulated conduct of war.[18] This decline is enhanced by a global sense of repudiation for wars fought by state powers such as the United States and Europe. One of the most popular fashion statements of the day is the peace symbol. This decline in war has reduced the number of combatants killed.

The reduction of war as a global social practice leaves an alarming social problem of violence and intimidation practiced by non-warring states against civilian subjects. This violence might well be termed its own type of warfare—but the relationship between perpetrator and victim is profoundly asymmetrical. Moreover, the perpetrator of genocidal violence is able to wrap himself in the international flag of sovereignty and demand deference to their "internal politics." Radical inhumane practices of force have privilege within the system of international law, which requires "respect" for states among states.[19] International experts have explored and worried that the preference for sovereignty may endanger individual human beings, but little progress seems evident in the public sphere. The most notable exception to this unfortunate rule is the work of Samantha Power in establishing a responsibility to protect doctrine (R2P) that is most apparent in the recent case of Libya deposing dictator Mohammar Qaddafi.[20]

A recent example of the remaining problem is seen in Sudan:

> Following the International Criminal Court's decision to issue a warrant for President Omar al-Bashir's arrest for serious human violation charges concerning the Darfur crisis, the Sudanese authorities are stirring up the issue of national sovereignty and dignity. This is an issue that cannot be subjected to discussions or doubts and no one can cast doubts at Sudan's independence and its right to preserve its sovereignty.[21]

For states such as Sudan, the rhetorical capacity to invoke arguments regarding international law and the preference for the integrity of state bodies over human bodies obviates the voice of the "community of the beloved."[22]

Vladimir Putin borrowed from this rhetoric in his *New York Times* editorial published on September 11, 2013, chastising President Obama's goal of military strikes against Bashar al-Assad for using sarin gas to kill civilian families in the suburbs of Damascus. Putin reminded Americans about the privileges of states, in his conclusion with this warning:

It is extremely dangerous to encourage people to see themselves as exceptional, whatever the motivation. There are big countries and small countries, rich and poor, those with long democratic traditions and those still finding their way to democracy. Their policies differ, too. We are all different, but when we ask for the Lord's blessings, we must not forget that God created us equal. [23]

Putin's language is a stark reminder of how international law works—preserving the autonomy and dignity of states while erasing and diminishing human individuals. According to Putin, God created states to be equal, not individual human beings. The dead civilian victims of the sarin gas attacks may as well have been microbes infecting the co-equal body/state of Syria. They made the civil body of Syria ill, the sarin gas was the cure. Dr. Assad administered the medicine to the body/state of Syria, in the form of sarin gas. States are all equal in God's eyes, but individuals are little more than microbial threats to the host.

THE ALTERNATIVE: FREEDOM SUMMER FOR THE WORLD

Utilizing Freedom Summer 1964 and its related civil rights era can serve as a model for rehabilitating the public sphere in the various states of the world and provide a pedagogical means for teaching about global human rights. A growing commitment in higher education and elsewhere to "understand the world around us" can bring with it capacities to transform regimes of localized prejudicial violence "into an oasis of freedom and justice." Several insights from that era can serve a twenty-first century pedagogy of argumentation dedicated to empowering advocates in the same way Freedom Summer volunteers did in 1964. Key elements of this analogy include: 1) breaking the silence, 2) educating about our common human dignity, and 3) understanding the positive role of outside intervention.

Public comments in an emerging global public sphere can break the silence surrounding state violence against individuals. Human rights activists from around the world need to know that individuals outside the sphere of oppression are speaking up and arguing on their behalf. In the case of Freedom Summer the larger apparatus of activity was designed by CORE founder James Farmer Jr. Farmer was trained as a debater and recognized in a 2007 film, *The Great Debaters*. [24] Farmer's argumentation and debate training prepared him for the difficult advocacy of Freedom Summer and similar projects by CORE. The training of Freedom Summer volunteers in Ohio and their travel to Mississippi to work with blacks in the state broke a sense of silence prevailing in that province. The murder of the three civil rights workers was an argument by the state of Mississippi for that continued silence. In various locales of global violence such as Burma or Sudan, individuals need to communicate a sense of concern for victims. Though the practical repeal, breakdown or reform of sovereignty is always unlikely, the underlying dignity of oppressed subjects is motivated by the shared sense of concern and is the catalyst to human imagination overcoming entrenched injustice.

Less noted in the activism of Freedom Summer volunteers was the establishment in Mississippi of freedom schools. Freedom schools worked to educate young blacks about their own inherent dignity. The public school system of Mississippi was two-tiered and provided such a weak support to the intellectual development of blacks that a pattern of discrimination was insured. The education of women in Afghanistan is an example of how the initial phases of justice are embedded in the intellectual processes of education.[25] In education, the mind explores the greater possibilities of the individual within a larger world. Without education, the limited mental scope provides a viable template for the social manufacture of injustice and oppression. Propaganda and related argument forms thrive in circumstances free from education, and the mind remains small enough to accept such feeble communication. A global pattern of education needs to emerge for various individuals of creative power to unravel the limiting discursive patterns of oppressive states.

Outside intervention, like that demonstrated in the Responsibility to Protect Doctrine (R2P), also remains the provocative option for resolving statist injustice against individuals. In the case of James Meredith, forty thousand federal troops intervened against local authorities in Mississippi to create a momentary glimpse of what integrated education might look like. That world would emerge over many years and remains with us in some forms today. The use of calculated force—the threat of violence by one state against another—provides a paradoxical impetus for the progression of justice. The Taliban were not going to tolerate a public sphere or broad based social education. The government of Saddam Hussein was not going to tolerate such practices. The government of Liberia was not going to tolerate such practices. The government of Sudan was not going to tolerate such practices. In each case, some measure of forceful intervention interrupted the sovereignty of the state to increase space for individual human expression and education. The stigma presently arrayed against "war" needs to be arrayed against genocide and the various practices of systemic violence expressed by the radical statists of the twenty-first century. Mickey Schwerner had said shortly before his death that "the Federal government would have to come to Neshoba county if negroes were to have justice there." The same can be said of so many oppressed individuals around the world.

Without a full consideration and implementation of these argumentation strategies so effectively implemented by James Chaney, Andrew Goodman, Mickey Schwerner, and leaders like James Farmer Jr., the world will remain a chilling status quo for the individual dissident and minority communities in far too many States. As serious students and teachers of communication and rhetoric we need to move beyond romanticism of the past into a practical implementation of the future. Equipping voices to argue for equal human dignity globally is a morally appropriate agenda for a field of rhetoric too often seen as divorced from ethics. The world is becoming more transparent, and with this, our eyes are being opened to oppression we may not have seen before. In our universities, we have students from all over the world— many aspiring to transform their own homelands. This can be a first important step in helping students and society speak out, argue, and break the silence that hurts these victims most.

NOTES

1. Wiesel, Elie. 1986. Foreword. *The Courage to Care*. Eds. Carol Rittmer and Sondra Myers, New York: New York University Press.
2. Foucault, Michel. 1977. *Discipline and Punish: the Birth of the Prison*, trans. A. Sheridan. New York: Pantheon Books.
3. Huie, William Bradford. 1965. *Three Lives for Mississippi*. New York: WCC books.
4. McPhail, Mark. "The Price of an Apology: Richard Molpus: Rhetoric of Reconciliation" Paper presented at the annual meeting of the NCA 94th Annual Convention, San Diego, CA. Accessed May 6, 2013. http://citation.allacademic.com/meta/p256357_index.html.
5. Lewis, John. "John Lewis." *Americans Who Tell the Truth*. Accessed September 21, 2013. http://www.americanswhotellthetruth.org/portraits/john-lewis.
6. Foucault, Michel. 1977. *Discipline and Punish: the Birth of the Prison*, trans. A. Sheridan. New York: Pantheon Books.
7. Power, Samantha. 2002. *A Problem from Hell: America and the Age of Genocide*. New York: Harper Perennial.
8. Totten, Samuel and William Parsons. 2012. *Century of Genocide: Critical Essays and Eyewitness Accounts*, 4th edition. New York & London: Routledge.
9. Huie, William Bradford. 1965. *Three Lives for Mississippi*. New York: WCC books.
10. Boustany, Nora. 2007. "Iran Cited Over Execution of Minors 71 Child Offenders Are on Death Row, According to Rights Group." the *Washington Post*. June 27. Accessed May 15, 2010. http://washingtonpost.com.
11. Lewis, John. "John Lewis." *Americans Who Tell the Truth*. Accessed September 21, 2013. http://www.americanswhotellthetruth.org/portraits/john-lewis.
12. MDAH Digital Collections. 2009. "Sovereignty Commission Online Agency History," Accessed June 2, 2009. http://mdah.state.ms.us/bugle/sovcom/scagencycasehistory.php.
13. MDAH Digital Collections. 2009. "Sovereignty Commission Online Agency History," Accessed June 2, 2009. http://mdah.state.ms.us/bugle/sovcom/scagencycasehistory.php.
14. Spain, David. 1964. "Mississippi Autopsy." *Mississippi Eyewitness*. Ramparts magazine special issue. Accessed June 1, 2009. http://mdah.state.ms.us/arrec/digital_archives/sovcom/result.php?image=/data/sov_commission/images/png/cd09/068354.png&otherstuff=10|60|0|30|49|1|1|67477|.
15. James Meredith and the Integration of Ole Miss. 2002. With James Meredith, Burke Marshall, and John Doar; Moderated by Juan Williams. John F. Kennedy Library and Foundation. September 30. Accessed June 2, 2009. http://www.jfklibrary.org.
16. Molpus, Richard. 2004. Remarks By Secretary of State Dick Molpus Ecumenical Memorial Service Mount Zion Church June 21, 1989. Accessed June 1, 2009. http://www.neshobajustice.com/pages/molpus89.htm.
17. CNN. 2005. "Former Klansman found guilty of manslaughter." Accessed September 21, 2013. http://www.cnn.com/2005/LAW/06/21/mississippi.killings/.
18. Goldstein, Josh. 2011. "Think again: War." Foreign policy. Accessed August 15, 2013. http://www.foreignpolicy.com/articles/2011/08/15/think_again_war.

19. Voth, Ben and Aaron Noland. 2007. "Argumentation and the International Problem of Genocide," *Contemporary Argumentation and Debate*, 28: 38–46.

20. Abramowitz, Michael. 2013. "Does the United States Have a Responsibility to Protect." *Washington Post*. September 6. http://www.washingtonpost.com/opinions/does-the-united-states-have-a-responsibility-to-protect-the-syrian-people/2013/09/06/5decf4c0-167d-11e3-be6e-dc6ae8a5b3a8_story.html.

21. Iskandar, Abdallah. 2009. Al-Bashir and Sudan's sovereignty. Al Arabiya. March 26. Accessed May 15, 2010. http://www.alarabiya.net./

22. Lewis, John. "John Lewis." *Americans Who Tell the Truth*. Accessed September 21, 2013. http://www.americanswhotellthetruth.org/portraits/john-lewis.

23. Putin, Vladimir. 2013. "A Plea for Caution from Russia." *New York Times*. September 11. Accessed September 17, 2013.

24. *The Great Debaters*. 2007, by Denzel Washington.

25. Wilkinson, Ian. 2009. "Taliban militants in northwest Pakistan kidnapped about 400 students from a military-run college on Monday along with their teachers and relatives." *The Telegraph*. Accessed June 1, 2009 http://www.telegraph.co.uk.

Chapter Three

Discursive Complexity as a Communication-Based Moral and Ethical Framework

To learn who rules over you, simply find out who you are not allowed to criticize.—Voltaire

One of most serious problems in developing an intellectual framework for resisting the problem of genocide is the absence of a moral and ethical foundation from which to begin our conversation. In many respects, this moral absence is what makes genocide possible and persistent. At present, academic disposition is profoundly distorted by valorized notions of culture.

Multiculturalism is an intuitive and worthwhile ethical insight that intellectuals study and promote in the academy. In essence, the ethics of multiculturalism are straightforward and easy to understand: all cultures are intrinsically valuable and equally worthy. The clear moral lines drawn by multiculturalism appear to thwart one of the more central motives of genocide: to destroy an ethnic group. Multiculturalism facially rejects the subordination of ethnic groups and calls upon all interested hearers to recognize the value of any such group. Communication theory often grounds ethics as inherently subordinate to culture.[1] Ironically, this commitment and practice leads us to the present twenty-first century impasse on the question of genocide.

If a culture defines itself in terms of annihilating others, how can we in an intellectual community of multiculturalists reject this definition and its inherent practices of genocide and eliminationism? There are no easy answers and the lack of answers is now so well observed that political groups exploit this in the public conversations about genocide. Was Nazi culture essentially German culture? Was the Khmer Rouge essentially the Cambodian culture?

Are all forms of resistance to the program of cultural purity undue interferences to culture? The straightforward problems inherent in these questions slowed to a dismal crawl the initial fervor to stop genocide, observed in phrases such as "never again," after the Holocaust. If perpetrators gown themselves in robes of multiculturalism and ask intellectuals to accept the perpetrators as the sovereign arbiters of culture, what ethical resistance can intellectuals and activists offer?

Is it fair to fear that cultures may define themselves in terms of annihilating the "other"? This appears reasonable and even probable. Rhetorician Kenneth Burke observed social penchants for scapegoating in his studies of communication and group identity. [2] Groups tend to select scapegoats as a way of organizing their identities. Rhetorical processes inexorably lead to public marginalization and even genocide. Because of this feature of cultural identity, we need useful alternatives for moralizing about genocide outside of the multiculturalist point of view.

An alternative to this point of view is discursive complexity. Discursive complexity can be defined and recognized as the capacity of an individual or group to encourage and allow dissent. [3] Furthermore, discursive complexity is a principal recognizing the value of various expressed viewpoints. The notion of discursive complexity is highly contrasted with a diminished notion of discursive simplicity whereby an individual or group demands or insists upon a limited capacity of expression. Argumentation inherently valorizes discursive complexity by emphasizing the study and teaching of contrasting and competing ideas. Discursive complexity represents a moral point of view since we can prefer individuals and groups that make greater provision for free expression. Such environments encourage critical thinking and diminish the expectation and need for violence.

Discursive complexity can be a tool for moral judgment. In reviewing ethnic disputes globally, it is possible to assess and review how competing powers practice free expression. Political powers that allow free expression ought to be preferred in disputes, and powers that limit free expression should be pressured to allow greater capacities to question authorities about the use of power. The initial phases of discursive complexity can be confusing at a moral level. We may become aware of a problem because of openness and conflate our awareness with a cause. If we suddenly uncover an ongoing genocide, we may mistakenly think we have regressed. Of course the world would be better without such a known crime, but awareness is a first step toward reducing and solving the problem. Our initial awareness of a problem is not a cause but a beginning toward taking action to reduce and minimize the problem. Openness can allow advocates to ask questions and clarify the violence in various global locations.

An incident involving Andrea Mitchell reporting in Sudan is illustrative. After a public press conference regarding genocide issues in the nation,

Mitchell sought to follow government entities into a meeting among various public figures. Before she could enter the meeting, Sudanese government officials grabbed her and forcibly removed her from the meeting. Mitchell verbally protested her treatment and demanded to be present. The Sudanese officials responded: "This is not America where you have press freedom. You will not be in this meeting."[4] The silencing and repression of inquiry by the Sudanese government is a candid admission that their larger policies surrounding important questions such as Darfur are morally illegitimate. Bashir's government of Sudan cannot allow inquiry about its policies. This is an indication of low discursive simplicity.

Drawing from this example, interested parties reviewing genocide claims should take into account the discursive complexity of competing agents. In a dispute between Russia and Georgia, which side seems more open to public inquiry about the dispute? It does seem that in South Ossetia that Russia had established a propaganda state wherein the operation of a free press was impossible.[5] This distinction should modify our judgment of potentially equal states fighting one another. We should favor states and groups with more systemic openness.

In one of the most polarizing political cases in the world, Israel, this idea of discursive complexity can be effectively demonstrated. Can a person go into the Gaza strip and shout in Arabic: "Israel has a right to exist!"? Conversely, can a person go into Tel Aviv and shout in Hebrew or English: "Palestine has a right to exist!"? The sense such individuals would have in each setting about the danger they face in free expression is a moral comment upon the society they are dialoguing with in their exclamation. In those places where physical threats against the individual reduce our willingness to speak freely, the morality of that society or group is rightly in question. The open society has a greater ethical status than the closed one.

The potential use of discursive complexity was apparent in the trial of Saddam Hussein in 2006. In the trial, defense attorneys argued rather artfully that Hussein's violence was justifiable action against known assassination threats coming from a small town in Iraq. According to the defense, the violence was no different than violence meted out by American soldiers in Fallujah acting in their own defense. According to Newton and Scharf, the prosecution did win their case but failed to highlight the absence of trials for the accused when Saddam summarily killed six hundred residents of the town, including children, in an insidious show of force that gave no recourse to residents in the way of trial or appeal.[6] The absence of discursive complexity differentiates the behavior of the Iraqi sovereign and offers a measure of moral clarity.

These examples provide us with some operational clarity of how a communication concept such as discursive complexity might be used to judge international affairs. It is, however, worthy to sharpen these examples into

steady empirical points of observation. Here are some criteria that can useful-
ly be applied to societies to assess the relative strength of discursive complexity:

1. Access to the internet
2. Number of newspapers
3. Number of cell phone users
4. Number of political parties
5. Number of participants in elections

Criteria like these can become a barometer of discursive complexity. They
can indicate the political weather of a community and how free individuals
are to register disagreement with political power. These criteria are an important early warning sign regarding a possibly impending genocide. Genocide
is not a crime that any authoritarian is ultimately proud of among the larger
global population. Hiding the crime and removing the ability to dissent are
important communication pieces in the puzzle of genocide. Keeping track of
these details can make genocide both more manageable and preventable.

Organizations such as Freedom House create some empirical measures
similar to the ones listed here. Here is an excerpt of their 2013 report on press
freedom for 2012:

> Of the 197 countries and territories assessed during 2012, a total of 63 (32
> percent) were rated Free, 70 (36 percent) were rated Partly Free, and 64 (32
> percent) were rated Not Free. This balance marks a shift toward the Not Free
> category compared with the edition covering 2011, which featured 66 Free, 72
> Partly Free, and 59 Not Free countries and territories.
> The analysis found that less than 14 percent of the world's inhabitants lived in
> countries with a Free press, while 43 percent had a Partly Free press and 43
> percent lived in Not Free environments. The population figures are significant-
> ly affected by two countries—China, with a Not Free status, and India, with a
> Partly Free status—that together account for over a third of the world's nearly
> seven billion people. The percentage of those enjoying Free media in 2012
> declined by another half point to the lowest level since 1996, when Freedom
> House began incorporating population data into the findings of the survey.
> Meanwhile, the share living in Not Free countries jumped by 2.5 percentage
> points, reflecting the move by populous states such as Egypt and Thailand
> back into that category.[7]

Gallup has related survey instruments that ask the public whether they have a
free press. Here is an example from 2013:

> In fact, a third or fewer adults in the Palestinian Territories (33%), Gabon
> (32%), Chad (32%), Zimbabwe (32%), and Belarus say the media in their
> countries have a lot of freedom. Expert evaluations of media freedom fall in

line with these public opinions. Ten out of the 13 countries with the lowest percentage of adults saying their media are free are rated "not free" according to Freedom House's latest evaluations of press freedom. [8]

Reports like these and possible improvements of these measures can become an intellectual marker for discursive complexity. It is important to maintain that this principal is not limited to groups but also a consideration for each individual. Do I consider the viewpoints of others? Consideration of other points of view is an intrinsic human value that has public and individual practice. Consideration of multiple points of view tends to encourage the moral practice of empathy.

The practical implementation of discursive complexity is also important. The American political model is important and globally active. The First Amendment to the United States Constitution is a clear, compelling, and empirically successful implementation of discursive complexity. Not only for American civics but for global idealists, the First Amendment is a practical call for individuals to be free in their consideration and dissemination of opinions.

As authored in 1791 by James Madison, the First Amendment says:

> Congress shall make no law respecting an establishment of religion, or prohibiting the free exercise thereof; or abridging the freedom of speech, or of the press; or the right of the people peaceably to assemble, and to petition the government for a redress of grievances. [9]

The amendment provides for five freedoms essential to human civics: 1) religion, 2) speech, 3) press, 4) assembly, and 5) petition. Each of these clear areas provide a civic pretext to the legitimate political world. For the United States, the founders viewed the amendment process as controversial since it called into question what the source of these freedoms might be. Had the government created these freedoms or was the government acknowledging that these rights were natural and inevitable prior to the emergence of the government? The later view was certainly intended but the amendment process arguably implied that governing authorities created them. It is quite likely that the First Amendment was drafted in reference to, its primacy. It was among the first concerns founders had for a government overreaching in power against its citizens. The amendment process also suggested that some notion of correction was needed to the original text and promise of the Constitution. This history is carefully examined and considered both inside and outside the United States and its practical relation to discursive complexity is immense. Human beings have an intimate expectation of being able to communicate their needs to those in authority over them. Without such channels, it is hard to imagine how the political body could be effective in policy. Moreover, the channels of communication are an ethical predicate. The possibility of communication enables resistance, reconsideration, and reinterpretation of events. Each of these freedoms deserves some distinct elaboration. The five arguably distinct aspects of discursive complexity are listed together like five fingers on a hand. They are not listed as separate amendments to the Constitution—suggesting they have some necessary relationship. The religion clauses are the most paradoxical and the only one that is listed with two phrases: an establishment clause and a free exercise clause—"Congress shall make no law respecting an establishment of religion nor prohibiting the free exercise thereof."[10] The two phrases create a practical tension between abolishing all aspects of civil religion and removing the bounds of individual exercises of religion. Somehow the state cannot collude with the organs of religion and it cannot make laws to inhibit individual practice of religion. The founders likely knew that human thoughts about religion were among the most powerfully held in our consciousness. A careful broker was necessary in this language. This would prove decisively distinct from the French Revolution that continues to promise more of a protection from religion's public encroachment than the kind of thorough free exercise imagined and practiced in the United States. This tension remains compelling for a global community that is far more religious than secular and yet clearly torn by sectarian strife. These matters go to the heart of genocide both with regard to how religion can be politically commandeered to implement a genocide and at the same time religious communities can become the identifiable scapegoat target receiving state sponsored acts of genocide. The First Amendment phrasing mirrors the human heart's habit of seeing an authoritarian vehicle in religion and a reliable scapegoat on other occasions. Somehow human beings must be mindful of both outcomes. This delicate balance begins the narration of the Bill of Rights to the U.S. Constitution.

Freedom of speech is one of the most well-known and cherished aspects of the American Constitution. It is one of the most distinguishing international features of the American civic character. Global protests regularly invoke the expectation of a "freedom of speech." Activists and dissidents practically demand the admiration of their American compatriots for the dangerous deeds they commit in the public square of tyrannical regimes. Freedom of speech is among the most individual, innate and discrete of expectations. It is not systemic and it is not dependent on a group. One person may assert, by speech and argument, a thought that may be picked up by others. One person may, by speech, influence others toward becoming a social movement. In this respect, the freedom of speech is the initial spark of discursive complexity. Whether Lincoln at Gettysburg, King at Lincoln's feet in DC, or Mandela upon release from prison, the collective imagination of the better world is generally emancipated in the initial utterances of an individual who somehow can see that transcendent better world that should be and can describe it with such vividness that it becomes captivating and inevitable. Freedom of speech is a mysterious yet essential core to the First Amendment and any primitive notion of discursive complexity. What can one voice do? We cannot know the answer if there is no freedom of speech. In fact, the appeal is so archetypal that it is difficult to imagine how any government can fully contain its possibility as dissidents like Alexander Solzhenitsyn so ably demonstrated. [11]

Freedom of press is a third yet equally compelling aspect of First Amendment civics. Freedom of press is profoundly important to the global questions of genocide because we rely upon the eyes and ears of journalists to have some sense of what is actually happening. The number of journalists killed each year in this important communication task is staggering. Seventy-three journalists were killed in the field in 2012. [12] Because journalists pose a direct challenge to the discursive complexity of genocidaires, they are common targets. The sacrifices of journalists to open up the public space for broader conversation are pivotal for meaningful debate and civic progress. It is not surprising that freedom of press is listed in the First Amendment guarantees. Technology is simplifying and bringing the role of journalism to average citizens around the world. Anyone can report news. Instilling a broader sense of the professionalism journalists expect and reducing the prospects of being used in abusive communication processes managed by the genocidaire remains important. Freedom of press is a vital component to discursive complexity.

Freedom of assembly is so intuitive in many contemporary societies that it is hard to fathom the necessity of a political statement guaranteeing it. However, in the most closed societies, it is illegal to congregate for unclear purposes. If the authorities have not deemed a meeting appropriate, it is considered "criminal." Authoritarianism and its genocidal byproducts recognize that assembling for causes unknown to the Sovereign or unsupported are profound threats. People should be free to gather and consider their common points of view. These views may put them at odds with government power. Despite its intuitive nature, this freedom is not as common as the public tends to expect.

Finally, a freedom to petition suggests that the subjects of government power should be able to formally register concerns with the government. In my own work with government groups, there is an intuitive frustration in 'hearing the public.' Whether at a city council meeting or a legislative hearing, the public wants to be heard. In many instances what is heard is unpleasant to those governing. The dialectic of petition between the citizen and the government constitutes a check on centralized power. The apparent confusion often seen in the varied opinions of the public is arguably a check against certitude that may render decisive government action marginalizing groups to the point of violent subjugation.

All five of these First Amendment freedoms act like fingers on a hand to equip individuals to resist the worst excesses of governmental power. Despite their American inception, they remain enticing global concepts and inescapable in the conversation of expectations about ending genocide. Genocide so often needs propaganda to create a facile army to "follow orders." The principals of the First Amendment arrest that process by keeping the public sphere open.

In sum, discursive complexity is a central and vital communication-based component for improving the human condition. We can individually adhere to this ethic. We can draw international standards for measuring it. We can point to compelling historical examples like the First Amendment to derive an empirical basis for expecting this better world. Discursive complexity is a foundational principal for moving the world away from genocide and toward peaceful co-existence in difference.

NOTES

1. Shuter, Robert. 2000. "Part II. CHAPTER TEN: Ethical Issues in Global Communication." In *Communication & Global Society*, 181–90. n.p.: Peter Lang Publishing, Inc., 2000. Communication & Mass Media Complete, EBSCOhost (accessed September 14, 2013).

2. Burke, Kenneth. 1941. "The Rhetoric of Hitler's 'Battle.'" *The Philosophy of Literary Form: Studies in Symbolic Action.* New York: Vintage, 191–220.

3. Voth, Ben. 2009. "Argumentation and the International Problem of Genocide," with Aaron Noland, *Contemporary Argumentation and Debate* 28, 2007, 38–46.

4. Mitchell, Andrea. 2005. "Sudanese scuffle symbolic of disregard for own U.S.-Sudanese disagreement over Darfur region expected to continue," MSNBC. July 21. Accessed August 1, 2005. http://www.msnbc.msn.com/id/8655411/.

5. Kucera, Joshua. 2008. "The World's Worst Spies." May 22. Accessed August 15, 2013. Slate. http://www.slate.com/id/2197134/entry/2191673/.

6. Newton, M. A. and Michael P. Sharf (2008). *Enemy of the State: The Trial and Execution of Saddam Hussein.* New York: St. Martin's Press.

7. Freedom House report. 2013. Middle East volatility amid Global decline. Accessed August 15, 2013. http://www.freedomhouse.org/report/freedom-press/freedom-press-2013

8. Lee Becker and Cynthia English. 2013. "Majorities in Most Countries Perceive Their Media as Free." Gallup. May 3. Accessed August 15, 2013. http://www.gallup.com/poll/162179/majorities-countries-perceive-media-free.aspx.

9. First Amendment to the United States Constitution. 1791.

10. Religion clauses of the First Amendment to the United States Constitution. 1791.

11. Solzhenitsyn, Aleksandr I. *The Gulag Archipelago.* Harper Collins: New York. 174.

12. CPJ. 2013. "73 Journalists killed in 2012." Committee to Protect Journalists. Accessed September 1, 2013. http://www.cpj.org/killed/2012/.

Chapter Four

The Cell Phone versus the AK-47

Metaphors are captivating terms of rhetoric. They tend to make obscure and confusing topics more salient and intuitive. It is that feature that I seek to encourage in this chapter by offering two compelling metaphors to anchor the competing epistemologies of the twentieth and twenty-first centuries: the AK-47 and the cell phone. These two "shooters" are the truth telling devices of the centuries we presently straddle.

We are at an epistemological tectonic moment where the competing views of the AK-47 and the cell phone meet. In many instances, we seek to interpret "earthquakes" of the closed society meeting the open society. The cell phone and the AK-47 are both shooters and they both have a capacity for disseminating the truth. The AK-47 establishes and stands for the rule of force. The cell phone with its camera and transmission capabilities is a force of revelation. It is useful to begin this review with an example of this struggle.

The 2008 Mumbai massacre is, in many respects, a violent communicative snapshot of the two metaphors in literal competition. Ten gunmen sought to kill as many Indians as possible as part of their interpretation of Islamic supremacy. The prospective victims primarily fought back against their attackers by using their cell phones.[1] One hundred and seventy-two people were killed in the attacks. Several of them were Muslim. One prospective victim, Anthony Rose credits his cell phone with saving his life. Relaying and receiving information allowed him to seek out the best means of survival during the attack. One news report conveyed the struggle this way with regard to the one gunman caught alive:

Pictures of the young gunman wearing a black T-shirt and toting an AK-47 rifle as he strode through Mumbai's train station were published around the

world — helping to secure his eventual conviction and death sentence in
August.[2]

The disturbing power and rhetoric of AK-47s expressed itself in mass killings conducted by the radical Islamist terror group known as Al- Shabab. The
killers entered a Nairobi mall in September of 2013 and asked shoppers if
they were Muslims. Muslims were allowed to escape while others were
shot.[3] Dozens of people were killed, and more than one hundred and fifty
people were injured. Al-Shabab used their twitter account to commend the
actions and claim credit for the killings. Although their twitter account was
suspended, the group immediately created a new account. They continued to
positively interpret their violent arguments in the mall. Their twitter messages said the killings were in response to Kenyan troop participation in
attacks on Al-Shabab in Somalia.[4] In both attacks, AK-47s were used and
cell phone technology was important to the struggle. It is useful to begin our
analysis with the epistemological technology of the twentieth century: the
AK-47.

THE AK-47

The AK-47 is an assault weapon originally manufactured by the Soviet Union. It is one of the most disseminated weapons of modern warfare in the
world. There may be as many as one hundred million such weapons circulat-
ing in the world today.[5] The weapon is emblematic of a world of force
wherein the holder of the weapon stands as a symbol of the public order. Its
capacity to fire many bullets at a high rate of speed constitutes a kind of mass
media in the message of death as a text. It is possible to kill many people in a
short amount of time with this weapon. The democidal barbarism of the
twentieth century is largely recognizable in this distinctive weapon. An individual holding such a weapon is recognizable—especially to civilians who
are unarmed. There is little reasonable prospect of evading or reasoning past
what the weapon can do to the human body. The holder of such weapons has
social authority and can preside over scenes of violence. The holder of such a
weapon can enact considerable steps toward the completion of genocide. An
unarmed public knows to remain silent or to repeat the desired convictions of
the authority in face of such a weapon. It is quite clear that the AK-47 is one
of the most decisive epistemological symbols of the twentieth century. It
established the "truth" in many parts of the world. The world today remains
substantially in its shadow. In many parts of the world, the weapon continues
to communicate the order of the day in given locales.

THE CELL PHONE

The cell phone is becoming one of the most common human accessories in the world. Since the turn of the century, the growth and sale of cell phones has grown exponentially. In 2014, there are nearly as many cell phones on the planet as there are people. More people have access to cell phones than clean water or basic sanitation. The essential function of a mobile or cell phone is to enable communication. The prospects for human isolation are fundamentally reduced by this technology.[6] The communication ramifications for this technology are multiple:

1. People can communicate with a more diverse set of individuals.
2. People can resist singular narratives common to state propaganda.
3. People can compare varying interpretations of events and information rather than relying on single sources.
4. People can create visual records of events.

All of these ramifications contribute to a greater sense of discursive complexity and greater ethical possibilities. This technology allows individuals to find a better source of information with regard to many questions they might have.[7] In some of the relatively remote parts of the world, human beings have mobile/cellular technology allowing them to make communication contacts beyond their immediate setting. Questions about personal health, employment, resource access, weather risks, and many more are accessible through this portable technology. Roughly 90 percent of the developing world has access to this technology currently.[8] This compelling rhetorical reality explains the pervasiveness of the technology.

The discrete aspects of this technology aid the human push for an end to genocide. In many respects, the cell phone is the weapon of choice to an individual resisting the common systemic violence from the twentieth century. Like the AK-47 that established the epistemological foundations of the previous century, the cell phone can shoot. It can shoot pictures. These pictures can be transmitted to the world. The ability to transmit immediate images of violence to the world limits the ability of perpetrators to be anonymous or to create false narratives defending their actions. Cell phones constitute a personal form of violence repellant. Whether taking a nighttime stroll through a shadowy park or hiding out from violent militias in a forgotten corner of the globe, the cell phone can aid the holder with a sense of security. These phones identify locations and have the potential to reach any point on the earth with an immediate message. As this technology becomes more inexpensive, humanity gathers more in urban centers, and technology reaches more hands the discursive complexity of the world dramatically increases, and the ability to create the grand scapegoating narrative is diminished.

THE VICTORY OF THE CELL PHONE

The cell phone is gradually, yet dramatically winning out as the new episte-mological center for humanity. Despite the pervasiveness of the AK-47, the cell phone is saturating a far larger population of individuals. There are at least sixty times more cell phones and mobile phones distributed globally than AK-47s. The practical reach of the gun is becoming limited. Cell phones provide a basis for warning and avoiding these centers of violence. In direct clashes, the cell phone records and establishes an accurate history of vio-lence. The phone can summon means for help or means for hiding and escape. All of these capacities are shrinking the epistemological space of violence.

As a practical example, in 2007, with my work at the United States Holocaust Memorial Museum in DC, we explained to survivors and the public that only one country in the world had not logged into the website available through the museum. That country was North Korea. North Korea was and remains one of the most deadly and inhumane governments in the world— operating brutal work camps throughout its sovereign space. As a practical extension of its radical sovereignty, internet technologies is strictly limited. In 2007, the supreme leader Kim Jong Il may have been the only North Korean with any meaningful internet access. Cell phones were prohib-ited. Today, there are two million subscribers to cell phone service in North Korea.[9] The content and access of this service is highly limited by the pro-vider and the North Korean state but it remains a distinct accommodation and change from only five years previously where cell phones were banned. North Korea now manufactures its own version of an android phone.[10] Phone service costs \$300–\$600 a month in a society where the average worker makes \$90 a month. The possibility of comparing life in North Korea with life in South Korea opens up a Pandora's box of communication possibilities within the closed society of North Korea. The risk that millions of cell phone users may begin to formulate a greater basis for an open mind beyond that designed by the intensively propaganda driven state is growing. As one of the most closed societies on the planet, North Korea is a model for where the world is headed in the twenty-first century. That direction is toward greater discursive complexity and the inability of dictators to maintain a holistic political message and facilitate the passive acceptance of brutal practices like the quasi-concentration camps of North Korea. Recently, 20,000 people were known to have disappeared from these camps.[11] Nearly two million people have starved to death in North Korea since the 1990s.

The archetypal trauma of the 911 hijacking of American airliners is also illustrative of the triumph of this technology. Nineteen terrorists established sovereign intimidation and control of four aircraft filled with captive sub-jects. Three airlines were initially directed by the hijackers to strike targets in

New York and Washington DC. In the two hours of this activity, phones played a decisive role in the outcome of the final aircraft. [12] The last aircraft was commonly thought to have DC as a target but passengers on Flight 93 knew from mobile phone conversations what had happened to the other hijacked flights. Passengers realized that their passivity would gain them no release from their captors. Consequent to this new information the passengers mounted an attack on their captors that factored into the aircraft failing to reach its intended target.

In the more recent example of Arab spring, cell phones continue to play a decisive role. [13] Protesters and activists across North Africa use cell phones to record attacks and organize resistance. They also report to the world through various social media. Governments such as Egypt react to such activity by trying to shut down the internet as a means of communication. All of this indicates that the cell phone plays an increasingly central role in the emerging global politics. The cell phone is the epistemological tool of this new century and it is erasing the shadows cast by its violent rival of the past—the AK-47.

NOTES

1. PBS. 2009. "Mumbai Massacre: Background information." November 24. Accessed August 15, 2013. http://www.pbs.org/wnet/secrets/features/mumbai-massacre-background-information/502/.

2. NBC News. 2012. "India hangs only surviving gunman of 2008 Mumbai attacks." November 12. Accessed August 15, 2013. http://worldnews.nbcnews.com/_news/2012/11/21/15328783-india-hangs-only-surviving-gunman-of-2008-mumbai-attacks?lite.

3. Gettelman, Jeffrey, and Nicholas Kulish. 2013. "Gunmen Kill Dozens in Terror Attack at Kenyan Mall." *New York Times*. September 21. Accessed September 23, 2013. http://www.nytimes.com/2013/09/22/world/africa/nairobi-mall-shooting.html?pagewanted=all&_r=1&.

4. Kulish, Nicholas. 2013. "Kenya Presses Assault Against Militants in Mall Siege." *New York Times*. September 22. Accessed September 23, 2013.

5. Chivers, Chris. 2010. *The Gun*. New York: Simon & Schuster.

6. Kavoori, Anandam. 2007. "The Word and the World: Rethinking International Communication." Conference Papers—International Communication Association 1. Communication & Mass Media Complete, EBSCOhost (accessed September 14, 2013).

7. Castells, Manuell. 2007. "Communication, Power and Counter-power in the Network Society." *International Journal of Communication*, 1: 238–66. Accessed September 14, 2013. http://ijoc.org/index.php/ijoc/article/viewFile/46/35.

8. Falk, Tyler. "There are (almost) as many cell phone subscriptions as people." *Smartplanet*. 2013. July 2. Accessed August 20, 2013. http://www.smartplanet.com/blog/bulletin/there-are-almost-as-many-cell-phone-subscriptions-as-people/23353.

9. Quartz, Leo Mirani. 2013. "Mobile Phones Are Booming in North Korea, of All Places." *Business Insider*. April 26. Accessed August 15, 2013. http://www.businessinsider.com/mobile-phones-are-booming-in-north-korea-of-all-places-2013-4.

10. Dobie, Alex. 2013. "North Korea unveils Android smartphone." *Androidcentral*. August 12. Accessed August 20, 2013. http://www.androidcentral.com/north-korea-unveils-android-smartphone.

11. Palmer, Ewan. 2013. "twenty thousand prisoners 'disappear' from North Korean camp." *International Business Times*. September 6. Accessed September 10, 2013. http://

www.ibtimes.co.uk/articles/504258/20130906/20000-prisoners-disappear-north-korean-camp-22.htm.

12. Slevin, Peter. 2004. "Outside the cockpit door, a fight to save the plane." *The Washington Post*. July 24. A10. Accessed September 24, 2013. http://www.washingtonpost.com/wp-dyn/articles/A10206-2004Jul23_2.html.

13. Duffy, Matt. 2011. "Smartphones in the Arab Spring." *IPI*. Accessed September 14, 2013. http://www.academia.edu/1911044/Smartphones_in_the_Arab_Spring.

Chapter Five

The Genocidaire

The Perpetrator

Thanks to ideology, the twentieth century was fated to experience evildoing on a scale calculated in the millions. This cannot be denied or passed over or suppressed. How, then, do we dare insist that evildoers do not exist? And who was it that destroyed these millions? Without evildoers there would have been no Archipelago.—Alexander Sohlzinestin[1]

Only the French seem to have a term for the perpetrators of genocide: the Genocidaire. This linguistic limitation is significant since from a Burkean standpoint, it limits our capacity to understand the agent and the act. The habit of viewing genocides as a scenic feature is detrimental to the victims and our capacity to seek justice. Media coverage tends to emphasize the place of genocide rather than the agents and agency. Tragedies in Sudan and Rwanda leave us more familiar with the place than the crime.[2] A scene/agency ratio creates a public impression that genocide is endemic to parts of the world.[3] "Africa will always be this way." "We cannot change Somalia, Rwanda, Sudan." "This is the way of Africa." The reduction of human actions to geographical motion is a selection and, therefore, deflection of reality. Individuals have chosen to give orders to kill. Individuals have taken arms in response to arguments for the purpose of carrying out genocides. It is possible to communicate with reference to agents and agency and re-establish the agent/scene ratio.

This distinction is vital to the operation of international law. Establishing motive and action remains a critical distinction in the prosecution of genocide as a crime. So long as perpetrators can rely upon communication patterns emphasizing the scene, they will know that their identity will be limited and risk of prosecution low.

The difficult struggle over naming the Sudanese violence came to an abrupt end in 2003 when U.S. secretary of state, Colin Powell, said to the U.S. Congress that the violence in Sudan constituted a "genocide."[4] In an instant, the scene/act ratio became act/scene. The world saw at least a public argument that the government of Sudan was committing genocide. The public argument stood in contrast to the State department's careful avoidance of the term during the 1994 Rwandan genocide.[5]

A consistent pattern of communicating about violence as instigated and caused rather than serially inevitable can convert "motion" back into the ideal of "action." The genocides in Africa and elsewhere do not arise out of the soil or elements of a continent. The genocides there and around the world are the consequences of public arguments made to individuals who then carry out the crimes—whether in Cambodia, Kosovo, Rwanda, Iraq, or Turkey.

Communication and argumentation scholars and students can identify proponents of genocide. Individuals can be named and the rhetoric they employ can be critiqued. Such an application can apply in cases such as Darfur. By emphasizing and personalizing Omar al-Bashir's role in the genocide, rather than the more oblique Sudanese government, it provides accountability, incentives to responsibility, and an anticipation of reform in government. This specificity should displace the pedestrian "place is violent" pattern which encourages students of the global public sphere to believe nothing can change.

DEFINING THE GENOCIDAIRE

It is immediately useful to begin the task of defining with some precision, the genocidaire. Recognizing the characteristics of the genocidaire allows for more pre-emptive resistance and it increases the chances that political solutions can work. These are the characteristics of genocidaires:

1. They are the sovereign. Sovereign is defined when used as an adjective as: "possessing supreme or ultimate power."[6] This is to say that their utterances constitute revealed "truths" about a geographic space. Of course distributed power reduces the risk of authoritarian and democidal slaughters. Experts should recognize how individuals constitute themselves as having all power over a geographic space. International law tends to consistently reify sovereignty as opposed to the sanctity of the individual.

2. The public sphere functions to amplify and reify the good character and absolutism of the genocidaire. The public sphere might contain opinions for or against the genocidaire. An abundance of such variety suggests discursive complexity. The deformed public sphere is like a

parabolic mirror making the authoritarian leader bigger than life—
more like a god than a human being. Individuals within a system of
propaganda gain rapid appreciation of the leader being near perfection
and without rival.[7]

3. The genocidaire presides over instances of mass killing. Hundreds,
thousands, tens of thousands, hundreds of thousands, and perhaps millions will die in the geography controlled by the genocidaire. Of
course these deaths will be offered as incidental and unrelated to the
genocidaire insofar as the global public sphere is aware of such mass
death. Starvation will seem "unforeseen." Mass executions will seem
"necessary" and an elaborated form of "self-defense." Despite the
vacuity, the deaths will be real and increasingly apparent. The sensation of mass death, while hidden, will tend to elicit migration from the
domestic civilians at the outset. There will be an effort to escape. It is
these migrations and escapes that tend to call into question the collective silence of the global community.

Ultimately the use of language and public argument is important to the end of
genocide. Naming misconduct and the demonizing language of genocide
proponents is vital to the project of ending death as a text. One of the most
pivotal advocates on this question, Samantha Power, faced a brief public
crisis on the power of such words.

A LESSON IN LANGUAGE: SAMANTHA POWER

The following is a rhetorical criticism written in 2008 during the height of a
presidential election. The analysis illustrates the important power of language and the rhetorical processes surrounding the hunt for genocidaires:

In the spring of 2008, noted genocide expert Samantha Power resigned from
her campaign post as an advisor for the presidential campaign of Barack Obama. Power resigned over the controversy created when she described democratic campaign rival Hillary Clinton as a "Monster." The unfortunate excess
of candor points to a larger problem of civility in public debate and its potential connection to the problems of global violence. Ironically and sadly, Power's words undermine the important task to which she has been so consistently
and effectively dedicated—the prevention of genocide.

The urgent need for civility in American political debate is in many ways a
function of how Americans find themselves as a relatively transparent model
demonstrating how political contests should be for the world. In demonstrating
our vigorous differences we hope to illustrate to the world the great possibilities arising from such debate. Power's use of the term "monster" poses unique
problems for her and the world in the context of this American presidential
campaign. Despite all the hyperbole of American political elections—to which

Power is only a minute contributor—none of the American political candidates or the current President are "monsters." The reckless work of the tongue which Power desperately sought to retract found its way into public dialogue, and culminated in a request for her resignation. Arguably, we could be ambivalent about global attitudes regarding our political dialogue. But the fact that Power's comments arose in an interview from the European press, suggests we are dangerously naïve to suppose there is neither value nor utility in recognizing the global reach of our discussions.

The misapplication of the term raises greater problems for the larger yet significantly connected problem of genocide. Who are the "monsters" in our moral universe? Is Kim Jong Il a "monster" for presiding over the starvation of more than 2 million North Korea citizens—reducing them to the desperate task of clawing bark off trees to feed themselves? Was Milosevic a "monster" for implementing the slaughter of thousands of Muslim men on soccer fields at Srebrenica? Is Bashir of Sudan a "monster" for unleashing the crucifixion of Christians and animists in southern Sudan and now the rape and annihilation of the western communities of Darfur? Was Saddam Hussein a "monster" for dropping chemical weapons on Kurdish villages, as so eloquently and desperately described in chapter eight of Samantha Power's Pulitzer Prize winning book?

If these men, responsible for the deaths of millions of innocents are indeed "monsters," we are substantially less capable in denouncing them today with the trivial use of this term applied to an American presidential candidate named Hillary Clinton. We hurt the cause of speaking truth to power when we slander one another in American political debates ideally designed to illustrate the virtue of civility as an alternative to the ultimate discursive violence—death. As one of our nation's most articulate spokespersons for the desperate case of global genocide, professor Power has taken an unfortunate misstep that can provide a productive lesson for us all: The civility of American political debate is one of the most important global messages we send on the matters of human difference. Death is not the answer, and the road away from this violence is guided by the disciplined precision of language. This world may indeed be haunted by monsters, and our capacity to name them is a vital first step in the necessary confrontation with them. Hopefully, we can take from this small unfortunate episode of American Presidential politics, a vital lesson in how political rhetoric shapes our most compelling options in confronting the terrible human reality of genocide.

"Monsters," *American Thinker*, March 9, 2008. http://
www.americanthinker.com/blog/2008/03/monsters_by_ben_voth.html

Samantha Power serves in the Obama administration and she worked with Secretary of State Hillary Clinton to confront the true "monster" of the world. The gradual transformation of their lives demonstrates how we can each individually overcome the hurt and misguided uses of words. As the ambassador to the United Nations, her carefully tuned rhetoric makes the case for human rights questions surrounding genocide. Her missteps can be vital lessons for any student of genocide.

APPLYING OUR KNOWLEDGE OF THE GENOCIDAIRE

Those dedicated to an end to genocide in the twenty-first century, must master the identification and elaboration of the genocidaire. Our communication must progress from a scenic notion of genocides that conveys to the public a "sad scene", Genocide must become more than a place. The present fixation on places blunts the necessary and difficult task of blame. By affixing the problem of genocide primarily to a place, we invite readers and a broader public to see themselves removed from the problem. The genocide may as well be on another planet because it is over "there." Burke's insights are profound. We can change from a scene/agency perspective where the place dominates the agency of a genocide. Rhetorical ratios such as agency/act and agency/scene need to inform readers and the public increasingly aware of these crimes against humanity. [8]

In many respects, the Kony 2012 campaign was a case study in how this should work. Prior to the proliferation of the YouTube video identifying Joseph Kony as the key advocate for mass violence in Uganda and central Africa, he was largely unknown, but the idea of missing children in a place within Africa was rather understood. Focusing on his name and pressing it forward in the public conscious put Kony on the run and galvanized public policy toward reducing the violence advocated and practiced by Joseph Kony. Most experts think that Kony has fled into the sovereignty of another genocidaire: Omar al-Bashir—the sovereign of Northern Sudan. [9]

The communicative results of the campaign are striking:

> According to Visible Measures, which has been tracking the Kony 2012 campaign's progress, Invisible Children posted the full 30-minute documentary on Joseph Kony at 3:00 p.m. on March 5, 2012. Roughly 13 hours later, in the early hours of March 6, the first video response to the group's campaign was posted, meaning a reiteration of the campaign that was not just a repost of the video. By the morning of March 8, 200 clips from the documentary had been posted by users on YouTube, with an average runtime of over six minutes. Seventy million people had viewed the video, many of them posting clips on their Facebook profiles or tweeting links to the documentary. By March 12, roughly 112 million people had viewed Invisible Children's video, with thousands more retweeting it as the data came in. To give a little comparison to how fast this viral campaign has grown, Visible Measures compared the Joseph Kony 2012 campaign's success with other viral hits, from social campaigns like Evian's Live Young to the Charlie Bit My Finger Again video and Justin Bieber's music video for Baby. The idea was to compare how fast the Kony video grew, achieving over 100 million views six days after going viral, with the heaviest hitters out there. The results were uncontested: Kony 2012 had broken all the records. [10]

Studies done after this campaign suggest that while Kony remains at large, the results are positive:

> According to a joint study from Invisible Children and another non-profit Resolve, more high-ranking LRA officials left the group in 2012 than in the previous three years combined. Two high ranking officials, Major General Ceasar Acellam and Lieutenant Colonel Vincent Binansio "Binani" Okumu were removed from the battlefield. LRA killings decreased 67% from 2011 to 2012. What's more, 51 civilians were killed by the LRA in 2012, compared to 154 in 2011 and 706 in 2010. While these numbers may not sound too significant, the U.N. estimates that 400,000 people have been forced to relocate, fleeing LRA activities. [11]

These figures do not include the large numbers of individuals who have escaped the control of the LRA. Both the leadership and membership of LRA has taken a severe hit from a communication rich environment that challenges the assumptions and rhetoric of Joseph Kony. At the center of the campaign is a strategic and theoretical communication reversal—emphasizing the perpetrator of crimes rather than the scene and its victims.

Even the disappointing case of Rwanda has practical insights on how this new knowledge works positively. A woman involved in carrying out the genocide of Rwanda was recently caught and sentenced in the United States. The media identified her as a "genocidaire." She will serve time for her role in trapping and killing Tutsis during the Rwandan genocide in the 1990s. [12] If genocidaires know they will be identified and publicized for their crimes they are less likely to give such diabolical orders and public exhortations for the killing of the "other." The fact that publicity can and should go beyond the easily controlled publics they manipulate is an essential communication process to the end of genocide in the twenty-first century. In the 1990s, the world struggled to name the crime in places like Rwanda and Yugoslavia. It was, in fact, properly called genocide. Today we need to take the next step in the rhetorical war against genocide. Advocates against genocide need to name names and facilitate the rhetorical processes of identification that can allow the public to imagine the end to these deadly deaths as texts still being woven by these leaders.

NOTES

1. Solzhenitsyn, Aleksandr I. *The Gulag Archipelago*. New York: Harper Collins. p. 174.

2. Kanuma, S. 2009. Rwanda: "My proudest achievement will be to hand over power, kagame." Accessed January 23, 2009. http://allafrica.com/stories/200901210722.html; "Sudan: Darfur suffers 'worst violence in a year.'" 2009. Accessed 01/29, 2009. http://allafrica.com/stories/200901290570.html; and "UN warned of south sudan violence." 2009. Accessed 01/07, 2009. http://news.bbc.co.uk/2/hi/africa/7815367.stm.

3. Burke, Kenneth. 1969. *A grammar of motives*. Berkeley: University of California Press.

4. Weisman, Steven. 2004. *New York Times.* September 9. Accessed September 23, 2013. http://www.nytimes.com/2004/09/09/international/africa/09CND-SUDA.html.

5. Tisdall, S. 2009. "Sudan fears US military action over Darfur: Clinton warns of 'need to sound alarm' over crisis: Obama urged to keep pledge to end genocide." *The Guardian* (London) - Final Edition. January 16. p. 24; and Power, Samantha. 2002. *A problem from Hell: America and the age of genocide.* New York: Harper Perennial.

6. *New Oxford American Dictionary.* 2013.

7. Fisher, Max. 2012. "The Emperor's Speech: 67 Years Ago, Hirohito Transformed Japan Forever." *The Atlantic.* August 15. Accessed September 23, 2013. http://www.theatlantic.com/international/archive/2012/08/the-emperors-speech-67-years-ago-hirohito-transformed-japan-forever/261166/.

8. Burke, Kenneth. 1969. *A grammar of motives.* Berkeley: University of California Press.

9. Odokonyero, Moses. 2013. "Joseph Kony losing control over the LRA." *Sudan Tribune.* July 31. Accessed September 10, 2013. http://www.sudantribune.com/spip.php?article47495.

10. Jones, Melanie. 2012. "Joseph Kony 2012 Campaign Now Most Successful Viral Video In History." *International Business Times.* Accessed September 17, 2013. http://www.ibtimes.com/joseph-kony-2012-campaign-now-most-successful-viral-video-history-423988.

11. Fox, Zoe. 2013. "Kony 2012 One year later: Success or Failure?" *Mashable.* March 5. Accessed September 17, 2013. http://mashable.com/2013/03/05/kony-2012-retrospective/.

12. Simon, Natalie. 2013. "Rwandan Genocidaire convicted, sentenced in the US." *SA News.* July 16. "Accessed September 23, 2013. http://za.news.yahoo.com/rwandan-genocidaire-convicted-sentenced-us-085715475.html.

Chapter Six

Christianity as a Critical Methodology for Moral Action

Christianity has functioned for the normative self-understanding of modernity as more than a mere precursor or a catalyst. Egalitarian universalism, from which sprang the ideas of freedom and social solidarity, of an autonomous conduct of life and emancipation, of the individual morality of conscience, human rights, and democracy, is the direct heir to the Judaic ethic of justice and the Christian ethic of love. This legacy, substantially unchanged, has been the object of continual critical appropriation and reinterpretation. To this day, there is no alternative to it. And in the light of the current challenges of a postnational constellation, we continue to draw on the substance of this heritage. Everything else is just idle postmodern talk.—Jürgen Habermas [1]

Christianity is the largest popular religion in the world. With more than two billion adherents, this community of faith has several important avenues relating to the problem of genocide: 1) prospects for being victim targets of genocide, [2] 2) prospects for rationalizing and asserting genocide, [3] and 3) the potential to resist and overcome both of these undesirable outcomes. The purpose of this chapter is to articulate an intellectual and academic vision for accomplishing this third way. The commentary here should be read as less of a theological statement and more as an even secular justification for fashioning a Christian critical rhetoric that resists the social progression of genocide and some of humanity's most nefarious habits of inhumanity.

Toward the goal of fashioning a critical Christian rhetorical theory, it is useful to begin with some academic understanding of critical theory broadly. Critical theory in its most elementary form can be described as follows:

a philosophical approach to culture, and especially to literature, that seeks to confront the social, historical, and ideological forces and structures that pro-

duce and constrain it. The term is applied particularly to the work of the
Frankfurt School.[4]

Critical theory is an important aspect of communication study. The Frankfurt
School, of which Jürgen Habermas was originally a part, surmised that communication played an important role in deceiving the public toward the acceptance of assumptions contrary to the goals of the Frankfurt School.[5] False
consciousness arising from notions of capitalism and patriarchy are regularly
critiqued within the academic practices of communication study and other
fields with a goal of liberating minds toward some "truer" notion such as
socialism or feminism. As this definition suggests, our assumptions are derived from communicative processes embedded in culture and controlled by
ideology. The most common convention of academia is to treat Christianity
as an object of critical scrutiny—suggesting in most cases that the Christian
church facilitates pathological assumptions such as capitalism and patriarchy. The approach offered here is quite different and turns academic convention on its head. This analysis offers Christianity as a long-standing and
intrinsic intellectual critique of human practices. Looking at the most seminal
basis of Christian doctrine, the Bible, it is possible to understand this theological approach as critiquing two important assumptions of human societies:
1) public killing of the innocent as social argument and 2) the subordination
of women as male subjects.

It is not necessary to repeat the earlier material of this book establishing
that public killing is indeed an important feature of human life both historically and sociologically as a phenomena in present political orders.[6] It is
important to understand two additional features of this violence with regard
to this critique: 1) killing is endemic to human nature and 2) many killings
are highly symbolic and constitute public performances designed to instill
fear and control in the general public.[7]

With regard to the first feature, there is some risk, and perhaps a desperate
hope, that public killing could be isolated as a cultural or historical phenome-
non. It is, however, clear both from historical studies and anthropological
studies that the performance of public killings is intrinsic to human nature.
Regardless of tribe, culture, education, science education, wealth, or status,
human beings demonstrate a willingness to move toward the most severe of
arguments in accomplishing their rhetorical goals.[8] The most severe argument is the public killing of an innocent individual. Whether by lynching,
crucifixion, burning at the stake, beheading, stoning, or the innumerable
other methods human beings have sadistically devised toward the public
Kill,[9] human beings want their fellow community members to feel the sting
of death in a way that not only removes another individual from membership
but creates the powerful chill that limits free communication within society.
It is worth some consideration to pause on the notion of the "innocence" of

victims. In most every case, the perpetrators of violence will describe the victim as guilty. With regard to genocide, the ethnic notions of guilt are quite viable and one can be guilty of being Jewish or Tutsi. In North Korea, one can remain guilty for generations after a father or grandmother has insulted the State. In all of these cases, the perpetrators—the genocidaires—symbolize the victim as guilty.

Here we encounter practical intellectual problems with secular assumptions. Can culture be a reliable epistemological arbiter? Can a culture define an individual as completely guilty and worthy of execution? The fact that most every historical and current society does do this remains disturbing and far from reassuring. Perhaps the innocent do die and perhaps the powerful of a culture do define and provide evidence in such a deceptive way that we might better recognize many victims as truly innocent. The very processes of rhetorical designation that make these individuals guilty serves as a larger social warrant for the control of the sovereign genocidaire. We could each find ourselves at the receiving end of violence because of the extensive epistemological resources of the genocidaire to name anyone guilty. This power is suggestive of a God-like power and intersects immediately with Judeo-Christian notions of idolatry. The genocidaire substitutes himself for God. The appeal of a theological reality recognizing the transcendent innocence of the locally accused is apparent to most human consciences—secular or religious. Perhaps God knows better and has more compassion. That possibility calls into question the tenacious processes of genocide ordered by the genocidaire.

The public nature of these killings is also important. Capital punishment is an obvious and important component of this discussion that largely illustrates many of the obvious ethical concerns. The need to hide such killings is important and is a distinction worthy of rhetorical reflection. What is the difference between those who kill in public and those who kill in relative secrecy? The audacity of public killing is important and signifies the position of the killer. Society approves of a vigilante killing as indicated by actions such as lynching in the United States during the early twentieth century. Public killings tell us about the extensive nature of social warrants where a notion of a trial to test the proposition of guilt seems incomprehensible. Individuals feel they must act upon social indoctrination of prejudices to such an urgent extent that procedures and communication safeguards for verifying accusations are abolished or foresworn. This kind of social abolition is a necessary pre-condition to genocide. Public killings, which in the modern age now include common practices of relaying such violence by mobile technologies such as cell phones, tell us a great deal about how immediate the risks of genocide are within a location.

Public killings are extensive and commonplace in sovereign spaces such as North Korea, Iran, and China. Iran has struggled with this practice due to international outrage against the practice. Hangings in Iran have at times displayed bodies at the ends of nooses on cranes.[10] The cranes are located in strategic locations throughout urban centers to communicate "death as a text" to large numbers of people. The implicit message of "this could be you" is graphic and relatively continuous. This differs rhetorically from the deaths that happen in government prisons from beatings and torture. Practically speaking such deaths are similar but tend to give rise to mysterious speculation about whether the victim has died. The impressive nature of the killing is diminished by not performing it broadly in public. Iran currently performs many executions by arranging nooses at highway overpasses. Buses are parked beneath the overpass and public victims are arranged on the top of the bus to be attached to respective multiple nooses. The buses are driven away from the overpass while blindfolded victims fall from the moving bus to deaths observable to the Iranian public. These extravagant arguments of the Sovereign communicate powerfully the desired conformity and contempt for the victims.

It is possible to elaborate with unending chronology and a great range of cultures the willingness of human societies to perform such sadistic and soul emptying rituals. That is not necessary to recognize the underlying exigency to Christianity and the inherent intellectual quality of a theological perspective to call a public killing process into question. Throughout history and cultures, individual human beings have watched those that they love be killed by the local Sovereign. There remains a consistent sense of horror and hurt across culture and time. This constitutes a fundamental rhetorical exigency for Christianity.[11]

The central contention of Christianity is that an innocent being, Jesus, was killed by the Sovereign State in a public crucifixion. That is hardly surprising nor particularly ironic given human tendencies already noted. The provocative twist is that days later, Jesus allegedly rose from the dead and restored himself to a community of love. This later allegation of faith critiques the basic logic of public killing. Public killings mean that the individual and those like them are forever banished from the social contract of community. In Christianity, this is no longer true. There is indeed a "community of the beloved" that despite such killings, persists eternally on the basis of faith that this single public deed in history failed in a dramatic and public way.

In the rhetorical perspective taken here, it is less important to establish the empirical underpinnings of this story. It is more important to recognize that the problem of public killing is sufficient to give rise to a persistent social desire to overcome this rather disturbing form of argument. In order for Christianity to stop being so globally compelling—as indicated by Christianity's broad global popularity—local sovereigns would need to reduce the public killing of innocent people in order to limit the exigency of Christianity's argument.

It is important to grasp the axiological significance of the crucifixion/ resurrection story within Christianity. The resurrection calls into question the fundamental premise of public killing as a reliable epistemological tool. We cannot know that the local Sovereign is completely correct in their Kill. Hope and community can persist within a rationale of faith. The centrality of this allegation within Christianity surpasses an array of additional narrative threads that remain speculative and significant: the healing of the sick, the destruction of evil, the feeding of the hungry, the yielding of nature's power and many more. None of these peculiar events and patterns rises to the central argumentative contention within Christianity, which states that Jesus rose from the dead after being killed in public. A secular sense of why that contention is important involves more than recognizing the event as an epistemological magic trick. The suggestion is powerful because the alternative—public killing of innocents as effective argument—is too disturbing to allow. From a secular standpoint, the contention that "death has lost its sting" is meritorious at a sociological level apart from the empirical demands, if society indeed needs an alternative to human habits of public killing to anchor sovereignty. Sociological advocates can recognize the inherent critique of public killing as argument seen in the narrative of Christianity. Recognizing this argument could leave open the larger theological allegations of proof so often demanded in other intellectual venues.

CHRISTIANITY AND PATRIARCHY

Of course this first assumption is supremely important but there is at least one other important assumption that Christianity challenges: the patriarchy. Much like public killing, it is hard not to see across time and culture that men enjoy a degree of privilege and power rarely surpassed by women. The topic and practice of genocide is itself dominated by male practitioners. There is no lack of evidence and emphatic proof demonstrating the reliable power of men over women in global societies. That power displays itself in cruelty directed toward women and children. Women and children easily exist as mere property subject to the epistemological determinations of men.

Ironically, Christianity may constitute one of the more staggering developments against the patriarchy in human history. This is ironic within intellectual and academic literature since current western literatures tend to define Christianity as a source of patriarchy rather than a challenge to it. Many of those claims are warranted by empirical actions of those acting in the name of Christianity. This section of analysis proceeds directly against that academic grain. Turning directly to the Bible as a central rhetorical vehicle for the practice of Christianity, it is possible to see something quite different and derive a powerful critique of the patriarchy.

The gospels (Matthew, Mark, Luke, and John) constitute the central narratives of the life of Jesus and consequently the primary arguments about who Jesus was. The telling of these stories are, therefore, important. Luke provides from the perspective of a doctor an explanation of the life of Jesus. The story begins in chapter one with a supreme patriarchal irony. A teenage girl is to be pregnant—outside of wedlock—and carry the child of God, Jesus. Evaluating this initial writing as deliberate fiction—as many skeptics often do—this first rhetorical move by the author is disturbing. Beginning the story of Jesus with pre-pregnancy conversations between the teen girl and God hardly ushers in the sense of a masculine champion more aligned to male patterns of narrative. In fact, chapter one of Luke is a flagrant violation of patriarchal custom and law. Joseph is a relatively distant and unassuming figure. Joseph is scared and must be told by angels what to do. Unlike the teen mother, Mary, he does not sing a jubilant and triumphant song about how God is with him. Joseph considers seriously the impending social sanctions against him and Mary and wants to "put her away." From the outset of this gospel story, the argument is proceeding in a supremely ironic way against the patriarchal grain of first century cultures. A woman who should have been stoned to death for sex out of wedlock is practically gloating about her pregnancy and championing God's purpose in her life. The current fascination with the Christmas story beginning in Luke chapter two is unfortunate since it fails to appreciate the true inception offered by Luke. God worked through a woman as a central heroic figure who was strong enough to say aloud the goodness of her blessed life while pregnant outside of wedlock. The exigency of this story in the twenty-first century remains salient. Public killings of women for sex outside of wedlock remain a common public practice around the world. [12] The need to prove themselves virgins remains a pivotal cultural standard that calls into question the lives of too many women. Luke's story of Jesus' inception is profoundly "wrong" in first century Judea. It remains unacceptable in the twenty-first century sexual politics of the world. Luke's portrayal of Jesus's birth mocks the paradigmatic norms of masculine culture demanding that earthly males control the family life. Mary's ongoing strength of character and the increasing invisibility of Joseph only presses this irony further until Jesus, at his crucifixion, is looking into the eyes of one of his few remaining public champions—his mother—while he dies a humiliating death at the hands of the state.

Here again, the empirical features are less important than the peculiar choices the author makes in revealing the character of Jesus. If such things did happen, they would have been better kept secret with regard to the patriarchal order. All of this is an affront to patriarchal culture and an incitement to sexual rebellion among women who might be suspiciously pregnant with "God's child."

The persistence of the narrative favoring women suggests a broad critique of the patriarchy by the gospel writer Luke. In chapter eight, Luke explains initially how women are funding and supporting Jesus' ministry. Later in the same chapter, he explains how a woman "with an issue of blood" is healed. The rapid-fire events of healing can leave us lost on the cultural significance of Luke's choices in narration. From the standpoint of various patriarchal norms, men are inherently clean and women are inherently less clean. Menstruation and other issues of blood were determinative socially with regard to the subordination of women.[13] Women could not touch a teacher—especially while having an issue of blood. Luke suggests that Jesus asked out loud, "Who touched me?" as he passed by this woman. It is a rather peculiar question given the suggestion of crowds and Jesus trying to travel through them. The public communication involved in this event is important and critical. Jesus's public question constituted a profound dilemma since the woman could no longer privately seek a solution. Her efforts to touch Jesus's garment suggest that she was trying to be discreet. This scenario offered by Luke tends to deconstruct the patriarchal practices of that day and present gender segregation. After the woman admits she touched him, despite Peter's insistence of the absurd nature of this conversation, Jesus replies: "Daughter, your faith has made you well; go in peace."[14] The woman by almost all known patriarchal notions should have been punished and rebuked, and certainly not healed by Jesus. Here again, we should ask a scholarly question about why this detail is provided by Luke. From the standpoint of patriarchy, it would be better to leave such details out of the story. This story argumentatively challenges patriarchal assumptions and makes women view themselves as more valued and cared for by God in the midst of patriarchal crowds.

The purpose of this critical theoretical review is not to isolate a cause in the past but to illuminate present gender struggles. This point of female access to knowledge and power is not lost on the twenty-first century that we might imagine as progressing beyond such logics. Globally the practice of hymenoplasty is a common rhetorical practice designed to deceive men into believing that women are absolutely the physiological virgins that they expect and require.[15] Plastic surgeons restore the appearances and sensations of "virginity" oftentimes to thwart patriarchal expectations that exist around the world. Cultures globally continue to expect to see bloody sheets from the marital bed to prove the moral character of a newly married woman. The absence of such rhetorical indications can bring severe punishments, and even death to women.

The rhetorical signification of menstruation also remains overriding. In a 2007 court in Bagdad a woman approaches the judge to seek justice. The first question he asks is, "Are you clean?" The indirect language is a prompt about menstruation. If a woman is menstruating, she is forbidden in twenty-first century legal practice of liberated Iraq from seeking justice in a court. She must wait and return to the court "clean." Menstruation remains a taboo inhibiting female participation in the public sphere around the world. [16]

It is little wonder in the twenty-first century that Christianity continues to be popular as an argument. It is also not surprising that Christianity is more popular among women than men. [17] Christianity clearly critiques many powerful aspects of masculine power and reaches into the most intimate aspects of sexuality to offer an alternative. This alternative is rather heroic and far from passive. The most pivotal aspects of the Christian story—Jesus's resurrection—rest primarily upon the testimony of women. The testimony of women in important public questions remains problematic culturally today. Here again, if those events were accurate, gospel writers then and apologists today would be socially well served to hide the role of women discovering Jesus's resurrection, and instead leave the pivotal epistemological claim to Peter. [18] Peter, as the founder of the Church, is a practical patriarchal figure. Jesus is recorded as saying that Peter's confession would constitute the cornerstone of his church. But when we compare the characters of Peter and Mary, we find such a shocking disparity of character and will that it is difficult to believe that the gospel writers were not calling into deep question the global reliability of male leadership.

Peter flounders again and again with the most elemental aspects of faith. Peter nearly drowns walking to Jesus on the water because of his lack of faith. [19] Peter lashes out at state authorities with a sword earning a sharp rebuke from Jesus. [20] Peter denies he even knows who Jesus is three times in a public square after Jesus is arrested. [21] Mary, on the other hand, champions Jesus and remains with him through death. [22] The standard notions of male leadership in the Christian church have tended to champion the idea of Jesus choosing male disciples and building his church on Peter's confession. These conceptualizations fail to appreciate the rather evident remediation the male disciples needed in order to understand theological suppositions immediately obvious to women. Structures of male leadership arguably exist to serve the weak rhetorical hold men have upon the gospel transcendentally evident in all aspects of the gospel story. For women, the gospel story critique of public killing and feminine marginalization proves more profound and real for them than men. The exigency of Christianity is experienced most directly by women as attested by their wider participation in the faith. [23]

This cursory review of the basic aspects of Christianity and how they might practically critique dangerous human habits constitute a framework for an intellectual critical Christianity. Regardless of any individual's theological commitments, the practical interpretation of Christianity to resist public killing as argument and the marginalization of women is socially desirable.

As a critical theory, its purpose is not to establish a stable hierarchical or normative view of historical practices as they may have existed in first-century AD. The purpose of critical approaches like this one is to establish liberating functions in social meaning so that marginalized communities can more fully participate in the present. It is possible to interpret Christianity toward genocidal ends and toward patriarchal ends. This however is not ideal. A "hermeneutic of faith" rather than a "hermeneutic of suspicion"[24] can be applied not only to Christianity but all religions as a means toward human empowerment and the positive reduction of harms associated with genocide and patriarchal roots of violence. There are many other examples of how to interpret religious texts in this critical manner.[25]

This review begins to find its way back to Habermas's radical assertion about Christianity. As a former member of the Frankfurt school and lifelong proponent of relatively secular notions of critical theory, it is important to grapple with why this assertion is made. Habermas's relatively idealistic view of key communication concepts such as the public sphere, have lead to serious criticisms of his work.[26] More negative explanations of human behavior common in materialistic explanations of human conduct often attack Habermas for failing to see the limitations of his view. Habermas's dramatic suggestion that communication is a central dynamic to the "evolution" of society remains provocative.[27] Some have disputed whether Habermas even made this statement about Christianity in the original interview where it appeared. Yet when asked about this quote, Habermas does not deny it.[28]

The problems of an exclusively secular worldview are summarized more recently by Habermas:

> What puts pressure on secularism then is the expectation that the secular citizens in civil society and the political public sphere must be able to encounter their religious fellow citizens at eye's level as equals. Were secular citizens to encounter their fellow citizens with the reservation that the latter, because of their religious mindset, are not to be taken seriously as modern contemporaries, they would revert to the level of a mere modus vivendi—and would thus quit the very basis of mutual recognition which is constitutive for shared citizenship. Secular citizens are expected not to exclude a fortiori that they may discover even in religious utterances semantic contents and covert personal intuitions that can be translated and introduced into a secular discourse.
>
> So, if all is to go well both sides, each from its own viewpoint, must accept an interpretation of the relation between faith and knowledge that enables them to live together in a self-reflective manner.[29]

The communication framework of discursive complexity provides the desired self-reflective relationship for all sides—the secular and the variety of religious viewpoints at play in the global public sphere. This chapter does not resolve questions of exclusivity surrounding Christianity and other religions.

Nonetheless, the time for reconsidering religion's role in the public sphere is
now.[30] Secular critiques of power do not guarantee the humane outcomes
that we so desperately seek—such as the end of genocide. Religious belief is
so pervasive and common that theorizing about a future world of secularism
seems implausible or at least long term. Habermas recognizes that our
present progress away from violence likely depends on deep motives—arguably theological—moving more profoundly than the presently understood
secular alternatives. Recognizing Christianity as a form of critical theory can
provide practical resistance to serious global problems of public killing of the
innocent and the marginalization of women.

NOTES

1. Habermas, Jürgen. *Time of Transitions*. Cambridge, UK: Polity, 2006. 150–51.
2. Khan, Ismail, and Salman Masood. "2013. Scores Are Killed by Suicide Bomb Attack at
Historic Church in Pakistan." *New York Times*. September 22. Accessed September 23, 2013.
http://www.nytimes.com/2013/09/23/world/asia/pakistan-church-bombing.html.
3. Huie, William Bradford. 1965. *Three Lives for Mississippi*. New York: WCC books.
4. *New Oxford American Dictionary*. 2012.
5. Internet Encyclopedia of Philosophy. Accessed September 23, 2013. http://
www.iep.utm.edu/frankfur/.
6. Wilson, E. O. 2013. *The Social Conquest of the Earth*. Liveright; Goldhagen, Daniel.
2009. *Worse Than War: Genocide, Eliminationism, and the Ongoing Assault on Humanity*.
New York: Public Affairs; and Rummel, Rudolph. 2002. *Power Kills: Democracy as a method
of non-violent action*. New York: Transaction publishers.
7. Voth, Ben. 2010. "Death as a Text: State Killings as Public Argument," in Dennis
Gouran, *The Functions of Argument and Social Context*, Washington: 16th Biennial Conference, National Communication Association and the American Forensic Association, 543–49.
8. Wilson, E. O. 2013. *The Social Conquest of the Earth*. Liveright.
9. Kenneth Burke explains in *The Philosophy of Literary Form: Studies in Symbolic Action
(1941)*, how the Kill is an important end to the rhetorical process of scapegoating. In pages
40–50 he discusses how this functions as a socially communicative act. The term "Kill" is
capitalized here to signify that unique communication process integral to the genocide process.
10. Iran "public hanging" video emerges. 2011. Telegraph. July 22. Accessed September 5,
2013. http://www.telegraph.co.uk/news/worldnews/middleeast/iran/8653780/Iran-public-hang-
ing-video-emerges.html.
11. Bitzer, Lloyd F. 1968. "The Rhetorical Situation." *Rhetoric: Concepts, Definitions,
Boundaries*. William A. Covino ed. Boston: Allyn and Bacon: 1995.
12. CNN. July 2012. "Taliban shoot woman 9 times in public execution as men cheer."
Accessed August 15, 2013. http://www.cnn.com/2012/07/08/world/asia/afghanistan-public-
execution.
13. Danby, Herbert. 1933. The Mishnah. Oxford University Press. 745–57; and Keener,
Craig. 1999. A Commentary on the Gospel of Matthew. Cambridge U.K.: William B. Eerdmans Publishing:
14. Scripture taken from the New American Standard Bible with permission from The
Lockman Foundation. http://www.lockman.org/tlf/copyright.php.
15. Boras, Scott D. 2006. "Rhetorical Limitations and Possibilities of Technological Embodiment and the 'Plastic Body:' A Critical Analysis of Cosmetic Body Alteration and the
Hymenoplasty Procedure." *Electronic Thesis or Dissertation*. Miami University. Accessed on
August 20, 2013. https://etd.ohiolink.edu/.
16. Thomas, Erika M. 2008. "The Rhetoric of the Modern American Menstrual Taboo."
Electronic Thesis or Dissertation. Miami University. https://etd.ohiolink.edu/

17. Britt, R. R. 2009. "Women more religious than men." *LiveScience.* February 28. Accessed on August 25, 2013. http://www.livescience.com/7689-women-religious-men.html.

18. Luke 24: 1–12.

19. Matthew 14: 28–30.

20. John 18: 10.

21. Matthew 26: 74–75.

22. John 19: 26–27.

23. Britt, R. R. 2009. "Women more religious than men." *LiveScience.* February 28. Accessed on August 25, 2013. http://www.livescience.com/7689-women-religious-men.html.

24. Ricoeur, Paul. 1975. *The Rule of Metaphor: Multi-disciplinary studies of the meaning in language.* Buffalo: University of Toronto Press.

25. Voth, Ben. 2007. "Toward a Critical Christian Rhetoric" Paper presented at the annual meeting of the NCA 93rd Annual Convention, TBA, Chicago, IL, Nov 15. Accessed September 12, 2013. http://citation.allacademic.com/meta/p191658_index.html

26. Palczewski, Catherine Helen, and John Fritch. 2013. "INTRODUCTION." *Argumentation & Advocacy* 49, no. 3: 228. Communication & Mass Media Complete, EBSCOhost (accessed September 14, 2013).

27. Habermas, Jürgen. 1979. *Communication and the Evolution of Society.* Beacon Press.

28. "Habermas on Christianity and Liberalism." 2008. *YouTube.* October 8. Accessed September 24, 2013. http://www.youtube.com/watch?v=SjfBqMlr4rk. A tremendous debate surrounds this quotation on the internet. There exist such a variety of secondary citations for the quote, along with a failure of Habermas to deny the quote, as found in this audio question to Habermas, that the quote is deemed reliable for a basis of discussion in this chapter.

29. Habermas, Jürgen. 2008. "A post-secular society: What does that mean?" *Dialogues on Civilizations* RESETDOC. Accessed September 5, 2013. http://www.resetdoc.org/story/00000000926.

30. Platt, Carrie Anne, and Zoltan P. Majdik. 2012. "The place of religion in Habermas's transformed public sphere." *Argumentation & Advocacy* 49, no. 2: 138–41. Communication & Mass Media Complete, EBSCOhost (accessed September 14, 2013).

Chapter Seven

Islam and the Rhetorical Construct of Islamophobia

All of us here today understand this: We do not fight Islam, we fight against evil.—President George W. Bush [1]

One of the most severe communication problems facing humanity in the twenty-first century is the achievement of a better understanding of Islam that will mitigate and reduce the risks of genocide. As the world's second largest religion, the risks are not unlike those noticed with Christianity. In fact, for all religions and thoughts, there is a risk of being eliminated and being the eliminator or genocidaire. The unique and distinct aspects of this generic problem deserve attention for Islam. One of the most significant problems hindering the emergence of a better understanding that reduces the risk of genocide for Muslims and non-Muslims is the intellectually constructed notions of Islamophobia under which we now labor. The long standing intellectual tradition of caution surrounding criticism of those espousing violence from an Islamic point of view needs careful reconsideration.

Criticism of individuals engaged in violence perhaps derived from an interpretation of Islam is often categorized as Islamophobia. From this intellectual standpoint, removing all criticism of negative public behavior of Muslims will eventually purge a cycle of fear that produces the common byproducts of terroristic violence well known throughout most of the world. Intellectuals controlling this flawed notion of Islamophobia condition communities to self-censor their concerns. Here in the United States, a disturbing case of violence against U.S. soldiers at Fort Hood Texas has been categorized as "work place violence" rather than as terrorism or an action of Islamic violence. [2] In Britain, Muslim violence is journalistically re-coded with terms such as "Asian" or "from South Asia" to blur and confound possible public interpretations that Islam plays a role in reported crimes or violence.[3] In the United States, Britain and elsewhere, the consistent re-coding of events to prevent potential backlash of hate crimes against Muslims appears on the surface to make sense.

Ironically, this interpretation—envisioned to protect Muslims from discriminatory or even violent backlashes—may hurt Muslims most. Our allies within Islam who support the ethical principal of discursive complexity are quite liable to face the vigorous death as text arguments against their perceived moderation. The Islamic radicalism that expresses itself in the form of terrorism and other forms of social intimidation hurts Muslims most. In the case of the Fort Hood shooting, re-coding the events as "workplace violence" from the paternal standpoint of preventing a public backlash ignores the direct victims of the violence at Fort Hood—who may or may not be Muslims themselves—and confers an aura of mysterious power to those globally who agree with Hasan Nidal's violent message expressed through his gunshots. Muslims are sidelined from a conversation about Nidal's interpretation of Islam, which he repeatedly expressed publicly as being incompatible with service in the U.S. military.

A new rhetorical framing of Islamic violence would recognize that Muslims are the foremost victims of the violent misinterpretations of this religion. The original liberation of Afghanistan in 2001 by the United States did not wrest control away from local Muslims and give it to non-Muslims. The Taliban were not directing their violent practices exclusively or even predominantly toward non-Muslims. Muslim women and children face the brunt of the supremacist interpretations offered by the Taliban and are evident in the relatively mild acts of violence like throwing acid in the faces of Muslims.[4] In Somalia, the Islamic supremacists Al- Shabab engage in the same deadly forms of argument—even burying teen-age girls up to their necks and then publicly killing them with stoning for crimes perceived, such as adultery.[5] The false rhetorical framing of protecting Muslims by hiding the sourcing of supremacist arguments impedes a critical process that must necessarily wrest Islam away from violent handlers. We must empower Muslim voices that affirm discursive complexity in the midst of violent supremacists who may denounce them as theological traitors.

A new rhetorical framing of these violent practices should acknowledge that on Friday afternoons around the world, men with violent visions interpret Islam in a way to favor their own power and ultimate capacity to marginalize and destroy those who disagree with them.[6] The political sensitivity built up around the thousands of lives lost in this question since 9-11 and before makes a new rhetorical frame challenging and daunting. We need to understand that the current flawed rhetorical model of "Islamophobia" poses the greatest risk and harm to Muslims themselves and does not advance toward a dialogue bounded by critical thinking and argument—greater discursive complexity. In an effort to move this communication process forward, some useful analogies are helpful. These analogies are designed to highlight and emphasize the themes of this book dedicated to reducing the risk of genocide by emphasizing that it is our communication habits that lead us to ultimate harm. It is not ethnicity, religion, gender, or some other human characteristic that leads us to genocide. It is our peculiar certitude that generates demands of annihilation known as genocide. By reforming our communication habits, we can arrest and reduce the global problems of genocide. The development of Islamic critical perspectives like the one outlined for Christianity is possible but not the focus of this chapter. In an appendix of this book, Shia Muslim student Basma Raza develops an initial empathetic framework for understanding dissident perspectives within Islam. In this chapter, I will examine some important historical analogs that can help us correct our currently narrow and endangering perspectives toward Islamic supremacism.

A first analogy is relatively contemporary and involves the practice of Shintoism. Shintoism was and is a relatively small religion among the various religions of the world. Though Shintoism is often described as a cultural practice, its primacy in Japanese culture and larger traditions of religious study have consistently placed it in lists of world religions.[7] It is not the purpose of this discussion to change or decide that rather important distinction between cultural practice and religion. Regardless of categorization, Shintoism as a social practice was and remains an important source of meaning in the world today. The favored people of Shintoism are the Japanese. An interpretation of Shintoism arose. It is important to pause here because we encounter in this short sentence the precise emergence of a problem that can be seen throughout religious practices globally. Religions are interpreted. How religions provide meaning socially is derived by *interpretations* that individuals make. This is not to say or problematize that God may ultimately speak or message meaning. It is to say that human beings interpret theological sources variously and are capable of grand misinterpretations. Interpretations of various religions are always arising. Sometimes the interpretations are good and sometimes they are bad. We must all be willing to face honestly the difficult task of recognizing when interpretations are bad without the fear that we are automatically essentializing an entire point of view. Earlier we established a principal of discursive complexity that provides a compelling guide for pursuing this important judgment.

Returning to the example of Shintoism—an interpretation of Shintoism arose that held that the emperor was essentially the God of Japan. Around this emperor began a military establishment dedicated to defending the notion and even asserting it beyond the island of Japan and onto the continent of Asia. By the end of World War II, decades of this interpretation lead to death as a text being articulated to more than twenty million people from

Korea to China.[8] The vicious interpretation of Shintoism produced dangerous deadly genocidal results for Asia that arguably surpassed the violence in
Europe being done through the lens of violent interpretations of German
nationalism.[9] The peculiar devotion to the Japanese Emperor, nurtured by
propaganda, created a rhetorical expectation that all one hundred million
Japanese subjects would die in suicide defense of his sovereignty.[10]

The hurricane-like rhetorical insularity of the emperor seemed to wind
tighter and tighter toward the end of the war in 1945. The diminishing sense
of discursive complexity revealed itself in the form of suicide or kamikaze
attacks. The devotion of Japanese military men expressed itself with radical
loyalty. In contemporary parlance, we might be tempted to ask an essentialist
question: Is Shintoism inherently violent and dangerous? That question
would badly miss the point. Shintoism had no profound relationship to the
questions of violence faced by the world in the mid 1940s. The *interpretation*
of Shintoism had everything to do with the questions of violence faced by the
world.[11] That inescapable communication maxim must be our guide out of
genocide questions rooted in relationships with all religion. The ultimate
surrender of Japan pivoted on at least one culturally intimate and difficult
question: Who is the emperor of Japan? The question was less one of basic
recognition and more a question of function. Admitting that the Emperor was
not God and that he was a human was the essential rhetorical catalyst that
energized the suicide clique surrounding the emperor for purposes of defeating this suggestion of mere humanity. That logic was apparent in the coup
attempts against the emperor as he began to takes steps toward surrender.

Shintoism continues as a cultural practice today. However, the urgency
and anxiety of violent misinterpretations is greatly diminished. The concerns
are certainly not fully abated on the continent of Asia, but the world observes
Shintoism as a rather different and more discursively complex interpretation
of Japanese life. The idea of Shintoism as inherently or essentially committed
to violence appears distant.

By way of analogy, Islam as a community must be supported in a quest
for more discursively complex interpretations. The motive for this interpretation need not be rooted in the needs of non-Muslims, but Muslims themselves. Like Shintoism, the various interpretations of Islam presently allow
for genocidal assaults on Muslim minorities such as Shia in places like Bahrain and elsewhere. It is unlikely that ultimately any Muslim can meet the
interpretive standards argued for by Al Qaeda, Hezbollah, Al-Shabab or any
number of supremacist groups using Islam as a basis for their radicalism.
Ultimately, all Muslims are jeopardized by these radical rhetorics.

A second useful historical analogy surrounds the political relationship
between the Barbary pirates of North Africa and early colonial America. This
relationship produced a compelling case study in how the rhetoric of religion
is managed in the public sphere. The events of more than two hundred years

ago suggest a steady basis for religious interpretations and the unique diffi-
culties of managing religious interpretations in any setting. From the standpoint of colonial America, the attacks of Barbary pirates from North Africa
were exacting an excruciating financial toll on ships traveling in the Mediterranean. The pirates viewed all commercial ships in the Mediterranean as "fair
game" in an elaborate extortion scheme that would trade captured ships for
ransoms paid by host governments. For the young sovereign government of
America, the problem of piracy was pernicious and difficult to manage. In
short order, the American government was paying much of its small $7
million dollar treasury to the pirates. As ambassador to France, Thomas
Jefferson met an emissary for the pirates and derived the following conclusion which he reported to U.S. Secretary of State John Jay:

> The ambassador answered us that [their right] was founded on the Laws of the
> Prophet, that it was written in their Koran, that all nations who should not have
> answered their authority were sinners, that it was their right and duty to make
> war upon them wherever they could be found, and to make slaves of all they
> could take as prisoners, and that every Mussulman who should be slain in
> battle was sure to go to Paradise. [12]

This was Jefferson's conclusion after speaking to Sidi Haji Abdul Rahman
Adja, Tripoli's envoy to London, in 1786. Ultimately, this conflict would
seek resolution in the form of a treaty. In the treaty, American diplomats
assured the government in Tripoli that:

> As the government of the United States of America is not in any sense founded
> on the Christian Religion—as it has in itself no character of enmity against the
> laws, religion or tranquility of Musselmen—and as the said States never have
> entered into any war or act of hostility against any Mehomitan nation, it is
> declared by the parties that no pretext arising from religious opinions shall
> ever produce an interruption of the harmony existing between the two coun-
> tries. [13]

The treaty constituted a rhetorical assurance that though the pirates interpreted American vessels as being from a Christian nation, this was in fact,
not the case. The government was not founded on the Christian religion and,
therefore, America and her mercantile vessels had no necessary conflict with
Muslim pirates of North Africa. It was an effort to persuade the pirates to
stop attacking the shipping of Americans in the Mediterranean. Jefferson
sought to better understand the pirates by gaining an English copy of the
Koran. His copy from England was among the first English translations of
the holy book typically provided in Arabic. Though often construed as a
gesture of intellectual deference, Jefferson likely sought the copy as a means
of reasoning with the political adversaries in North Africa. The treaty was a

major rhetorical strategy toward persuading the pirates to stop their attacks. Ultimately, the pirates were not convinced that "the United States of America is not in any sense founded on the Christian Religion," because the attacks continued. Ultimately, as President of the United States, Jefferson would order the newly constituted U.S. Marines to go and sack the pirate bases at Tripoli. The effort is commemorated to this day in the Marine Battle hymn that intones "from the halls of Montezuma to the shores of Tripoli."

The protracted rhetorical exchange and argument between American and North African emissaries and institutions is illuminating to the interpretations of the Islamic world today. Interpretations of Islam in the late eighteenth and early nineteenth century held that the financial plundering of non-Muslim vessels was both politically legitimate and desirable. In fact, similar acts of piracy continue to this day from parts of northern Africa.[14] The struggles predated the more recent practices of colonialism and other forms of political structuralism that are often asserted as "underlying causes" of violence between various parts of global sovereignty. To some extent, it is possible that base motives of profit encourage the "interpretations of Islam" that lead to the practice. This historical anecdote suggests the following key implications toward interpreting Islam today:

1. Violent struggles between Muslims and non-Muslims is not historically unique or limited to the present time.
2. The causes of these struggles cannot be located or limited to more recent historical phenomena such as colonialism, globalization, climate change, or American hegemony.
3. Secular avowals are not a clear means of political insurance against violent attacks rooted in religious interpretation.
4. Religious based argument was an important component of these conflicts.

Noted author on these events, Joshua Londons, explained: "It's a little bit ludicrous to say religion doesn't enter into it if everyone at the time understood religion was a factor."[15] Here again the complexity of Islam is evident. While the government of Tripoli offered Islam as its reason, American forces that attacked Tripoli were composed of Christians and Muslims.[16] With every religion, there exists a complex array of interpretations, and these are often dedicated to political outcomes such as the practices endorsed by the government in Tripoli. American forces attempted regime change in 1802, but were ultimately content with another peace treaty with Tripoli. Rendering the conflict only as a battle between Christianity and Islam fails to appreciate the rhetorical complexities of religious arguments on both sides and their inherent relationship to struggles today.

MISINTERPRETING ISLAM

The flood of information and the increasing vividness of international politics lend itself to considerable confusion and misunderstanding about Islam and global politics. In teaching about these topics on college campuses, I have found several insights helpful to promoting discursive complexity and higher-level debates for all concerned communities. These are lecture concepts that I raise in international communication classes:

1. The two largest Muslim countries by population are not in the Middle East.

I sometimes challenge students to name the largest Muslim countries by population on quizzes. This is fairly difficult for most to do, and rather surprising given all the controversy surrounding Islam in twenty-first century politics. Indonesia and India are the two largest countries by population for Islam. Both countries have distinct interpretations of Islamic practice that inherently encourage a consideration of discursive complexity surrounding the religion rather than the monolithic views that tend to dominate our current headlines. Indonesia practices Islam in a way that allows for cross-dressing males in beauty pageants. [17] That does not prevent non-indigenous Muslims from objecting, but the practice does call into question what "normative" Islamic interpretations are. India is interesting because it is not predominantly Muslim despite having the second largest population in the world. Consequently, India's struggle over Islam and politics is much larger and longer than that with the West. Their struggles call into question common East/West conceptualizations of Islamic politics offered by thinkers such as Edward Said. [18] Both countries are good starting points for complicating rather than over-simplifying Islam.

2. America has made profound political sacrifices to help Muslims.

Like many genocidal ideologies, Islamic radicalism utilizes scapegoats to manipulate its audience. America and Israel are the nearly literalized devils for the genocidal leaders of this movement. Because this demonization is so apparent and operant globally, it is important to know how to deconstruct this rhetorical action. After a young Jordanian man was arrested in Dallas for attempting to blow up the largest building in the city in 2009, I asked my debate class if they could think of any good things the United States has done for Muslims. I pressed this question because I wondered if they had encountered the grievance-inspired man, could they reason with him not to destroy the building. The class was largely unable to offer reasons. That led to lectures and an article about what America has done for Muslims. Of course the Koran does not say anything about how Muslims should feel specifically about America. That is an interpretive question. The list of ten things America has done for Muslims include:

1. The largest global aid package in the world to Indonesia in the aftermath of the deadly tsunami.
2. The creation of a Muslim community in Europe through military force known as Kosovo.
3. The liberation of Kuwait by military force from the secular Baathist government of Saddam Hussein.
4. The largest economic transfers of wealth in human history in the form of free trade for oil that provides nearly $1 trillion per year to largely Muslim countries.
5. Violating international law to rescue Muslims being slaughtered at Srebrenica in Yugoslavia.
6. Removing secular Baathist Saddam Hussein from power in 2003 to allow the installation of a predominantly Shia Muslim government.
7. Billions of dollars in annual private remittances provided by domestic Muslims to their home communities in the Islamic world.
8. The war against the Taliban in 2001 removed a government that violated the human rights of Muslims in Afghanistan.
9. The U.S. War on Terror killed Islamic Supremacists in Yemen, Somalia, the Phillipines and elsewhere who often focused their killings on unorthodox Muslims.
10. The Unites States guarantees and observes freedom of religion for Muslims inside the United States in contrast to many Islamic theocracies that punish both the practice and conversion to other religions with death. [19]

All of the positive outcomes listed constitute not a normative stance, but an opportunity for debate on the question of America and an Islamic interpretation. Without this information, the vacuum invites supremacists to dictate the initial terms of conversation and bypass discursive complexity. In many instances, like the one in Dallas, individuals are manipulated by way of the internet to a one-sided conversation about global political realities. Every student of genocide should be able to consider multiple sides of a question.

The fact that individual Muslims today and yesterday object to and resist theocratic implementations of Islam is an important clarification to the present public concern about Islam. [20] The solution of discursive complexity that encourages complex views of the question and recognizes the inherent aspiration of individuals to be free in their interpretations is apparent and necessary. [21] The appendix essay provided by Basma Raza in this book is an important step in that direction.

Both of these historical anecdotes deconstruct a monolithic view of Islam or any other theocratic system of thought. The rhetorical assumption of theology to deprive individuals of interpretive options is a pattern leading to danger and necessarily human violence. Recognizing the dissidents within such patterns is important in constraining the genocidal response impulse. "All of this religion must go or be destroyed." Such a view is not compatible with discursive complexity or general human well being. Nonetheless, the rhetoric couched in religious language—Islamic or not— that requires ethnic annihilations or subordinations must be confronted specifically and challenged. These challenges can take place at the individual, social, political, and geopolitical levels.

SAMPLE RHETORICAL CRITICISM

The following is an example of rhetorical criticism offered to encourage discursive complexity within the interpretation of Islam. The piece analyzes re-emergent anti-Semitism and its use in various global locales under the guise of promoting an interpretation of Islam. This essay was published in 2009 by the National Communication Association's Communication, Research, and Theory Network in response to an academic presentation of anti-Semitic arguments in a professional listserv. The title, "Hitler's Battle Part 2," refers to Kenneth Burke's well known essay "Hitler's Battle":

> Elie Wiesel famously observed that what hurts victim most is not the physical cruelty of the oppressor but the silence of the bystander. This past week CRTNET published to its listserv a plainly anti-Semitic piece regarding Jewish control of global affairs. This allegation is an ancient and deadly piece of rhetoric that many hoped had reached its nadir in the Holocaust. As a communication and argumentation scholar I have continuously believed that in some sense we were collectively humanity's firehouse—ever ready to pour water on the raging infernos of rhetoric that could so easily destroy human life. Its not simply the silence of our discipline but the fact that we now seem to have so many arsonists who delight in fanning the flames of human hatred so innocent human beings can be incinerated. The silence of our community on global anti-Semitism is deafening, Thursday noted genocidaire Omar al-Bashir, the Sovereign leader of Sudan said the following: "There is one battle—in Darfur, in Iraq, in Gaza, in Somalia, in Afghanistan—against the Jews and we are fighting one enemy."[22]
>
> In the world today, David Duke and far too many others know that there is only one enemy in the world. Consequent, to this misguided rhetoric, the incitements and acts of violence against Jews continue. The passivity of our discipline accentuates its ascendancy in Europe and the indispensable role it plays in Islamic radicalism. We are content to bide our time until something catastrophic happens.

Of course speaking out is complicated. Presently, hundreds of Palestinians have died and are dying in the Gaza strip. If we speak out against anti-Semitism, are we devaluing those lives? No.

Hamas, Hezbollah and the radical Shia government of Iran have developed a new bullet proof rhetorical armor. Shahid. Any innocent woman or child who dies in the war against the Jewish state has glorified Hamas's interpretation of Allah. Hamas fighters have this past month gone into hospitals and shot "traitors" at point blank range as they lay in hospital beds. [23] Throughout much of the world, it is easy to bring violence to a human being by suggesting that they "collaborate with Jews." The death of innocents in Gaza is part of the reification of Hamas and their profound militant counterparts. The reason Hamas initially annihilated Palestinian Fatah members and their families when Hamas took power was because of their perceived failure to fight against the Jewish state.

Anti-Semitism like we see from David Duke is sadly not eccentric or even unusual. It is globally normative. It is reasonable. The fabric of its reasonability has been created by our silence and refusal to criticize it for the bigotry that it is. Anti-Semitism is a reliable rhetorical trope that can rescue any foreign leader from the exigence of criticism. Whether Hugo Chavez, Ahmadinejad, or Bashir, the common enemy of the Jews makes all abuses of human dignity a delightful sacrifice in our common struggle against the Enemy.

Until communication and argumentation scholars are willing to step forward and rhetorically pierce the armor of anti-Semitism, the innocent will be strapped to the chests of human aggressors eager to annihilate "Jewish collaborators." Global rhetoric spins on an axis connected by two points: hatred of the Jewish state and hatred of the demonic collaborator—the United States. This week Iranian protestors have already burned large posters holding the image of President-Elect Barack Obama. [24] Those protests are carefully instigated and conducted by the government of Iran. The government of Iran believes, just as David Duke, that the one essential evil in our world is the Jewish state of Israel. Among 192 nations there are dozens of ethnic-religious states, but there must not and cannot be even one small Jewish nation. If appealing to multiculturalism can accomplish this erasure, then let anti-Semitism ride on its back.

In personally working with Jewish Holocaust survivors, I know they actually hold back from the full explanation of anti-Semitism—particularly as it relates to Israel. The perverse conspiratorial logic that envelops these public servants remains astounding to me despite its pedantic patterns. As someone not of the Jewish background, it shocks me to see how mild the public sphere is about such apparent bigotry.

Kenneth Burke's article, "Hitler's Battle" is not a great article simply because it was accurate. It was a great article because it was timely. He spoke prior to the inception of a profound moral tragedy that began not as militarism but as rhetoric. We as scholars can do more to help humanity out of its lowest points. What I read on Thursday on CRTNET was demoralizing. Anti-Semitism is used as a rhetorical trope to kill Palestinians, Sudanese, Lebanese, Americans, Somalis and an array of other innocent human beings.

The painful irony noted by others about this being attached to a call for hate speech syllabi is an indication of our disciplinary detachment. We can do much better.

NOTES

1. "Remarks by President George W. Bush to the Warsaw Conference on Combating Terrorism." November 6, 2001. http://georgewbush-whitehouse.archives.gov/infocus/ramadan/islam.html.

2. New York Post. 2012. "Fort Hood: diversity rules." October 29. Accessed September 15, 2013. http://nypost.com/2012/10/29/fort-hood-diversity-rules/.

3. Fisk, Robert. 2013. "We British go out of our way to avoid using the word 'Muslim.'" *The Independent*. July 7. Accessed September 15, 2013. http://www.independent.co.uk/voices/comment/we-british-go-out-of-our-way-to-avoid-using-the-word-muslim-8693702.html.

4. Brinkley, Joel. 2010. "Why the Taliban is killing unarmed Muslims." *San Francisco Gate*. November 7. Accessed September 15, 2013. http://www.sfgate.com/opinion/article/Why-the-Taliban-is-killing-unarmed-Muslims-3167043.php.

5. Gettelman, Jeffrey and Nicholas Kulish. 2013. "Gunmen Kill Dozens in Terror Attack at Kenyan Mall." *The New York Times*. September 21. Accessed September 23, 2013. http://www.nytimes.com/2013/09/22/world/africa/nairobi-mall-shooting.html?pagewanted=all&_r=1&.

6. Williams, Ian. 2007. "Death to America." *NBC News*. March 17. Accessed September 15, 2013. http://dailynightly.nbcnews.com/_news/2007/03/17/6536180-death-to-america?lite.

7. BBC. 2011. "Shinto at a glance." Accessed August 15, 2013. http://www.bbc.co.uk/religion/religions/shinto/ataglance/glance.shtml.

8. Spitzer, Kirk. 2012. "Japan is still not sorry enough." *Time*. December 12. Accessed September 15, 2013. http://nation.time.com/2012/12/11/why-japan-is-still-not-sorry-enough/.

9. Kennedy, David. 1998. "The Horror: Should the Japanese atrocities in Nanking be equated with the Nazi Holocaust?" *The Atlantic*. April 1. Accessed September 23, 2013. http://www.theatlantic.com/magazine/archive/1998/04/the-horror/306532/.

10. Fisher, Max. 2012. "The Emperor's Speech: 67 Years Ago, Hirohito Transformed Japan Forever." *The Atlantic*. August 15. Accessed September 23, 2013. http://www.theatlantic.com/international/archive/2012/08/the-emperors-speech-67-years-ago-hirohito-transformed-japan-forever/261166/.

11. Rummel, Rudolph. 2004. Death by Government. London: Transaction Publishers.

12. Rizvi, Ali. 2103. "An Atheist Muslim's Perspective on the 'Root Causes' of Islamist Jihadism and the Politics of Islamophobia." *Huffington Post*. May 3. Accessed August 25, 2013.

13. "Treaty of Peace and Friendship, Signed at Tripoli." November 4, 1796, Accessed August 25, 2013. http://avalon.law.yale.edu/18th_century/bar1796t.asp.

14. Crompton, Paul. 2013. "Mideast task force needed to fight Somali piracy, says expert." *Al Arabiya*. September 13. Accessed September 23, 2013. http://english.alarabiya.net/en/News/middle-east/2013/09/17/Mideast-task-force-needed-to-fight-Somali-piracy-says-expert.html.

15. Drye, Willie. 2005. "Pirate Coast Campaign was U.S.'s First War on Terror, Authors Say." *National Geographic*. December 2. Accessed September 1, 2013. http://news.nationalgeographic.com/news/2005/12/1202_051202_pirate_coast_2.html.

16. Dwyer, John. 2005. "No subsitute for Victory." *American Thinker*. November 24. Accessed September 1, 2013. http://www.americanthinker.com/2005/11/no_substitute_for_victory.html.

17. Kortschak, Irfan. 2007. "Defining Waria." *Inside Indonesia*. October–December. Accessed September 16, 2013. http://www.insideindonesia.org/weekly-articles/defining-waria.

18. Said, Edward. 2003. *Orientalism: Western Conceptions of the Orient*. London, UK: Penguin Books.

19. Voth, Ben. 2010. "Top ten things America has done for Muslims." *American Thinker.* Accessed   September   15,   2013.   http://www.americanthinker.com/2010/08/ top_ten_things_america_has_don.html.

20. Rizvi, Ali. 2103. "An Atheist Muslim's Perspective on the "Root Causes" of Islamist Jihadism and the Politics of Islamophobia." *Huffington Post.* May 3. Accessed August 25, 2013; and Avraham, Rachel. 2013. "Prominent Muslim doctor speaks out against radical Islam." *The Jewish Press.* September 16, 2013. Accessed September 16, 2013. http:// www.jewishpress.com/blogs/united-with-israel/prominent-muslim-doctor-speaks-out-against-radical-islam/2013/09/16/.

21. Ali, Hirsi. 2013. "Ayaan Hirsi Ali: The Problem of Muslim Leadership." *Wall Street Journal.* May 27. Accessed September 15, 2013. http://online.wsj.com/article/ SB10001424127887323475304578503613890263762.html.

22. "Sudan Bombs Darfur Rebels." 2009. *Agency France Press.* January 14. Accessed March   10,   2009.   http://www.google.com/hostednews/afp/article/ ALeqM5jiSwZhWIQAzCfAKGGGi4GK2RUH0g.

23. Bronner, Ethan, and El-Khodary, Taghree. 2008. "No Early End Seen to 'All-Out War' on Hamas in Gaza." *International Herald Tribune.* December 29. Accessed September 10, 2013. http://www.iht.com/articles/2008/12/29/mideast/gaza.php.

24. "Iranian protesters back Gaza and burn Obama pictures." 2009. Reuters. January 13. Accessed   September   15,   2013.   http://uk.reuters.com/article/UKNews1/idUKTRE 50C4IQ20090113.

Chapter Eight

Global Anti-Semitism

The Persistent Genocidal Trope

There is one battle—in Darfur, in Iraq, in Gaza, in Somalia, in Afghanistan— against the Jews and we are fighting one enemy.—Omar al-Bashir, the sovereign leader of Sudan, speaking in 2009 [1]

The issue of anti-Semitism is increasingly salient and critical to our global community and the larger questions surrounding genocide. Anti-Semitism is conventionally thought of within American circles as an archaic and idiosyncratic bigotry. Despite our cultural and intellectual triumphalism over the Nazis, there is increasing evidence of a new and virulent contemporary anti-Semitism. This chapter provides a current review of an increasingly significant global argument. The symbolic assignment of dangerous traits to the ethnic and religious community of Jews is being rapidly and significantly deployed in a variety of global circumstances and rallying forces of oppression and repression.

In 2006 and 2007, I worked as a public speaking consultant at the United States Holocaust Memorial Museum, working with Holocaust survivors toward improving their public voice. This project started shortly after the President of Iran began emphasizing publicly and politically his firm belief that the Holocaust did not happen. Moreover, the former President of Iran expressed a desire to erase Israel from the map, and international experts remain increasingly concerned that a nuclear power program would provide the weapons for accomplishing this second holocaust.

A variety of instances point to the ominous threat of contemporary anti-Semitic argumentation: the Egyptian President's public "amen" to "Jews as enemies," capital punishment for selling land to Jews, carving stars of David

77

into the backs of Jewish sympathizers, and a block-buster Turkish movie (Valley of the Wolves) with American icons Billy Zane and Gary Buse promoting the age old notion of blood libel.[2] Argumentation scholarship has the potential to identify and prepare audiences to resist the insidious dimensions of this rhetoric. Classic studies like those of "Hitler's Battle" provided by Kenneth Burke[3] provide something of a model on how rhetorical and argumentation studies can undermine pathological viewpoints. This ancient trope organized genocides in the past and is being reenergized to the same type of genocidal activity today.

This chapter presents a model on how the disciplinary practice of argumentation study takes human form to resist contemporary anti-Semitism and reverse the cruel maxim: those ignorant of history are doomed to repeat it. Contemporary intellectuals such as Paulo Freire[4] emphasize the role that education should play in practical resistance to modern practices that undermine the human community. Michel Foucault[5] has noted the praxis of the "specific intellectual" dedicated to exposing the relations of power in the immediate situation and circumstances they find themselves. Argumentation and communication study should be engaged to inform humanity of cruel hoaxes in argument which break down the bonds of human community. This chapter provides a review of the workshop procedures that implemented rhetorical and argumentation instruction for Holocaust survivors to make it possible for them to effectively give voice to their personal narratives and confront skeptical audiences that occasionally resist their advocacy. Argumentation and forensics pedagogy can be used to empower the human voice toward a critical practice of communication that is both liberating and educational.

UNDERSTANDING THE CONTEMPORARY
PROBLEM OF ANTI-SEMITISM

Jews, like many other groups, have served as convenient scapegoats for the global elite. The famous example of the German Nazis was a strategic amplification of latent attitudes toward Jews that existed for hundreds of years.[6] The dominant educational approach within the United States treats anti-Semitism as a largely historic problem, which rose and fell with the Third Reich. Nonetheless, Jews continue to serve as a rhetorical scapegoat globally as indicated by the widespread sale of common anti-Semitic propaganda such as "The Protocols of the Elders of Zion."[7] This book, created in Russia during the early twentieth-century, has been widely reproduced throughout the Middle East and the world. The book details a conspiracy by Jewish leaders to control the world and, despite its fictional content, it is widely held as a factual representation of Jewish motives.

Common stereotypes such as blood libel—which suggest that Jews enjoy drinking the blood of innocents—continue to be utilized throughout the world. In 2007, a Turkish filmmaker employed American actors Billy Zane and Gary Buse to describe how a Jewish doctor (Buse's character) was shipping organs of Iraqis to Jews around the world in Israel, New York, and London. The film's plot was built around global antagonism toward the U.S. war in Iraq. In the storyline of the movie, organs were harvested from innocent Iraqis in the notorious Abu Ghraib prison. The film was a huge financial success in Europe where British and German media conceded its clear anti-Semitic content.[8] Noted civil rights activist Andrew Young scandalized the American public sphere with arguments that Americans should appreciate Wal-Mart putting Jewish, Korean, and Arab merchants out of business. He would later describe his own remarks as "demagogic" and an unfortunate lapse.[9] Ward Churchill's notorious post 9-11 accusations against World Trade Center victims was anchored in a repudiation of Nazi officer Adolf Eichmann's active role in the Holocaust.[10] His comments posed not simply a problem for lost American lives but the potential lessons of deadly anti-Semitism from the past.

Unfortunately, anti-Semitism is being deeply amplified in Middle East cultures. Direct English translation services of Middle East media such as MEMRI.org provide the international community with an opportunity to observe the anti-Semitic rants of religious and political leaders in the region. In 2007, strong objections were lodged against Hamas programming in the West Bank that had a Mickey Mouse like character singing about killing Jews with AK-47s. More recently, during Ramadan 2013, Arab TV aired a show called "Khaybar." Khaybar is the historical Jewish community conquered by the Prophet Mohammed in 628 CE. The show explains Jewish community activity as inherently dangerous. An actor, Ahmad Maher, portraying a Jewish character for the show explained how he and the show's screenwriter viewed the argument:

> "History has shown that the Jews are a people with no moral values, who do not honor their agreements." According to him [Maher], screenwriter Yusri Al-Gindi "created a historical document showing how these people are oppressors, who do not honor their agreements. History shows that they are the people who disputed Allah. They are the slayers of prophets."[11] The TV shows appeals to an Arab audience with an appetite for anti-Semitism.

A 2008 global survey of public attitudes toward religious groups, demonstrates the serious problem of anti-Semitism within the Middle East. The radically low favorability ratings of Jews in places such as Lebanon, Pakistan, Jordan, and Egypt suggest that public argument is being constructed to discourage positive attitudes towards Jews.

This table indicates how various local populations view Jews. It is worth
noting that in Jordan, Lebanon, Egypt, and Pakistan, less than 5 percent of
the population holds a favorable view of Jews. In contrast, the lowest favorable view toward Christians among seventeen nations surveyed, was 10 percent in Turkey. The lowest favorable view of Muslims was 20 percent in
China. It is clear from this information that there is a unique public and
cultural argument being made against the moral character of Jews in the
nations listed in this table 8.1.

The international nature of anti-Semitism is not limited to the Middle
East. Jews are a minority in most every nation they live. Consequently they
make convenient political scapegoats. In Honduras, in 2009, Manuel Zelaya
was struggling to hold onto power after the Court invalidated his election.
His media mouthpiece, David Romero, news director of the pro-Zelaya
Radio Globo, described Jews as "people that do damage in this country" and
mused, "After what I have learned, I ask myself why, why didn't we let Hitler
carry out his historic mission?"[12] The population of Jews in Honduras is less
than 5 percent of the population.

Here in the United States, President Obama's former pastor would blame
Jews for the lack of access to the White House after the election: "Them Jews
ain't going to let him talk to me. I told my baby daughter that he'll talk to me
in five years when he's a lame duck, or in eight years when he's out of
office."[13] Pastor Wright would later apologize for this explanation he provided to the media.

Hate crimes with a religious target chose Judaism 70 percent of the time
in 2005 according to the FBI.[14] That compares with 11 percent choosing
Islam as a target. This means that the FBI logged approximately one thousand federal hate crimes against the Jewish community in the United States

Table 8.1.   Favorability of Jews by Nation

	Favorable	Unfavorable
Turkey	7	76
Pakistan	4	76
Indonesia	10	66
Lebanon	2	97
Jordan	3	96
Egypt	3	95

Source: *Pew Research Global Attitudes Project.* 2008.
Note: This appears to be the last date Pew asked this survey. Beginning in 2013, Pew
asked similar types of questions about political groups such as Hamas, Israel, and political
leaders. The regular surveys about attitudes toward Jews appear to have stopped at Pew
Research.

for 2005. In 2007, there were 969 reported hate crimes committed against Jews, according to the FBI, constituting 12.7 percent of all hate crimes reported and 69 percent of religious bias hate crimes reported. In 2011, the FBI broke down the categories of anti-religious hate crimes this way:

RELIGIOUS BIAS

Of the 1,482 victims of an anti-religion hate crime (19.2 percent of all hate crimes):

- 63.0 percent were victims of an offender's anti-Jewish bias.
- 12.5 percent were victims of an anti-Islamic bias.
- 5.7 percent were victims of an anti-Catholic bias.
- 3.4 percent were victims of an anti-Protestant bias.
- 0.3 percent were victims of an anti-Atheist/Agnostic bias.
- 10.5 percent were victims of a bias against other religions (anti-other religion).[15]

The FBI data continues to demonstrate dramatic and profound problems with anti-Semitic violence even in the United States and the trend does not suggest easy or substantial reductions in the problem. Anti-Jewish hate crimes dwarf other religious categories.

A local St. Louis news station reported a provocative example of these statistics—though the story received little national attention:

> Alaa Alsaegh says that two cars followed him as he drove on Compton. The drivers cut him off and Alsaegh says he pulled over. That's when two men got out of a car, armed with a handgun. They got into Alsaegh's car and attacked him with a knife.
>
> Alsaegh showed us a photo that his friend took at the hospital. More than a month later, Alsaegh still has scars. News 4's camera captured the outline of the Star of David, visible on Alsaegh's back.
>
> Alsaegh is a Muslim from Iraq. He says he recently posted a poem, online, expressing support for Jewish people in Israel. Alsaegh says that his attackers told him not to publish any more poems.
>
> St Louis Police confirm that officers responded to a call for help around 10:45 a.m. on August 14th. The department referred News 4 to the local FBI office. Spokeswoman Rebecca Wu responded via email saying, "The FBI cannot comment."[16]

The unusually vicious nature of inscribing a large Star of David into someone's back is highly symbolic and clearly communicative.

The popular internet site Wikipedia, has an entry for "New anti-Semitism" which states:

> New anti-Semitism is the concept of a new 21st-century form of anti-Semitism
> emanating simultaneously from the left, the far right, and radical Islam, and
> tending to manifest itself as opposition to Zionism and the State of Israel. The
> term has entered common usage to refer to what some writers describe as a
> wave of anti-Semitism that escalated, particularly in Western Europe, after the
> Second Intifada in 2000, the failure of the Oslo accords, and the September 11,
> 2001 attacks.[17]

The concept generally posits that much of what purports to be criticism of
Israel by various individuals and world bodies is, in fact, tantamount to
demonization and that together with an international resurgence of attacks on
Jewish symbols and an increased acceptance of anti-Semitic beliefs in public
discourse, such demonization represents an evolution in the appearance of
anti-Semitic beliefs.

The most recent State department report on anti-Semitism continues to
show explosive examples of the argument within the global public sphere:

> On October 19, President Morsy [Egyptian President] said "Amen" during
> televised prayers in Mansour after an imam stated, "Oh Allah . . . grant us
> victory over the infidels. Oh Allah, destroy the Jews and their supporters."
> This is a common prayer in Egyptian mosques and came in a litany of other
> prayers. Also in October, Muslim Brotherhood Supreme Guide Mohamed Ba-
> dei made several anti-Semitic statements, including saying in a sermon that
> was also published online that "It is time for the Muslim [nation] to unite for
> the sake of Jerusalem and Palestine after the Jews have increased the corrup-
> tion in the world. . ." He added that "Zionists only know the way of force." In
> Iran, the government regularly vilified Judaism. President Mahmoud Ahma-
> dinejad continued to question the existence and the scope of the Holocaust,
> and stated that "a horrendous Zionist clan" had been "ruling the major world
> affairs" for some 400 years, while Vice President Mohammad-Reza Rahimi
> publicly blamed the "Zionists" for spreading illegal drugs around the world.[18]

The report further noted: "In France, an Islamist extremist killed a rabbi and
his two children, along with another student, outside a Jewish school in
Toulouse." The report made no statistical claims but the report makes clear
that public contempt for Jews in the global public sphere is normative in
many communities.

THE PROBLEM OF ISRAEL

Zionism, or the political belief there should be a sovereign state for Judaism
known as Israel, has become the rhetorical buffer term for rejecting many
accusations of anti-Semitism. This logic suggests that the unjust imposition
of the state of Israel within the larger Middle East constitutes an objection-
able act to which the warrant of anti-Semitism is inaccurately attached. The

underlying exigency of the Holocaust was a powerful motive to the creation of Israel in 1948. From a rhetorical standpoint, it is not surprising that some political antagonists would deny that the event took place in order to delegitimize the state of Israel.

There are many reasons for rejecting the rhetorical buffer that anti-Zionism is not anti-Semitism. The best reasons are delineated by thinkers such as Alan Dershowitz[19] and Natan Sharansky.[20] Their work suggests that political critiques of Israel inherently hold this state to a unique set of double standards in regard to common complaints. Complaints of imperialism, colonialism, injustice, and violence have a unique application that is not apparent in public argument about surrounding states that border Israel or among other nations—with the exception of the United States. This logic was apparent in the 2007 decision by the United Nations Human Rights Commission to dismiss all cases of potential human rights abuses—save those pertaining to one nation—Israel.[21] The relentless critique of Israel as the paramount abuser of human rights cannot be divorced from a larger global agenda of anti-Semitism. Given its small size, small population, and repeated invasion by outside sovereigns, it is not reasonable to conclude that a strong majority of UN resolutions are directed at this single state among 192 were it not for underlying suspicions aroused by the existence of a Jewish state. In the Gaza strip, selling land to "Jews" is a crime punishable by death. "Jewish collaborators" in Gaza are publicly executed, and their bodies are dragged behind motorcycles to communicate the desired political message to the community.[22]

Greater study and consideration of public sphere arguments surrounding Israel is important for argument scholars. In my own work with Holocaust survivors, I observed a common desire to speak in defense of the state of Israel, but an awkward dilemma for the institution of the museum, which seeks to reduce the political profile of controversies like Israel to preserve its core mission—memory of the Holocaust. Survivors clearly felt a tension about how to speak out about this contemporary historical problem, which seems to so clearly relate to the ongoing struggle of anti-Semitism.

RHETORICAL SOLUTIONS

What can be done to diminish the global reach and power of the New Anti-Semitism? This has been a growing concern for me as I have worked with Holocaust survivors on how to make memories matter and their recitation to become a basis for moral action. A measure of solution has been achieved through workshops designed to: 1) instill basic public speaking mastery so memories can be conveyed to audiences, 2) review audience identification strategies to enhance rhetorical effect of these memories, 3) connect individual messages to institutional commitments such as the Holocaust Museum in

Washington D.C., and 4) relate memory to contemporary problems of anti-Semitism and genocidal activity like that of Darfur. These four goals were treated in four different workshops, and they raised the capacity of Holocaust survivors to amplify from the standpoint of enactment[23] the horrors of the Holocaust as a warning to audiences that they should remember and resist the return of history. Dozens of survivors participated in this pedagogy and dramatically increased the Museum's capacity to put a human face and voice on the trauma of the Holocaust.

Despite this positive pedagogical practice, the personal encounter with the survivors left me wanting more. What further could be done to reduce the current threats that genocide in general and anti-Semitism in particular would return with a true vengeance to contemporary global politics? What actions can we take as argumentation scholars to prevent the return of dangerous politics dominated by ethnic scapegoating?

One interesting alternative is the comic frame. Kenneth Burke's notion of reversing the tragic field of rhetoric with a comic frame is widely understood as a useful alternative to scapegoating strategies. Jews have become involved in comedic depictions of themselves designed to transcend the absurd caricatures of their alleged malevolence. The comic frame does have rhetorical potential to work as an argument to reduce the success of anti-Semitic communication.[24] By creating a sense of absurdity, it might destabilize the serious intentional designs of hatred. Nonetheless, serious risks do remain. Baron Cohen's comedic work in "Borat," which appeals to international stereotypes, might work to undermine prejudice. Cohen's work does contain risks that communities may misinterpret the work as an affirmation of their prejudices. This has led some opinion leaders to caution about the comic frame created by advocates such as Cohen.

Ultimately, the use of positive rhetorical models may be the best approach in overcoming arguments for anti-Semitism. In this view, members of confederates are demonstrated as acting in the heroic role of resistance to prejudice. For example, there are instances of Muslim communities offering refuge and sanctuary to Jews during Nazi hostilities.[25] These examples juxtapose contemporary anti-Semitism being cultivated within the Muslim community against resistance to anti-Semitism being implemented by the Nazis. This offer of positive dilemmas provides a measure of irony attractive to the postmodern mind without the same slippery slope of sarcasm wherein receivers may interpret the argument as an endorsement of prejudice.

CONCLUSION

Anti-Semitism continues to be a major argument in the global public sphere. The deadly bigotry of the Third Reich is re-introducing itself with a vengeance. Anti-Semitic films such as "Valley of the Wolves," reproductions of *The Protocols of the Elders of Zion,* and anti-Semitic Arab TV shows, suggest that Jews are a new rhetorical scapegoat that galvanizes violence against them and their alleged collaborators. The global antagonism toward the political state of Israel has conflated anti-Zionism and anti-Semitism to an extent that it is difficult to distinguish the two. Treacherous rhetoric such as Ward Churchill's suggestion that the World Trade Center victims are "little Eichmann's" demonstrates how the tragedy of the Holocaust is being erased and potentially re-inscribed on the state of Israel. The merging of victims and villains creates the moral ambiguity to tip the balance of rhetorical coherence toward chaotic violence directed at ethnic targets like the Jews.

The peculiar irony of history so transparently trying to repeat itself is an exigence to academics that must derive the argumentation solutions to resist the return of the "Final Solution." Kenneth Burke has well warned us about the perpetual human fascination with the scapegoat. It is desirable to create a public sphere that recognizes this prejudicial scapegoating rhetoric and offers positive alternative frameworks to ethnic annihilation. In so doing, argumentation scholars can increase the range of the human voice rather than standing by silently as groups of voices are annihilated and lost. Kenneth Burke's article, "Hitler's battle" is not a great article simply because it was accurate. It was a great article because it was timely. He spoke prior to the inception of a profound moral tragedy that began not as militarism but as rhetoric. Anti-Jewish sentiments dwarf hostility toward other religious groups such as Christians and Muslims. Our silence on this question is as serious as the false charges themselves. We as scholars must do more to help humanity out of its lowest points. Anti-Semitism remains an increasingly powerful rhetorical trope to kill Palestinians, Sudanese, Lebanese, Americans, Somalis, and an array of other innocent human beings.

NOTES

1. Sudan Bombs Darfur Rebels. 2009. *Agency France Press.* January 14. Accessed March 10, 2009. http://www.google.com/hostednews/afp/article/ALeqM5jiSwZhWIQAzCfAKG GGi4GK2RUH0g.

2. Özdemir, C. 2006. "Controversy over Turkish movie: Beyond the Valley of the Wolves." Speigel online. February 22. Accessed August 1, 2007. http://www.spiegel.de/international/0,1518,401565,00.html.

3. Burke, K. 1941. "The Rhetoric of Hitler's 'Battle.'" *The Philosophy of Literary Form: Studies in Symbolic Action.* New York: Vintage, 191–220.

4. Freire, Paulo. 1970. *Pedagogy of the Oppressed.* New York: Continuum Publishing Company.

5. Foucault Michel. 1988. "Politics and Reason," in Michel Foucault: *Politics, Philosophy, Culture: Interviews and Other Writings: 1977–1984,* trans. Alan Sheridan et al., ed. Lawrence D. Kritzman, New York: Routledge.

6. Hentoff, Nat. 2006. "The World's oldest hatred hasn't gone away." *Aspen Daily News* online edition. August 20; and Krieger, H. 2006. "Jewish world marks rise in antisemitism." *Jerusalem Post* online edition. August 1.

7. Hanscom, A. 2007. "Confronting a Worldwide Jew-Hatred." Accessed September 19, 2013 Frontpage.

8. Özdemir, C. 2006. "Controversy over Turkish movie: Beyond the Valley of the Wolves." *Speigel* online. February 22. Accessed August 1, 2007. http://www.spiegel.de/international/0,1518,401565,00.html.

9. Page, Clarence. 2006. "Learning from Andrew Young's Blunder." *Chicago Tribune.* August 21.

10. *NBC News.* "Professor fired after 9-11, Nazi comparison." 2007. Accessed September 24, 2013. http://www.nbcnews.com/id/19940243/ns/us_news-education/t/professor-fired-after—nazi-comparison/#.UkJL8RY9roM.

11. Yehoshua, Y. 2013. "The Image of the Jew in the Ramadan TV Show 'Khaybar'–Treacherous, Hateful of the Other, Scheming, and Corrupt." *MEMRI.* July 10. Accessed September 24, 2013. http://www.memri.org/report/en/0/0/0/0/0/51/7279.htm.

12. Keating, Joshua. 2009. "Blaming the Jews for the Honduras Coup." *Foreign Policy.* Accessed September 19, 2013. http://blog.foreignpolicy.com/posts/2009/10/05/blaming_the_jews_for_the_honduras_coup.

13. Memmot, Mark. 2009. "Rev. Wright: Them Jews ain't Going to let him talk to Obama." *NPR.* June 11. Accessed September 24, 2013. http://www.npr.org/blogs/thetwo-way/2009/06/rev_wright_jews_aint_going_to.html.

14. Hate Crime Statistics 2005 U.S. Department of Justice—Federal Bureau of Investigation Release Date: October 2006.

15. Hate Crime Statistics 2011 U.S. Department of Justice—Federal Bureau of Investigation Release Date: October 2012. Acccessed September 24, 2013. http://www.fbi.gov/about-us/cjis/ucr/hate-crime/2011/narratives/victims.

16. Zoga, Diana. 2011. "Man says hes the victim of a hate crime." *KMOV.* September 27. Accessed September 21, 2013. http://www.kmov.com/news/local/St-Louis-man-says-hes-the-victim-of-a-hate-crime-130680978.html.

17. Wikipedia (2007). "New anti-semitism." Accessed May 15, 2007. http://en.wikipedia.org/wiki/New_antisemitism.

18. "International Religious Freedom Report." U.S. State Department. 2012. Accessed September 24, 2013.http://www.state.gov/j/drl/rls/irf/religiousfreedom/index.htm#wrapper.

19. Dershowitz, Alan. 2004. *The Case for Israel*. Hoboken, NJ: Wiley.

20. Sharansky, Natan. 2006. *The Case for Democracy*. New York: New Leaf.

21. *International Herald Tribune.* 2007. "EU says U.N. human rights watchdog can do job despite flaws."

22. Rudoren, Jodi. "Collaboration in Gaza leads to grisly fate." 2012. *New York Times.* December 2. Accessed September 24, 2013. http://www.nytimes.com/2012/12/03/world/middleeast/preyed-on-by-both-sides-gaza-collaborators-have-grim-plight.html?pagewanted=all&_r=0.

23. Campbell, K. K and S. Huxman, 2003. *The Rhetorical Act*, 3rd Edition. Belmont, CA: Wadsworth.

24. Smith, Chris, and Ben Voth. 2002. "The Role of Humor in Political Argument: How 'Strategery' and 'Lockboxes' Changed a Political Campaign," *Argumentation & Advocacy*, 39 (2): 110–30.

25. Satloff, Robert. 2006. "Among the Righteous: Lost Stories from the Holocaust's Long Reach into Arab Lands." Public Affairs: New York.

Chapter Nine

James Farmer

A Model for Human Freedom

Upon completing college, James Farmer Sr. asked his son what he wanted to do with his life. His son responded with two words: "Destroy Segregation." [1]

The American Civil Rights movement represents one of the more iconic and successful efforts to end an extensive practice of ethnic hatred embodied in law and social practice. The heroic figures like Martin Luther King Jr. are known around the world, and they continue to inspire individuals today. As the fifty-year anniversary of key events from this era pass, it is an ideal moment to consider what lessons from that struggle can help us today in the twenty-first century. This chapter elaborates on pedagogy for the oppressed rooted in new understanding of the classic human rights struggle. [2] Though many figures of the civil rights movement are understood, there is one that provides a compelling example today from his too neglected past and missed contribution to the success of this movement: James Farmer Jr.

If Martin Luther King Jr. was the voice of the civil rights movement, James Farmer Jr. was its hands and feet. Among the giants of the civil rights movement he was arguably the largest. By age twenty-two, Farmer founded the *Center for Racial Equality* that would later become the *Congress of Racial Equality*. While MLK was still a child, Farmer would lead protests in Chicago against segregated restaurants. Those efforts in the 1940s were the foundational preludes to the key actions and civil rights strategies of the 1950s and 1960s.

The glaring spectacle of success can blind us to the difficult individual and intellectual disciplines necessary for historic events like the 1964 Civil Rights Act to come to pass. Farmer lived a life that offers more than interesting history, he offers a model for present action for the further repeal of injustice against its most vicious and thorough implementation: genocide.

James Farmer Jr. was born in 1920 in Marshall, Texas. He was born without an official birth certificate, and one was created for him later. As a young boy, Farmer reports being especially formed by an incident with his mother. While shopping, he asked if he might get a Coca-Cola. His mother warned him sternly that he could not have one. When he complained that he saw another boy get one at the store, his mother explained that he could not get one because he was not white. Farmer found this to be his first memory of segregation and its painful exclusions. The memory was so traumatic that years later he doubted if he understood the events properly. He would ask his mother about it and she confirmed that indeed those moments had transpired and that when she got home she went to her bedroom to sob about the pain of the day's events.[3]

Years later, as a successful college debater at Wiley College, Farmer would describe his oratorical skills regarding segregation this way:

> One night, the subject of segregation came up. I took the floor. I must have spoken for twenty minutes, and in that little speech I destroyed segregation, I killed it, buried it, delivered its epitaph. I was very proud of myself. Couldn't wait to tell Tolson [his college debate coach]. A few evenings later I was over at his house. I said, "You would have been very proud of your debater," and I told him how I'd taken the floor and killed segregation, reduced it to ashes and buried its corpse, mindless of the mixed metaphor. Tolson smiled and said, "I see, Farmer." He said, "I hear there's a good movie downtown." "Yes I saw it." "You saw it? Where did you see it?" "At the Paramount." That was the only theater in town. "How did you like it?" "Oh, it was a great movie." He said to me, "Now, let me get this straight. On Thursday night in your bull session you tore segregation to bits. Then on Saturday afternoon in the pitiless glare of the sun, you walked downtown in Marshall, Texas, to the Paramount Theater, went around to the side entrance, climbed the back stairs, and sat up in the buzzards' roost. Am I correct?" "Yes." "And you watched the movie. Not only that, you enjoyed it! You had killed segregation two days before. And now, you not only allowed yourself to be segregated, but paid your father's hard earned money for the privilege. And you enjoyed it!"
>
> He reached up on his shelf of books, pulled one down, and tossed it across the room to me. It was the writings of Henry David Thoreau. I opened it to where the blue divider ribbon already was, the essay "Civil Disobedience." A passage was marked, and it went like this: "What I have to do is see, at any rate, that I do not lend myself to the wrong which I condemn." I got up to leave, and as I walked across the campus, I wondered, "What has happened to me since that day when I was three and a half years old and was cut up inside to realize that I couldn't go into a drug store and get a Coca-Cola?"[4]

Melvin Tolson was a profound intellectual force at Wiley and nationally. His legacy reached beyond Farmer and remains an important lesson today. David

Gold, a professor of English summarized Tolson's approach and effect in an article designed to re-discover Tolson's brilliance:

> Yet in and out of the classroom, his blend of racial pride, radical Christianity, philological rigor, and liberatory rhetoric changed students' lives; several went on to become key figures in the struggle for black civil rights. Nearly forty years after his death, his former students still speak of him with reverence and awe. How did he manage such a delicate balancing act between rigor and nurture? And how can we?[5]

Farmer's formative experience in debate unlocks several important lessons about the rhetorical study of debate. Debate forms the mind for action by opening us to alternative realities. It cannot, however, substitute for the action necessary to create those new and better realities. Farmer's coach, Melvin Tolson, guided the young debater toward the larger understanding with the writings of Henry David Thoreau. This evidently laid the groundwork for the kind of activist James Farmer Jr. would become. Though debate cannot alone change an unjust world, it can prepare a mind for the long difficult struggle inherent in changing the many human minds that compose injustice. Farmer's intellectual growth as a debater was indispensable to the later task of becoming a civil rights leader.

Farmer also embodied the difficult reconciliation between idealism and pragmatism. After his undergraduate education, he planned to go into the ministry. He ultimately decided that he could not serve as a Christian minister in a segregated world. His Christian idealism motivated and challenged him, but it also compelled him to a journey of personal sacrifice toward serving others trapped in the cruel world of segregation. After graduating from the Howard University School of Religion in preparation for ministry, Farmer remarked: "I didn't see how I could honestly preach the Gospel of Christ in a church that practiced discrimination."[6] The action of "destroying segregation" required a steadfast determination that only fierce idealism could maintain. For at least two decades, James Farmer balanced his practical skills in rhetoric within a framework of fierce idealism to affect some of the most profound changes known to American society.

The formative aspects of college debate are worthy of attention. Among the group recently heralded by filmmaker Denzel Washington as *The Great Debaters*, Farmer grew up as the son of the university president at Wiley College. His unique situation allowed him to enter college early and pursue the tutelage of the popular and well-known debate coach Melvin Tolson. Attending Wiley during the late 1930s, Farmer was an unusually young college student. He was an alternate on the debate team when Wiley achieved its ultimate success—defeating national champions USC on their home campus in California. An audience of two thousand people watched the debate, and it was another chapter in the many successes of debate coach Melvin

Tolson. Tolson lead the first African-American team against a white college in March of 1930 when Wiley defeated Oklahoma City University on their campus. In describing his education at Wiley, Farmer explained that the most significant aspects of his education were not "sports, dances, fraternities or sororities but what he learned under the leadership of Melvin Tolson."[7]

The stunning vigor of Farmer's activism upon graduation from higher learning is startling. In 1943, Farmer would initiate a non-violent civil rights action against a Chicago restaurant known as *Jack Spratt*. Farmer explained what transpired there:

> We went in with a group of about twenty—this was a small place that seats thirty or thirty-five comfortably at the counter and in the booths—and occupied just about all of the available seats and waited for service. The woman was in charge again [the manager they had encountered on a previous visit]. She ordered the waitress to serve two whites who were seated at the counter, and she served them. Then she told the blacks, "I'm sorry, we can't serve you, you'll have to leave." And they, of course, declined to leave and continued to sit there. By this time the other customers who were in there were aware of what was going on and were watching, and most of these were university people, University of Chicago, who were more or less sympathetic with us. And they stopped eating and the two people at the counter she had served and those whites in the booth she had served were not eating. There was no turnover. People were coming in and standing around for a few minutes and walking out. There were no seats available.[8]

After the owner acceded to their demands for desegregation, the group moved on to other actions for civil rights. The action was part of a long-term commitment of leadership that Farmer would make to the *Committee of Racial Equality* and a group known as *Fellowship of Reconciliation*. Farmer championed the ideas and actions of Ghandi as a pacifist approach for social change. While Martin Luther King Jr. was still a child, Farmer was leading the way for destroying segregation through his non-violent campaign.

Farmer's biography, shaped intrinsically by the communication and rhetorical study of debate, remains a standard for consideration of how the twenty-first century might overcome the death as text found in genocide. While the emancipation of Negroes under Lincoln established a legal framework for the American promise of equality, a reign of systemic violence endured, especially in the Southern United States, to prevent the practical emergence of equality among blacks even in the 1960s. While segregation of blacks at that time did not constitute the formal practice of genocide, the pervasive acts of public violence and terror remain analogous and informative of precursors to global genocide practices today. Commentators and observers of the violence in Mississippi in the 1960s often compare the systemic violence to past injustices such as the Holocaust.[9] Farmer's strategic senses and peculiar persistence were formed by the pedagogical method of debate. His techniques remain a viable model for overturning various forms of segregation that exist throughout the world rationalized by states in various practices often reinforced by public violence. [10]

The difficult social norms of apathy and violent defense of social tradition combined to make the civil rights struggle implausible in a manner not unlike our current apprehensions about systemic global violence. Debate is a vital civic pole that props up discursive complexity in trying social conditions. James Farmer's preparation in the crucible of debate prepared him for the difficult trials of civil rights activism. Recognizing the grim exigency for civil rights can bolster the possibility that such actions might be modeled elsewhere for the same positive results of human equality.

One of the more profound strategic campaigns engineered by Farmer, was the Freedom Rides. The Freedom Ride campaign sent integrated buses of blacks and whites from northern locations through the south. The campaign took advantage of larger federal guarantees of desegregation for interstate commerce to create a practical political struggle for greater integration in the South. In May of 1961, activists loaded buses in Washington DC for travel that would end in Jackson, Mississippi. The rides were designed to test the federal promises of integration as the buses came and went from increasingly segregated communities in places like Georgia, Alabama, and Mississippi. Farmer left the bus upon news of his father's poor health and impending death. This left his subordinate, James Peck, in charge of the bus at a time of increasing danger for the travelers as they continued to move south. Farmer was deeply torn before and after the rides given the incredible violence that would ultimately transpire. [11]

Upon arrival in Anniston, the bus was met by an angry white mob. Though prevented from entering the bus, the mob did considerable damage to the bus—breaking windows and slashing tires. They made violent threats to the freedom ride passengers. After many minutes, the police arrived and dispersed the crowd without arrests. [12] A police car escorted the battered Greyhound bus to the edge of town before it was stopped again. The bus was followed by dozens of cars full of angry segregationists. Many were dressed for church on that Mother's Day, and a few had their children with them. When the bus stopped to tend to flat tires, a violent mob formed to attack the bus. The mob demanded the riders disembark and receive the violence planned for them, but the riders remained on the bus. Ultimately, the attackers chose to fire bomb the bus to force out the occupants. The mob attempted to keep the riders trapped in the burning bus to die. But frantic riders began to escape: Thomas, the first Rider to exit the front of the bus, crawled away from the doorway, a white man rushed toward him and asked, "Are you all okay?" Before Thomas could answer, the man's concerned look turned into a sneer as he struck the astonished student in the head with a baseball bat.

Thomas fell to the ground and was barely conscious as the rest of the exiting
Riders spilled out onto the grass. [13]

Arsenault documents a critical communication junction in the violent
annihilation that freedom riders faced:

> Rowe and several others, however, were preoccupied with Webb and contin-
> ued the attack until a news photographer snapped a picture of Rowe and the
> other Klansmen. As soon as the flashbulb went off, they abandoned Webb and
> ran after the photographer, Tommy Langston of the *Birmingham Post-Herald*,
> who made it to the station parking lot before being caught. After one man
> grabbed Langston's camera and smashed it to the ground, Rowe and several
> others, including Eastview klavern leader Hubert Page, kicked and punched
> him and threatened to beat him with the same pipes and baseball bats used on
> Webb.

The presence of media, and the possibility of recording the violence done to
the freedom riders, motivated the attackers to leave. The practical social
maintenance of silence was in question when the reporter took out the camera. The attackers sought to send a message not only to the riders but a broader
community of resistance that objected to segregation. The violence of 1961
remains analogous to struggles globally, where violent beatings and broader
social intimidation remain common.

Farmer viewed this event as his most important life accomplishment:

> In the end, it was a success, because Bobby Kennedy had the Interstate Com-
> merce Commission issue an order, with teeth in it, that he could enforce,
> banning segregation in interstate travel. That was my proudest achievement. [14]

Farmer and CORE were foundational to the growing struggle of non-vio-
lence against segregation. Thousands of individuals—many of them young
people—joined the ranks of the cause. By the summer of 1963, the movement was ready to make a larger national statement with a march on Washington. The massive event would gather tens of thousands of people on the
National Mall to demand firmer national resolve and action to end segregation. Civil rights leaders were collaborating and forming this national statement. Several speakers were slated to speak for what would turn out to be an
historic day—August 28, 1963. King's dream speech is famous and well
known. Less known is the role of the civil rights leader who did not rise to
speak that day despite having his name on the program. Farmer was to be the
eighth speaker at the podium—in the middle of a program that would end
with King's speech.

Farmer was arrested for civil rights activism in Plaquemine, Louisiana,
well before the national event. Though his celebrity and national status allowed him to skip out of jail, Farmer chose to stay in jail wishing for solidar-

ity with other local activist who had no such luxury or option to escape the cell. Farmer sent a letter that was read at the March. Farmer's letter, though overshadowed by the thundering live conclusion by King, outlined a broad vision for the civil rights movement. Farmer saw their work as reaching the entire world. Farmer believed that the work in the United States would serve as a model for global action. This vision touched on global scourges such as disease and hunger and with regard for every ethnic group.

Farmer's vision and the larger civil rights movement were jarred by the deaths of activists James Chaney, Michey Schwerner, and Andrew Goodman less than a year after that pivotal march on Washington. Schwerner and Chaney were CORE members. In the summer of 1964, CORE activists gathered in Oxford, Ohio—the same place Farmer had originally been inspired to pursue civil rights activism [15]—to train for the difficult activism planned for the state of Mississippi. As an African-American from Mississippi, Chaney was an important figure in the famous trio that would ultimately pay with their lives for the idealism they were acting upon. Chaney knew the local conditions better than the northern activists like Goodman and Schwerner. After traveling from Ohio to Mississippi to begin their work, and during the course of investigating a church burning, the three men were arrested in Philadelphia, Mississippi. After being released from jail, the three were abducted by the Klan, beaten with chains and shot. Local authorities originally insisted that the three men simply snuck out of Mississippi. Federal intervention in Mississippi lead to the discovery of their bodies on August 4. Freedom Summer was a pivotal national event. Two young white men died in the South at the hands of radical segregationists. Young people from the north were increasingly drawn to the cause and movement lead by those like James Farmer. The media attention surrounding these deaths was a powerful rhetorical force in pressing the case for federal laws against segregation policies.

These events constituted some of the most pivotal in the long career of activism by James Farmer. What he did in the aftermath remains important and suggestive to racial politics in America today. Farmer would run as a Republican for Congress and lose to an African-American female candidate Shirley Chisolm. Farmer endorsed a Republican for senate in New York at the same time he backed Hubert Humphrey—a Democratic candidate. Farmer ultimately took a job in the Nixon administration despite much criticism from civil rights leaders who disapproved of his cooperation with a Republican administration. Farmer became increasingly distant to the "jacobins" of the civil rights movement. [16] Farmer opposed interjecting the Vietnam War into the civil rights message and he was alarmed by civil rights support of Marxist organizations in Angola. [17] He was a moderating force between the political sides of American civil debate. As the civil rights movement moved more exclusively to the left, Farmer was pressed to the margins. Farmer later summarized his situation this way: "I lived in two worlds, one was the

volatile and explosive one of the new black Jacobins and the other was the
sophisticated and genteel one of the white and black liberal establishment. As
a bridge, I was called on by each side for help in contacting the other."[18]
Ultimately that bridge would fail to reach both sides. Farmer resigned from
CORE's leadership in 1965 over disagreements between these two groups—
especially the interjections of foreign policy. Farmer's historical cooperation
and collaboration with Republicans in the 1960s and 1970s is largely lost and
fosters the present illusion that only one party worked toward civil rights
progress in America.

Upon Farmer's death in 1999, the *New York Times* summarized the pivotal nature of his work this way:

> CORE under Mr. Farmer often served as the razor's edge of the movement. It
> was to CORE that the four Greensboro, N.C., students turned after staging the
> first in the series of sit-ins that swept the South in 1960. It was CORE that
> forced the issue of desegregation in interstate transportation with the Freedom
> Rides of 1961. It was CORE's James Chaney, Andrew Goodman [sic] and
> Michael Schwerner—a black and two whites—who became the first fatalities
> of the Mississippi Freedom Summer of 1964.[19]

Farmer raised up tens of thousands of activists from all over the United
States and from many ethnic groups. Farmer provided the bodies—the hands
and feet of the civil rights movement at the critical moments we now celebrate. Farmer expressed the theological underpinnings of his work rather
ironically when describing to a reporter a near death experience in civil rights
activism: "Farmer said instead of seeing St. Peter at the end of life, he saw
the Devil." And he said, "Oh, my God, don't let this nigger in! He'll organize
a resistance movement and try to put out my fire."[20]

DEBATE AND COMMUNICATION
STUDY'S ROLE IN MAKING FARMER

Farmer's education and preparation for later activism demonstrates several
key lessons about the important rhetorical study known as debate: 1) debate
prepares the mind for the encounter of opposing points of view that are
continually apparent and at work in society, 2) debate illuminates the practical tensions between knowledge and moral change, 3) debate rehearses the
communication skills necessary for leadership and the actions of social
change, 4) debate galvanizes the soul and protects it from natural erosions of
apathy and resistance to social change, and 5) debate stretches us ethically
and cognitively so we can reach across far partisan divides. Farmer's experiences should not be seen as unique or lost to an historical era. The appreciation of debate, the instruction in it, and the social practice of argument are the

evident social guide rails toward a world without genocide. Farmer's experiences are illuminating to this point.

James Farmer is an important pedagogical model for consideration of how twenty-first century resistance to genocide might proceed. In Farmer, we see how the general idealism of youth is shaped by education. We see how the particular educational practice of debate introduces powerful aspects of critical thinking so that idealism can pursue practical and humane outlets. We see in Farmer how collective formations like CORE can translate individual idealism into a social movement. We see in Farmer's biography useful non-violent strategies designed to challenge entrenched power at a rate that is sufficient to propel change while stifling the prospects of further genocidal backlash.

Farmer was a visionary leader. He saw his arguments as proceeding beyond the provincial boundaries of America and reaching a world of injustice. In the next three chapters, we will see how the same kinds of injustices pertaining to genocidal violence in the world, are being confronted and resolved. In many respects, individuals like Farmer are rising in the twenty-first century to confront and repeal their own dangerous worlds of "segregation." Our teaching and learning about argumentation, communication, and rhetoric can solidify the processes whereby these injustices are destroyed as Farmer imagined they would be.

NOTES

1. Gubert, Betty. 2004. "James Farmer." *African American Lives*. Eds: Henry Louis Gates and Brooks Higginbotham. New York: Oxford University Press. March 23. 287.
2. Freire, Paulo. 1970. *Pedagogy of the Oppressed*. New York: Continuum Publishing Company.
3. Farmer, J. 1985. *Lay Bare the Heart: An Autobiography of the Civil Rights Movement*. Fort Worth: Texas Christian University Press.
4. Scherman, Tony. 1997. "The Great Debaters," *American Legacy*. Spring.
5. Gold, David. 2003. "'Nothing Educates Us Like a Shock': The Integrated Rhetoric of Melvin B. Tolson" CCC 55:2. December. 226–253.
6. Farmer, J. 1985. *Lay Bare the Heart: An Autobiography of the Civil Rights Movement*. Fort Worth: Texas Christian University Press.
7. Farmer, J. 1985. *Lay Bare the Heart: An Autobiography of the Civil Rights Movement*. Fort Worth: Texas Christian University Press.
8. Raines, H. 1977. *My Soul Is Rested: Movement Days in the Deep South Remembered*. New York: Penguin Books; and Farmer, J. 1965. *Freedom When*. New York: Random House.
9. Huie, William Bradford. 1965. *Three Lives for Mississippi*. New York: WCC books.
10. Bruschke, Jon. 2012. "Argument and Evidence Evaluation: A Call for Scholars to Engage Contemporary Public Debates." *Argumentation & Advocacy* 49, no. 1: 59–75. Communication & Mass Media Complete, EBSCOhost (accessed September 14, 2013).
11. Farmer, J. 1985. *Lay Bare the Heart: An Autobiography of the Civil Rights Movement*. Fort Worth: Texas Christian University Press.
12. Gross, Terry. 2006. "Get on the Bus: Freedom Riders of 1961." *NPR*, http://www.npr.org/2006/01/12/5149667/get-on-the-bus-the-freedom-riders-of-1961.

13. Arsenault, Raymond. 2006. *Freedom Riders: 1961 and the Struggle for Racial Justice.* New York: Oxford University Press.

14. Severo, Richard. 1999. "James Farmer, Civil Rights Giant In the 50's and 60's, Is Dead at 79." *New York Times.* July 10. Archives. Accessed August 2, 2013. http://www.nytimes.com/1999/07/10/us/james-farmer-civil-rights-giant-in-the-50-s-and-60-s-is-dead-at-79.html?pagewanted=all&src=pm

15. Farmer, J. 1985. *Lay Bare the Heart: An Autobiography of the Civil Rights Movement.* Fort Worth: Texas Christian University Press.

16. Farmer, J. 1965. *Freedom When.* New York: Random House.

17. Severo, Richard. 1999. "James Farmer, Civil Rights Giant In the 50's and 60's, Is Dead at 79." *New York Times.* July 10. Archives. Accessed August 2, 2013. http://www.nytimes.com/1999/07/10/us/james-farmer-civil-rights-giant-in-the-50-s-and-60-s-is-dead-at-79.html?pagewanted=all&src=pm.

18. Farmer, J. 1985. *Lay Bare the Heart: An Autobiography of the Civil Rights Movement.* Fort Worth: Texas Christian University Press.

19. Severo, Richard. 1999. "James Farmer, Civil Rights Giant In the 50's and 60's, Is Dead at 79." *New York Times.* July 10. Archives. Accessed August 2, 2013. http://www.nytimes.com/1999/07/10/us/james-farmer-civil-rights-giant-in-the-50-s-and-60-s-is-dead-at-79.html?pagewanted=all&src=pm.

20. Farmer, J. 1985. *Lay Bare the Heart: An Autobiography of the Civil Rights Movement.* Fort Worth: Texas Christian University Press.

Chapter Ten

Gendercide

Sex Selection Abortion

As I left the congressional hearing room, two questions burned in my mind: How can this inhumane crime be stopped? When will this inhuman crime be stopped—Chai Ling, Tiananmen Square and human rights activist [1]

The most successful form of violence against women today is sex selection abortion. No other form of violence mounts the same staggering toll of bodies lost. This is important because the world remains principally held in a patriarchal grip. Politics favor men, and the margins of human existence are dominated by the presence of women. This topic is unusually ironic, and perhaps, an indication of how insidious patriarchal logic can be. Abortion is conventionally understood—especially among academics and intellectuals—as a necessary and primal aid to the well being of women. The absence of abortion is a standard signifying marker globally for discrimination against women.

Despite these rhetorical conventions propped up firmly by intellectuals, abortion is disproportionally directed against females. The direction is not subtle or something to be relegated to environmental causes. Too many women are convinced in the twenty-first century that the future will be best served with more male children than female children. That logic is now so indisputable that massive sovereign governments have adopted prohibitions against this logic in desperate hopes of righting a global skewing of the human gender balance. [2]

As a matter of perspective, there are approximately fifty million abortions performed every year in the world according to the United Nations Family Planning Association. [3] This means that in a world of equal chance twenty-five million boys and twenty-five millions girls are lost in this practice. That is not, however, the random logic of human behavior, and regardless of how one feels ethically about the action of abortion, the practice itself is profoundly gendered.[4] The global animus toward women is pressed most effectively within the womb of mothers.

The profound manifestations of this problem are most evident in India and China. Those two countries contain about one-third of the human population and they are rising global economies. Both societies feel the strain of sex selection abortion, and have in recent years enacted formal bans on the practice in order to discourage the over-riding cultural urge that continues despite the prohibition.[5] Each nation has a distinct practice of the problem.

For China, the sex selection abortion process is accentuated and accelerated by the Communist party dictates of a one-child policy that has dominated the nation for decades. Parents remain compelled to accept a family size of one child—though exemptions are increasingly possible and practiced.[6] The painful choice of limiting family size to one has accentuated the standard social preference for boys. Boys in China represent an important maintenance of the family and they are necessary for the care of parents as they age. This is the predominant cultural convention of people in China and the convention has savaged the ranks of female children. Female children are not only disproportionate targets of abortion but they also are abandoned as infants in greater numbers.

The statistical reality of this social persuasion is staggering. Normal sex gender ratios across the globe are 105 girls for every one hundred boys born. Experts pay close attention to how high the boy number in this ratio rises around the world. For parts of China, the ratio is over 130 in several Chinese provinces from Henan in the north to Hainan in the south.[7] By 2005, the number of excess males under twenty in China was over thirty million. Ninety-four percent of unmarried people aged twenty-eight to forty-nine in China are males.

In India, a similar problem is apparent and has also been banned. Nonetheless, the strong social preference for boys continues, and the financial burdens of having a girl remains considerable. The practice of dowries paid by families with girls to families with boys constitutes a profound social hurdle in a nation home to millions of poor. The current imbalance is as bad as it has been in fifty years. On average, there are 914 girls for every one thousand boys in India. In many parts of India, the problem is far worse. In one urban area the ratio was 882 girls for every one thousand boys.[8] Sex preference is so acute that hundreds of girls participate in public ceremonies to change their given names of Nakusa—meaning unwanted—to other more desirable names.[9]

Most surprising in the case of India is the role that education and income are playing in this crisis. When the problem became more evident in the 2000 census of India, experts believed that rising incomes and education would reverse a problem that was trending for decades. The 2011 census was a devastating setback to this secular premise for saving women. Similar trends are found in China where ethnic groups of Han tend to practice more sex selection despite their higher average incomes and education. [10]

Thought the most pronounced effects of the global preference for boys are seen in China and India, the total effect has been estimated to be one hundred million missing women from the world. Across Asia, the problem is noticeable. It can be seen in former Soviet Republics such as Georgia. Studies of sixty-one countries globally showed that half of them already practice increased activity of sex selection and surveys suggest there is growing demand in other countries to engage in this practice. [11] It is clearly a global problem. Even in the United States and other nations where gender imbalance is not strongly evident, there are increasing indications of this practice. [12] Gender selection abortions take place in the United States and Britain. [13] The United States maintains the legality of sex selection abortion. [14] Studies throughout the world of second and third children tend to dramatically demonstrate the sex selection process particularly among immigrant populations from societies that strongly prefer males.

IMPLICATIONS

In a world that is becoming more male everyday, the ramifications are profound. Shortages of women, theoretically, provide an increased value for the lives of women. That competition has tended to show itself in the form of violent activity. [15] The most obvious forms of violence include rape but extend to broader practices such as sexual slavery. Men cannot marry in many of these more disparate gender location, yet they resort to sexual liaisons that have nefarious social effects for women. Sociologists suggest that men may be more prone to crime and other restless acts of violence. With diminished social responsibilities, single men pursue their own ends unconcerned about ramifications for a wife and children. In fact, men may seek to be more assertive to demonstrate their male characteristics. The gender imbalance today is so bad that experts see themselves in uncharted waters with regard to the potential dangers of this problem:

> The social manifestations are also abhorrent from a feminist standpoint. As the number of women has declined within these societies, the scarcity of females has contributed to a dramatic rise in anti-woman behavior in these societies. Of particular note are forced female prostitution and female slavery. Because these societies increasingly lack the females to make conventional human marriages of men and women, they facilitate sexual arrangements that demean and destroy women. Abortion is the critical catalyst toward a run-away cycle

of violence against women. Women become subordinate to a political and social majority of men who see them as means to their own ends. Any feminist notion of patriarchy could have no greater ally in the perpetuation of female abuse than the sociological meat-grinder of sex-selection abortion. These practices are well documented by the international community and offer a compelling basis for representing abortion as a means to oppress women.[16]

From the standpoint of democracy, there are fewer women in society participating, voting, and giving voice to the needs of women. This enhances the social preferences of men in the marketplace, the public square and the civic realms. The decision to stigmatize public conversations about unborn children and veiling the rhetoric in euphemisms such as "a woman's choice," stifles our collective ability to resolve this growing problem. It will likely take decades to convince many cultures that girls are as valuable as boys. Pretending that unborn children lack meaningful human political content misses the profound point that unborn girls are being actively discriminated against because of their sex. Technology identifies and communicates their sex to doctors and parents who are participants in biased hostility against them.

POSSIBLE SOLUTIONS

The obvious need and solution to this problem is convincing the public, mothers in particular, that girls are as valuable as boys. Some public education, particularly in India has begun to focus on communicating this message. Public officials for the past decade have increasingly agreed that the trend is dangerous and must be not only stopped, but also reversed. Fortunately, the prospects for a solution are not as dismal as the data for China and India suggest. South Korea stands out as a remarkable reversal of fortunes on this question. The problem of gender imbalance of South Korea skyrocketed from 105 to 117 boys per one hundred girls between 1960 and 1995. South Korea's gender imbalance was following a similar trajectory and value to China. However, in 1995 South Korea, unlike most of Asia and the world, experienced a dramatic and sharp reversal away from gender imbalance. In the early twenty-first century the ratio is approaching the normal range of 105.[17]

Experts tend to assign the growing South Korean economy as a primary cause of this ideal correction. This does not fit well with the economic growth propelling both India and China. Deeper cultural reasons beyond money and resources are clearly at work. Most distinct and unique to South Korea compared to the rest of Asia is the dramatic growth of Christianity. Moving markedly away from Confucianism and toward Christianity, the South Koreans appear to have absorbed a change in the appreciation of girls for offspring. Somewhere between 30 and 40 percent of South Koreans identify as Christian. North Korea by contrast has a tiny, almost unknown, population of Christians. Across Asia, Christian populations tend to be less than 8 percent of the population. The recent and explosive growth of Christianity in South Korea over the past two decades fits well with the unusual reversal of gendercide. Whatever the cause, South Korea is unique in the global effort to sharply reverse gendercide.

The story inside India remains profoundly disturbing in provinces such as Jammu, Kashmir, Maharashtra, Uttar Pradesh, and Lakshadweep where sex selection accelerated in the past ten years. In fact in two of these provinces female births fell dramatically from above average to below average. The imbalance of births increased rather than decreased from 2001 to 2011 despite the dramatic increase in incomes and education for these communities.[18] In 1961, 974 girls were born for every one thousand boys. The ratio was 926 in the 2001 census. In the most recent census that number has fallen on average across India to 914. It is a staggering loss of females. Money and education not only failed to reduce the imbalance, it arguably accelerated the process as parents became more savvy and financially capable of executing their preferences.[19]

An energetic and compelling rhetorical leader on this question is an activist named Chai Ling. Ling was among dozens of activists who organized the Tiananmen Square protests of 1989. She fled China for America after the government sought to further its punishment and incarceration of these activists. Recently, she created an activism group known as *All Girls Allowed* designed to encourage greater global acceptance of female births. Her unique biography and compelling vision make her a positive example of how this global problem might begin to reverse and allow for a more female world. In her book, "Heart for Freedom," Ling documents her progression in thought from 1989 to her present work in the United States.[20] Work like hers is important to arrest and reverse the problem of sex selection abortion. Presently, the world is racing daily toward greater masculinity. The global intellectual silence surrounding the choice to end female life in the womb is creating a catastrophic gender schism in the world that we are only beginning to understand.

NOTES

1. Ling, Chai. 2011. *A Heart for Freedom*. Carol Stream, IL: Tyndale. 287–88.

2. Vogel, Lauren. 2012. "Sex-selective abortions: no simple solutions." *CMAJ*. 2012 February 21; 184(3): 286–88. Accessed September 23, 2013. http://www.ncbi.nlm.nih.gov/pmc/articles/PMC3281151/.

3. UNFPA. 2013. "Reproductive health: Ensuring every pregnancy is wanted." Accessed September 23, 2013. http://www.unfpa.org/rh/planning.htm.

4. Devine, Daniel. 2013. "The female holocaust." September 11. *World*.

5. Vogel, Lauren. 2012. "Sex-selective abortions: no simple solutions." *CMAJ.* 2012 February 21; 184(3): 286–88. Accessed September 23, 2013. http://www.ncbi.nlm.nih.gov/pmc/articles/PMC3281151/.

6. Kohm, Lynne Marie. 1997. "Sex Selection Abortion and the Boomerang Effect of a Woman's Right to Choose: A Paradox of the Skeptics," *Wm. & Mary J. Women & L. 4:* 91. Accessed September 16, 2013. http://scholarship.law.wm.edu/ wmjowl/vol4/iss1/3; and Junhong, Chu. 2001. "Prenatal Sex Determination and Sex-Selective Abortion in Rural Central China." *Population and Development Review,* 27: 259–281. doi: 10.1111/j.1728-4457.2001.00259.x.

7. "India and South Korea." 2011. *ScienceDaily,* March 15. Accessed September 5, 2013.

8. Asokan, Shyamantha. 2013. "India's rising middle class prefers sons." *The Washington Post.* January 11. Accessed August 20, 2013. http://articles.washingtonpost.com/2013-01-11/world/36272355_1_middle-class-indians-sons.

9. Myers, Christine. 2012. "Sex Selective Abortion in India." *Global Tides* 6:3. April 1. Accessed August 10, 2013. http://digitalcommons.pepperdine.edu/cgi/viewcontent.cgi?article=1049&context=globaltides.

10. Eberstadt, Nicholas. 2011. "The Global War on Baby Girls," *The New Atlantis; A Journal of Technology and Society.* Fall. Viewed January 25, 2012 at http://www.thenewatlantis.com/publications/the-global-war-against-baby-girls.

11. "Gendercide in the Caucauses." *The Economist.* September 21, 2013. Accessed September 25, 2013. http://www.economist.com/news/europe/21586617-son-preference-once-suppressed-reviving-alarmingly-gendercide-caucasus.

12. Vogel, Lauren. 2012. "Sex-selective abortions: no simple solutions." *CMAJ.* 2012 February 21; 184(3): 286–88. Accessed September 23, 2013. http://www.ncbi.nlm.nih.gov/pmc/articles/PMC3281151/.

13. Mason, Rowena. 2013. "The abortion of unwanted girls taking place in the UK." *The Telegraph.* January 10. Accessed September 16, 2013. http://www.telegraph.co.uk/news/uknews/crime/9794577/The-abortion-of-unwanted-girls-taking-place-in-the-UK.html.

14. Sidhu, Jasmeet. 2012. "Gender Selection Has Become A Multimillion-Dollar Industry." *Slate.* September 7.

15. Khazan, Olga and Lakshmi, Rama. 2012. "10 reasons why India has a sexual violence problem." *The Washington Post.* December 29. Accessed September 23, 2013. http://www.washingtonpost.com/blogs/worldviews/wp/2012/12/29/india-rape-victim-dies-sexual-violence-proble/.

16. Voth, Ben. 2004. "Making the best argument for unborn life: Understanding the racist and sexist assumptions of abortion," *Life and Learning XIII: Proceedings of the Thirteenth University Faculty for Life Conference,* ed. Joseph W. Koterski, S.J.

17. "India and South Korea." 2011. *ScienceDaily,* March 15. Accessed September 5, 2013.

18. Asokan, Shyamantha. 2013. "India's rising middle class prefers sons." *The Washington Post.* January 11. Accessed August 20, 2013. http://articles.washingtonpost.com/2013-01-11/world/36272355_1_middle-class-indians-sons.

19. *BBC.* 2011. "India's Unwanted Girls." May 22. Accessed August 20, 2013. http://www.bbc.co.uk/news/world-south-asia-13264301; and Sidhu, Jasmeet. 2012. "Gender Selection Has Become A Multimillion-Dollar Industry." *Slate.* September 7.

20. Ling, Chai. 2011. *A Heart for Freedom.* Carol Stream, IL: Tyndale.

Chapter Eleven

Giving War a Chance

Critical Theory and Genocide

Those who "abjure" violence can only do so because others are committing violence on their behalf.—George Orwell[1]

A global anti-war movement, traceable to the Vietnam era is a powerful global argumentative force for limiting American military actions in the world. Operating from a rhetorical binary of war and peace, the arguments by anti-war activists have suggested that if American military aggression is stopped then peace in the world will necessarily increase. The alleged zero sum relationship between American military attacks and global peace is a symbolic association highly worthy of scrutiny. This analysis finds that the anti-war movement identified in advocates as diverse as Michael Moore, Medea Benjamin, and Noam Chomsky are increasing global violence as expressed in terms of genocide rather than advancing a global circumstance of peace.[2] There are three primary ways that anti-war rhetoric contributes to the global prevalence of genocide: 1) the distortive binary of war and peace, 2) constraining military punishment of genocide agents, and 3) distorting the meaning of genocide terms.

UNDERSTANDING THE SUBTEXT: GENOCIDE

Usually unspoken in the debate about war is the general global violence that pervades present political life on the planet. Genocide is a term used to describe the systemic, deliberate, and targeted killing of groups of people. Such violence typically occurs to facilitate larger social goals. The genocide of Jews in Nazi Germany is a classic template for contemporary understanding of the concept of genocide. We established this definition previously. [3]

Genocide has been a matter of increased focus in international law circles as a result of the genocide in Hitler's Germany. Despite the obvious moral repugnance of such acts, genocide is a matter of growing concern within the community of sovereign nations.

The audacity of these crimes makes measure difficult. Bassiouni, one of the foremost contemporary experts on the subject, suggests that the twentieth century amassed 170 million deaths attributable to genocide. [4] These numbers are confirmed by a variety of other scholars including R.J. Rummel, Samantha Power and Daniel Goldhagen. [5] This genocide statistic stands in contrast to forty million deaths resulting from war. According to these numbers, the average global citizen is more than four times as likely to die of genocide as result of war. Given such staggering numbers, one might expect public sphere debate to be focused upon the optimal resolution of such a problem. Nonetheless, recent debates about Afghanistan, Iraq, Syria, and North Korea suggest a primacy to war deaths with little or no emphasis upon deaths attributable to genocide.

The salience and presence of genocide as an argument invites some historical review in order to grasp the propensities of it and the ultimate argument relationship behind the binary of war and peace. A summary of some prominent genocides with regard to military intervention from the past sixty years is a useful reminder.

A casual observation of life on earth suggests that for the average human being, genocide is one of the most systemic, practical, and brutal threats they face to their existence. Samantha Power, [6] documents the rapid pace of genocide in her Pulitzer Prize winning book. Power is currently the U.S. ambassador to the United Nations and leads American global efforts against genocide. Her ascendancy has added practical political weight to the struggle against genocide.

The global reality of genocide remains obscured by the western focus on a binary of war versus peace. The ideal reality is peace. War is to be avoided and severely scrutinized whenever it is initiated by Western powers such as the United States or Israel. The anti-war movement, beginning with the Vietnam War in the 1960s, has come to hold significant public sway in Western societies. Anti-war movements focus on the innocent lives lost as a result of war actions taken by western powers, particularly the United States.

Initially, anti-war activists such as ANSWER, Code Pink, Michael Moore, Ramsey Clark, and Noam Chomsky describe human options within a symbolic order of "war" and "peace." Audiences are asked by these advocates to consider whether they would prefer the world to exist in peace or war. War is the negative term and peace is the positive term. The withdrawal or failure to use military force will result in peace according to these acti-

Table 11.1.

Place/Leader	Time	Numbers Killed	Military Intervention
Russia/Stalin	1940s	17 million	No foreign military intervention
China/Mao Tse Tung	1950s	10 million	No foreign military intervention
Germany/Hitler	1930s	6 million	US and allies interrupted genocide late
Cambodia/Pol Pot	1970s	3 million	US military action ended prior to genocide
Sudan/Bashir	1990s	1-3 million	No foreign military intervention
Rwanda/Hutus	1990s	800,000	No foreign military intervention
Bosnia/Milosevic	1990s	200,000	Interrupted early by US led intervention
North Korea/Jung II	2002	2 million	No foreign military intervention

Source: Bassiouni, 1998; Scharf, 2000; Ratliff, 1999; Kelly, 2002; and Gordon, 2002.

vists. The presence of military force is symbolically strategic. American military force is noticeable and therefore achieves presence[7] in their arguments. Conversely, in an abundance of human slaughters the domestic uses of military force—against civilian populations in South Vietnam after U.S. forces withdrew, against the domestic populations of Cambodia by Pol Pot, against the domestic populations of Iraq by Saddam Hussein, against the domestic populations of Syria by Bashar al-Assad—have been largely rationalized. Because the sovereign attacks of domestic dictators against their own civilian populations is not within the symbolic order of "war" (two sovereign nations fighting each other), these events necessarily fall into the category of "peace" (sovereign nations not fighting each other). Consequently, the killing of millions in Rwanda, Sudan, North Korea, and Syria are rhetorically rendered as "peace." Military force is not used against these governments; therefore, "war" is avoided and "peace" is preserved.

This symbolic order also has a jingoistic alignment. As the principal global military power, the United States is presently an important agent for the possibility of war. Constraining U.S. military activity is significant to anti-war activists. In order to argue against the wars in Iraq, Afghanistan and elsewhere activists argue for pulling out U.S. troops in order to save their lives. The apparent sympathy for American troops solves domestic suspicion that the anti-war movement is unpatriotic and provides a rhetorical basis for ending U.S. military operations. The positioning is jingoistic since it appeals to base nativism by suggesting that the death of American soldiers is inherently more significant than the death of foreign soldiers or domestic civilians left to fight and resist the domestic terrorists alone. It is peace for me and not for thee.

Because the United States has the largest military force in the world, anti-war activists focus on it as the basis of stopping war in the world. The United States exists militarily like a Gulliver among Lilliputian powers. International law and advocacy groups must establish arguments to constrain U.S. military action. In so doing, the primary practical basis for stopping genocide is also constrained. As in the classic case of World War II where millions were slaughtered in Nazi death camps up until the liberation of camps by allied armies, genocides have little chance of ending without outside military force. The constraint of American military forces serves the interests of genocidal leaders such as Kim Jong Un of North Korea, Omar al-Bashir of Sudan, and Bashar al-Assad of Syria, by preserving their sovereign autonomy to kill people in their assigned geographic space. In his classic anti-war tale "Fahrenheit 9/11" Michael Moore narrates the dramatic moment of U.S. military invasion in Iraq by intoning that America "attacked the sovereign nation of Iraq." By noting it as a "sovereign nation" Moore was appealing to a set of international laws and norms, which accords privileges to self-assigned leaders that preside over various geographical spaces in the world. The United States disturbed that moral order with its military attack and the internationally sanctioned political functions of Saddam Hussein were interrupted. Saddam Hussein's role as the sovereign leader of Iraq was "unjustly" interfered with, and Moore argued that moral indignation should be directed to the warlike activities of the United States. Presiding over placid scenes of kite flying in Baghdad, Saddam Hussein's ongoing extermination of domestic Shiites and Kurds was understood by Moore and other anti-war advocates as reasonably within Hussein's peaceful symbolic order. For anti-war activists, the shattering of the genocidaire's symbolic order is the violation that audiences must focus upon not the inherent injustice of the genocidaire's domestic political practices in places like Syria, Iraq, North Korea and Sudan.

A similar set of rationales was used recently to stop a military strike against Syria. Syria's government under the leadership of Assad has killed tens of thousands of its citizens since 2011. Most notably, in the summer of 2013, the government ordered sarin gas attacks on communities in Damascus killing more than one hundred civilians including women and children. Despite the widespread consensus against using chemical weapons against civilians, a strong global public sphere argument emerged to "protect the sovereignty of Syria."[8]

The reification of international law is part of a moral component in anti-war arguments. The sanctity of international law provides a moral backdrop upon which to portray American military actions as "out of bounds" and subject to public censure. The United Nations is the principal locus of international law and anti-war advocates appeal to its functions as the proper basis of global governance. The forums and international traditions are offered as inherently ideal pretexts to global living. Essentially, the UN and other forms of international consensus maintain ideal civic conduct, and aggressive rivals such as the United States and Israel can disrupt this ideal political life. From this perspective, the United States is typically understood as a rogue state unwilling to submit to the benign global order. Empirically, this global order has shown little or no willingness to act on questions of genocide. Not only that, but international forces like those offered by the UN have systemically engaged in sexual abuse of local populations they were sent to serve and protect.[9] Several years ago, the United Nations released a report explaining how ongoing atrocities in Sudan and Darfur did not meet international legal agreements that define genocide.[10] In the 1990s, the UN did not approve of NATO and U.S. military action in the Balkans aimed at protecting Muslim minorities in Serbia. The inaction of the UN in Rwanda is powerfully observed in the film *Hotel Rwanda*. The simple reality that a single member of the five nation security council can negate a plan for military intervention became an overwhelming reality against any idealism toward stopping genocidal violence. This pattern of veto at the security council has entered into the global calculation of genocide perpetrators, as such dictators manipulate the public forum processes surrounding the UN to facilitate their own grotesque efforts. Samantha Power acknowledged this problem in the recent struggle to punish Syria militarily for chemical weapons use.[11] Iraq was able to lure France and Russia with oil contracts during UN debate on the Iraq war. Sudan has successfully wooed China to veto action in that region by providing 7 percent of China's national oil consumption.[12] Oil contracts for Security Council members have given new meaning for the anti-war cliché "blood for oil." Political leaders committing genocide utilize anti-war arguments to manipulate the public processes surrounding international consensus about violence against civilians. Sudanese leaders appealed to the global public that "the United States not be allowed to steal Sudan's oil."[13] The remarks were borrowed from numerous anti-war activists critiquing the U.S. war in Iraq. Such arguments came despite the purchase of China's UN influence with oil contracts from the Sudanese government.

A third reason that anti-war arguments lead to genocide is the misuse of genocide as a metaphorical term. Anti-war activists will tend to bolster arguments against military action by describing war as comparable to genocide. Military commanders at various levels are compared to historical genocide leaders. The most basic and intrinsic genocide comparison is the Nazi leader, Adolf Hitler. As a democratically elected figure of the most notorious genocide of the twentieth century, Hitler's invocation in argument is irresistible to many advocates including the anti-war community. It is noteworthy that moveon.org pulled a web site commercial created for its community competition for anti-Bush ads during election 2004. The ad directly compared Bush to Hitler. The overuse of Hitler as an argument is not particularly interesting; however, certain instances can be strategic in diluting the power of genocide as a moral concern. It is has been observed that the persistent tendency in the European press to refer to Israeli leaders as a Nazi or Hitler[14] is a not so subtle effort to re-rationalize the European origins of Hitler's powerful anti-Semitism. As the leader of the Jewish state, we are encouraged to see the Holocaust as an inevitable reality of global violence and not the peculiar targeted savagery of the innocents. If the Jewish state established as relief to the holocaust is now perpetuating a holocaust in Palestine, surely the German final solution can be seen as relatively harmless. This rationalization shows the insidious potential of genocide comparisons. The symbolic break down between government targeting of unarmed civilians and military targeting of combatants serves to move genocide victims into an acceptable scene within political dramas. Nothing can be done. War is genocide. Genocide is war. Military force aiming to interrupt such activity is rendered symbolically meaningless.

THE MILITARY INDUSTRIAL COMPLEX

A prominent meme within this opposition to war is a notion of a "military industrial complex." Drawn from President Eisenhower's farewell address as president, advocates against American war derive from this term the complete subordination of public discourse. All reason is being subverted by a military industrial complex composed of Haliburton, GE, and an array of arms suppliers who will profit from "this war." The overarching power of this dystopian fantasy draws all rhetoric supporting military actions into a larger subterfuge that only the activist can see clearly. "All arguments for military action are for the senseless profit of the war machine." It is useful to ask who is benefiting financially from the world of "peace"? In the early dialectic of the twenty-first century surrounding genocide in Sudan, this hue and cry was heard, and it was enhanced by the "blood for oil" mantra that suggested that part of the profit motive to the "war machine" is cheaper oil flowing from nations attacked by the United States. Who benefits from "peace"? In the case of Iraq, Saddam Hussein made extensive agreements in the decade before the U.S. invasion, with various national governments such as Russia to buy oil in violation of sanction agreements. Oil flowed freely in secret international arrangements from Iraq into the hands of those "enforcing the peace." When international action was sought in the early twenty-first century on Sudan, China was easily able to prevent UN authorization of military action. China would gradually develop a relationship allowing it to draw a substantial national oil supply from Sudan in defiance of international sanctions designed to "preserve the global peace."[15] Billions of dollars in oil money profits are easily discernible in the discursive formation of "peace" described and defended by advocates.

VIETNAM NOSTALGIA

An important characteristic of contemporary anti-war rhetoric is its conservative framing. Anti-war rhetoric is organized around the protests of the 1960s aimed at ending U.S. military action in Vietnam. The conservative nature of current anti-war argumentation means that advocates seek to preserve the sensations of that 1960s era. A LexisNexis search of news articles for the first week of the second Iraq war in March 2003 revealed more than three hundred news articles utilizing the words Iraq and Vietnam in the same sentence. A similar search for the first month of military action in Afghanistan revealed 291 articles with Afghanistan and Vietnam in the same sentence.[16] Numerous analogs also indicate the conservative thread of anti-war activism that aims to preserve 1960s experiences as normative to our present understandings of war.

Because Vietnam is such an organizing argumentative metaphor in anti-war discourse, it is useful to examine the genealogy of Vietnam conflict.[17] Though the historical treatments of Vietnam are so varied and formed by ideology, it is possible to observe some genealogical developments within the consistent nature of Vietnam narratives. The consistent telling of the failed American military mission describes the unilateral power of the United States gradually being dragged into a quagmire of ever increasing demands. Military advisers grow to combatants and ultimately an imperialist hegemon imposing themselves in a domestic dispute. Anti-war protests at home derailed the political future of Lyndon Johnson and the larger Democratic Party in 1968. Rhetorical resistance by the anti-war movement continued into the second term of Nixon when U.S. forces finally withdraw in defeat from Saigon. Because the story ends with the triumphant consummation of the anti-war movement, it is difficult to appreciate rhetorical factors larger than the story. Nonetheless, the subtext of genocide can be observed.

The expansion of the Vietnam War into Cambodia was an important impetus to anti-war efforts. Protests about American bombings of civilian populations in Cambodia reenergized anti-war sentiment. These protests were an important factor of Nixon's ultimate withdrawal from Vietnam and Cambodia.[18] The absence of U.S. military force resisting the Khmer Rouge in Cambodia is an important basis for the ascendancy of the genocide subtext. Experts consider the Cambodian genocide to be one of the most efficient genocides[19] of the twentieth century:

In the first few weeks after Cambodia fell to the Khmer Rouge in April, 1975, the nation's cities were evacuated, hospitals emptied, schools closed, factories deserted, money and wages abolished, monasteries emptied, and libraries scattered. Freedom of the press, movement, worship, organization association, and discussion, all completely disappeared for nearly four years. So did everyday family life. A whole nation was kidnapped [sic.], and then besieged from within. . . Democratic Kampuchea was a prison camp state, and the 8 million prisoners served most of their time in solitary confinement. And 1.5 million of the inmates were worked, starved, and beaten to death. Seeking a resurrection of the Cambodian race cleansed of all impurities, Pol Pot's regime launched a countrywide purge of foreign-educated intellectuals, Buddhists, non-Cambodian ethnicities, and finally his own people. This amounted to several religious or ethnically-driven genocides within the larger context of the atrocities that were perpetrated by the Khmer Rouge during its reign of terror. [20]

The appalling tale of Cambodia cannot be chronologically disconnected from the end of the Vietnam War and the role of American peace activists in bringing "peace" to Southeast Asia. Anti-war commentators such as Chomsky denounced evidence of impending genocidal slaughters by the Khmer Rouge as right wing propaganda designed to re-start war in Southeast Asia. A chorus of American editorial writers and U.S. Congressional members joined Chomsky in his charges. [21] Cambodians barely survived the "peace" that came while thousands of Vietnamese set to desperate boat flights in the ocean to escape similar annihilation in neighboring Vietnam. In four years following the Vietnam War, more than three hundred thousand Vietnamese accepted asylum provisions from the United States though many thousands more wanted in as well. [22] The departure of American military personnel from Southeast Asia played an important role in facilitating this new twentieth-century notion of "peace."

Rhetorical strategies noted thus far reduce the public capacity to view the subtext of genocide beneath "global peace" since war and genocide are apparently the same thing. The detention of combatants is indistinguishable from the detention of children such as Anne Frank or the Cambodian practice of having children execute their own parents under Pol Pot. The various conflations by anti-war activists of war and genocide are bountiful and serve to erode the distinction between the two. In so doing, the public is increasingly unable to recognize genocide as a salient concept and the sense of urgency toward military intervention arising from apparent scenes of genocide is ameliorated by the sensation that wars to stop genocide are the same as genocide. We are assured by anti-war arguments that military force is genocide and standing by passively is the best and most reasonable course of human action. The victims of state on civilian violence get far less empathy and play than human beings dying from outside military interventions by the United States.

A COMMUNICATION SOLUTION

In order to solve the problem of genocide globally, we must confirm some communication-based solutions regarding how we "talk" about genocide locally. A deconstructive critical move must be made to elevate the subtext above the current noisy dialectic of war and peace.

As seen in figure 11.1, we presently conduct our simplistic discourse along a binary of war versus peace. "Who wants peace?" and "Who wants war?" become the dialectic encampments of public opinion. This is enshrined in international law by protecting states from the risks and rhetorical ruptures associated with war. This simplistic communication paradigm that limits public discussion must be replaced with a new perspective that acknowledges the centrality and importance of genocide vis-à-vis war and peace.

In figure 11.2, we see the new symbolic arrangement that lifts genocide out of the unspoken subtext of the current war/peace binary and allows us to focus on the massive numbers of civilian victims left in "peaceful" exercises of "sovereign states." The new rhetorical logic that acknowledges that genocide is the unspoken reality of peace allows all actors—individual or state—to recognize and construct responses to that reality. The avoidance of war and the political scoring that treats this as an inherent victory is rhetorically driving victims into the arms of the genocidaires. This logic remains plain within the peaceful state relations ongoing with Syria. No nation is at war

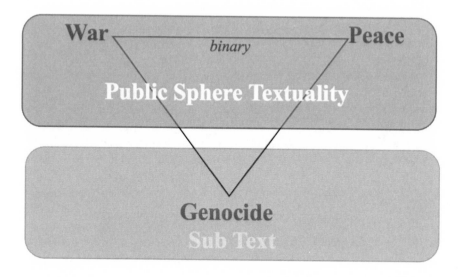

Figure 11.1.

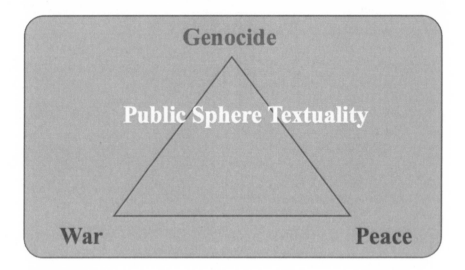

Figure 11.2.

with Syria. Syria is at peace—and yet two hundred thousand have died—and more will die in ethnic elimnations defined presently as peace.

Harvard scholar Daniel Goldhagen lodges an important academic step in this necessary moral communication endeavor in his work entitled: "Worse than War." The title and ultimate critical problem resolved, is the urging of political scientists to recognize that there is something worse than war at work on humanity. Goldhagen terms this genocidal practice eliminationism though he connects it to existing literature on genocide. Goldhagen's important recent work confirms that our current reviews of international politics and the deeper problem of genocide have missed the moral reality that genocide is worse than war. In continually safeguarding the State in international political science reviews of public policy, we have doomed millions of individual civilians to internal annihilations that are dishonestly signified as "peace."

This analysis recognizes this problem and centers it within the realm of communication. We must change how we talk about genocide in relation to war and peace. The figures 11.1 and 11.2 detail how genocide must be elevated in our discourse and this higher discursive complexity will aid in reducing the problem of genocide. The current angst was acutely felt in the Rwandan genocide of 1995 when Clinton's press secretary strained not to say the "G-word." More pressing was the Clinton administration perception of war fatigue in the American public surrounding the failed 1993 military mission in Mogadishu, Somalia, that provided sensational imagery of a U.S. soldier being dragged through the streets of Mogadishu by another combatant. That problem was overcome from a communication standpoint in 2004 when Secretary of State Colin Powell used the "G-word" to describe the international crisis in Sudan. This paved the way for current solutions that save millions in Southern Sudan.

A second deconstructive move surrounds the public depiction of soldiers. The anti-American war movement has problematized the symbolism surrounding American soldiers. During World War II, soldiers were portrayed empathetically by journalists such as Ernie Pyle. [23] Today our intellectual culture led by journalistic practice locates the American soldier on a Vietnam inspired continuum of victim or villain. They may be a disabled vet crippled by a roadside bomb that draws the empathy as a symbolic victim of "bad policy." Or they may be the villain of Abu Ghraib who tortures and demeans good citizens of another country like Lynndie England. American soldiers primarily exist within this symbolic order and this blocks them from the status of "hero," which tends to inspire and confirm public support for military action. These depictions are not accidental and their purposeful designs demoralize the effort to militarily contain or overcome genocide.

As noted in the symbol triangles of figures 11.3 and 11.4, the triad of victim, villain, and victor constitute inevitable interpretive possibilities for understanding American soldiers. The purposeful celebration of victors in heroic roles elevates military service and allows the public to see how genocides from Auschwitz to Somalia to Baghdad can be stopped and revered for the positive acts that they are. Many skeptics of this depiction suggest that this is dishonest, propaganda, whitewashing crimes of soldiers. But in what sense are the present negative depictions of American soldiers not the very same thing? Negative depictions of American soldiers make a principal rhetorical staple of radical genocidal governments from Tehran to Pyongyang. Are these depictions of American soldiers more honest and candid? A global blockbuster film from Turkey in 2007 entitled "Valley of the Wolves" made huge sums of money in global movie houses. The film depicted American soldiers as blood sucking Jewish doctors and ruthless killers of innocent human beings. American movie stars Gary Buse and Billy Zane depicted American military personnel and military contractors as deeply evil. The movie never appeared on American screens but was shown almost everywhere else despite its unapologetic usages of anti-Semitic tropes. [24] A moral interrogation of how American soldiers are depicted in the United States and globally is long overdue. If people can be expected to volunteer for the supremely dangerous task of donning a uniform to protect civilians from radical social nihilists around the world then the public should have communication access to the validation of their good efforts. Left unchecked, these global nihilists do develop statist tools to carry out eliminationism, genocide, and democide. The antagonists of American soldiers quite often refrain from the communication symbolism of uniforms, thereby conferring an opportu-

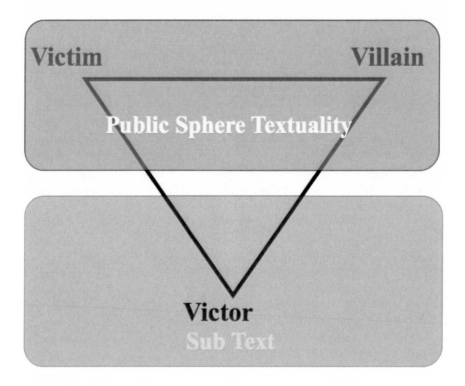

Figure 11.3.

nity for American skeptics to depict them as civilian innocents. American soldiers consistently take the ambitious and idealistic communication stance of identifying themselves as combatants. Mediators of the public sphere need to take a more honest stance about when and where the designation of "hero" might be more readily applied to the global sphere if we are to muster the necessary resources to combat genocide. One of the most surprising aspects of my work at the Holocaust museum in Washington DC was seeing and hearing how much survivors venerate and appreciate American soldiers. Much of their work involves speaking to military personnel. They consistently refer to service members as "liberators"—a term I had discarded within the academy as cynically impossible. I believe I was wrong in that judgment. I believe all students of genocide would do well to recalibrate their consideration of the symbolic triangle of victim, villain, victor. There is no need to burden these arguments with ideological labels such as liberal or conservative. There are practical human concerns that are diminished by continually preferring a symbolic construction of "peace" that misses the state violence against individuals that begins in the same kind of systemic preferences seen

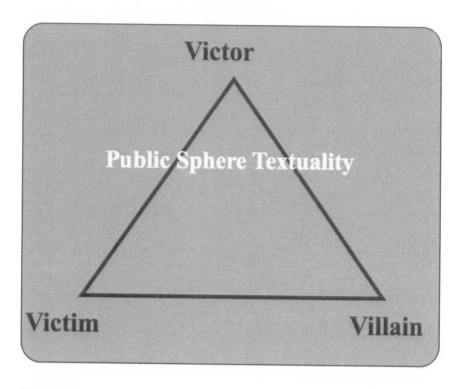

Figure 11.4.

in Farmer's segregated South but ends in extensive genocidal slaughters like those in Syria.

CONCLUSION

Michel Foucault urges that intellectuals need to take on the role of specific intellectuals—working within their own spheres of activity.[25] The killing of innocent civilians should be a constant academic concern—not a strategic rhetorical form for reassuring our American sense of peace. The ascendancy of the genocide subtext from beneath the rhetorical binary of war/peace suggests that the twenty-first century will be a rhetorical struggle over whether voiceless victims of genocide will return to the public gaze as gaudy victims of American imperialism or hapless members of the human family seeking help from the strong. Since the international community first swore at Nuremberg in 1948 to never let such atrocities happen again, more than 150 million people have been killed in war crimes, genocide, and crimes against humanity.[26]

After the world pontificated about the complexities of stopping a dictator in 2003 that killed more Muslims than any other human being in history,[27] it is useful to reflect on the shallow application of multicultural values on our campuses. No innocent civilians were killed by American military bombs in Rwanda's genocide of 1994. The two hundred thousand Muslims who died prior to American military intervention in Kosovo never had to worry that they would be hit by American bombs. None of the more than two hundred thousand Syrians deaths were caused by American cruise missiles. Presumably, these instances were "peace" at its finest. Yet ethnic groups were dying in those moments of "peace." The powerful interests of peace have consistently re-situated themselves within American and European intellectual cultures to facilitate realms of pleasure and ambivalence about the larger realities of global existence. The cliché of military industrial complex needs to be met in the public sphere by the more dominant peace industrial complex that acknowledges the dishonest political shadings of peace. Arms are sold as readily in peace as in war and in the twenty-first century, the arms sales in peace bolster to practice and provinces of genocidal activity. It is my personal hope that argument and communication scholars and students will come to see past the rhetorical binary of war and peace to understand the more meaningful trauma of human genocide.

NOTES

1. George Orwell, "Notes on Nationalism (1945)," in *Fifty Essays*, Project Gutenberg of Australia, 2010. Available at http://gutenberg.net.au/ebooks03/0300011h.html#part30.
2. Chomsky, Noam. 2001. *9-11*. New York: Seven Stories Press.
3. Convention on the Prevention and Punishment of the Crime of Genocide (1948). Article II.
4. Bassiouni, M. Cherif. 1998. "The Normative Framework of International Humanitarian Law: Overlaps, Gaps and Ambiguities," *Transnational Law & Contemporary Problems*, 8.
5. Power, Samantha. 2002. *A problem from Hell: America and the age of genocide*. New York: Perennial; Goldhagen, Daniel. 2009. "Worse Than War: Genocide, Eliminationism, and the Ongoing Assault on Humanity." New York: Public Affairs; and Rummel, Rudolph. 2002. "Power Kills: Democracy as a method of non-violent action." New York: Transaction publishers.
6. Power, Samantha. 2002. *A problem from Hell: America and the age of genocide*. New York: Perennial.
7. Dearin, Robert. 1982. "Perelman's 'Quasi-logical argument': A critical elaboration," in J. Robert Cox and Charles Arthur Willard, "Advances in Argumentation Theory." Carbondale: Southern Illinois Press, 78–94.
8. Campos, Paul. 2013. "Striking Syria is completely illegal." *Time*. September 5. Accessed September 25, 2013. http://ideas.time.com/2013/09/05/obamas-plan-for-intervention-in-syria-is-illegal/.
9. MacFarquhar, Neil. 2011. "Peacekeepers sex scandals linger, On Screen and Off." *New York Times*. September 7. Accessed September 25, 2013. http://www.nytimes.com/2011/09/08/world/08nations.html?pagewanted=all.
10. Leopold, Evelyn. 2005. "UN envoy says deaths in Darfur underestimated." *Reuters*. February 1.

11. Stolberg, Sheryl. "A New US player, Put on the World Stage by Syria." 2013. *New York Times*. Accessed September 25, 2013. http://www.nytimes.com/2013/09/23/world/a-new-us-player-put-on-world-stage-by-syria.html?pagewanted=all&_r=0.

12. Crilly, Rob. 2005. "Chinese seek resources, profits in Africa." *USA TODAY*. June 22 p. 4B; and Nanda, Ved P. 2005. "Global response to Darfur pitiful U.N., superpowers not doing enough after Sudan genocide." *The Denver Post*. June 26. p. B-07. Accessed August 15, 2005. http://www.denverpost.com/opinion/ci_2804617.

13. Deen, Thalif. 2004. "Politics: Annan asks more funds for Darfur-bound African force." *IPS-Inter Press Service*. September 2.

14. Smith, Craig S. 2005. "Ruling seen as victory, but not for a free press." *The International Herald Tribune*, June 28. p. 7. Accessed September 16, 2013. http://www.nytimes.com/2005/06/27/world/europe/27iht-france.html.

15. "Asian Nations lead the charge for exploration and exploitation." 2006. *Summit Reports*. March 7. Accessed September 25, 2013. http://www.summitreports.com/sudan/foreign.htm.

16. Voth, Ben, and Aaron Noland, . 2006. "Vietnam as Paradigmatic Metaphor," *Controversia: An International Journal of Debate and Democratic Renewal* 5(1). Fall. 57–84.

17. Der Derian, James. 2001. *Virtuous War: Mapping the military-industrial-media-entertainment network*. Boulder, CO: Westview Press.

18. Power, Samantha. 2002. *A problem from Hell: America and the age of genocide*. New York: Perennial.

19. Ratliff, Suellen. 1999. "UN Representation Disputes: A Case Study of Cambodia and a New Accreditation Proposal for the Twenty-First Century." *California Law Review*, 87.

20. Kelly, J. Michael. 2002. "Can sovereigns be brought to justice? The crime of genocide's evolution and the meaning of the Milosevic trial." *St. Johns Law Review*, 76, 257–332.

21. Power, Samantha. 2002. *A problem from Hell: America and the age of genocide* New York: Perennial.

22. Gee, Harvey. 2001. Book Review: *The Refugee Burden: A Closer Look at the Refugee Act of 1980*, N.C.J. Int'l L. & Com. Reg, 26. Spring.

23. Kuypers, Jim. 2014. *Partisan Journalism: A History of Media Bias in the United States*. Lanham, MD: Rowman & Littlefield.

24. "Audiences cheer Anti-American prejudice." 2006. *The Washington Times*. 14 February. Accessed December 11, 2013. http://www.washingtontimes.com/news/2006/feb/14/20060214-104958-5445r/.

25. Foucault, Michel. 1977. *Discipline and Punish: the Birth of the Prison*, trans. A. Sheridan. New York: Pantheon Books.

26. Scharf, Michael. 2000. "Post-cold war international security threats: terrorism, drugs, and organized crime symposium." *Michigan Journal of International Law*, 21. Spring.

27. Issa, Darrell. 2003. "Arab Americans Must Reject Tyranny." *Los Angeles Times*. 21 March. p. 15.

Chapter Twelve

Winning Wars against Genocide

We are preaching hope, standing on the bones of the past.—John Rucyahana,
The Bishop of Rwanda[1]

A vital aspect of repealing genocide is recognizing the empirical basis of success. Proving the negative is an inherently impossible task but it should not prevent reasonable observation of how genocide is prevented in recent political actions globally. This chapter examines three important examples of how political and military actions work in concert to stop genocide. The slippery and vague sense of inevitability surrounding the topic of genocide is a major component of its cause. Perpetrators need a reliable sense that the global community is "frustrated and exasperated" with the possibility of confrontation and prevention. The sense of moral malaise and inevitability conditions us toward silence enabling the genocidal process. Three key recent examples in the twenty-first century suggest that genocide can be stopped: Sudan, Iraq and Liberia.

SUDAN

Sudan has since 1989 been governed by sovereign leader Omar al-Bashir. The brutal progression of his rule has all the features and details of genocide. Decades of debate on who to hold responsible culminated in a conviction of genocide by the ICC in 2009. An arrest warrant was issued for Omar al-Bashir.[2] That conviction was based upon the gathered evidence suggesting that Bashir's unique Islamist supremacist interpretation of governance dictated the killing of more than two million Sudanese human beings. Those killings had savage and brutal features that clearly communicated not only a sense of war, but also an attitude of cultural intimidation.

Sudan is culturally and religiously divided between north and south.[3] The north is principally Arab and Muslim while the south is principally dark skinned African and Christian/animist.[4] Victims in the south have consistently complained that the genocidal actions of Khartoum were motivated by skin color and religious supremacism.[5] Most of the deaths in Sudan took place in the south during the 1990s. In this era, international resistances to the activities of genocidaire Omar al-Bashir were highly constrained.

American military failures in nearby Somalia accentuated the demoralized attitude dominating the international sphere toward stopping local forms of militarism on the continent. Commentator Samantha Power isolated the crushing symbolism of American deaths in Mogadishu as an important precursor to the Rwandan genocide and the awkward stammering of the Clinton administration that could not name the swift killing of nearly one million Tutsis in three months— a genocide.[6] The genocide in Rwanda typified the immobilization of the United States and a broader community concerned about genocide. That sense of malaise and futility was an important aspect of keeping the world safe for genocide. The belief that, "military intervention is always wrong and doomed" leads to accepting genocide as practically necessary. The 1990s indicated a common pattern of intervention that sees military action followed by interpretations of failure as a license toward inward isolationist focus by the United States and other major powers such as the United Nations. In the late 1990s, President Clinton ordered cruise missile strikes into Sudan to destroy chemical weapons production.[7] The military strikes were debated as distractions or misguided—particularly in the domestic preoccupation with the Monica Lewinsky scandal. The strikes did not galvanize public opinion toward reducing or even focusing on Sudan as a serious genocide problem. Bombings of embassies in Africa also did little to shift the public mood toward empathy or concern.

Of course the aftermath of 9-11 radically interrupted this malaise and shattered the pacifist mythology in the United States that ignoring the world could produce greater tranquility. An emerging War on Terror found Sudan again in the headlines as a place at least visited, and perhaps frequented, by Osama Bin Laden. An American African command emerged on the continent with a purpose of thwarting terrorism in locations such as Sudan and Somalia.[8] The American war footing brought international focus to domestic hearts and minds. The Bush administration maintained a broad argument that poverty and tyranny encouraged the emergence of terrorism. Though Sudan was not included in the "Axis of Evil"—recognized as Iran, North Korea, and Iraq—the sense that terrorism had many homes was an increasingly common thought.

Public pressure built to recognize political activities in Sudan as a genocide. The Secretary of State Colin Powell was pressed publicly on whether circumstances in Sudan could be called a genocide. The template of Rwanda was clearly in play. Would the new secretary of state refuse to name a genocide for the killing of two million people in Sudan? Powell declaring Sudan a "genocide" during Congressional hearings was a marked departure from the Rwandan era.[9] The naming of genocide escalated the priorities of the State Department and the United States toward diplomatic pressures aimed at curbing the violence in Sudan. This is an important juncture for observing how communication works. Questions about Sudan prompted response from the State Department. The State Department definition of genocide was applied. The larger international apparatus began to work against the genocide in Sudan. This did not involve any military action by the United States. Fighting directly in Afghanistan and ultimately in Iraq suggested limits to American power. Discussions of no-fly zones like those that once existed over Iraq were discussed but not implemented. In this era, the sovereign of Sudan Omar al-Bashir increasingly found himself answering questions and defending the social practices of Sudan. Sudan was becoming a known place in the lists of genocides in global history.

Instead of an American force, the United Nations and the African Union began constituting military forces. American pressure and guidance for an international military force defused one of the common tropes in preventing successful military intervention: the imperialism card. Anti-war activists regularly invoke the specter of imperialism as a reason indigenous militarism should remain unchecked.[10] International forces—principally from African Union nations—checked back rhetorically Bashir's ability to describe the "imperialists coming for his oil." The United States in direct contradiction to ongoing memes about "blood for oil" instituted an embargo against Sudan. All the while, China began to trade more freely with Sudan and drew 7 percent of its oil supply from the willing genocidaire. The murky arguments of "capitalist imperialism stealing the oil" of discriminated nations did not ring with truth in Sudan. Ultimately, a military force of seventeen thousand troops would build into Sudan.[11] Their focus became the western portions of Sudan known as Darfur. Within the Bush administration era, public awareness of Darfur would grow to one of the most well-known genocide events. Public protests were held, and a variety of public campaigns drew attention to the violence there. One of the most problematic aspects of the call to action was an inability to pinpoint the number of deaths in Darfur. Estimates of killing ranged from one hundred thousand to six hundred thousand and almost two million refugees.[12]

Frustrated advocates like Nicholas Kristoff may not have appreciated how the communication principals were actually working as they should. Public attention was thwarting the genocidaire's ability to easily gather and marshal forces for further ethnic cleansing as he had done with such ease and rapidity in the 1990s. The defeat of anti-American war forces globally with regard to Sudan, along with the use of African indigenous forces is an important lesson in the current progress made on genocide. Coalitions of willing partners opposed to genocide can defeat the binaries offered by anti-American war opponents. Africa policy critic Mahmood Mamdani grudgingly admits that South Sudan is the one success of the Bush foreign policy.[13] While Mamdani's general appreciation of Africa policy is debatable his grudging acceptance of what transpires in Sudan as a success is an important rhetorical marker of success against genocide.

Alongside the outside efforts to establish military counters to Bashir's military policies inside Sudan, indigenous movements in the South began to press for independence. In January of 2005, a peace agreement between the North and South of Sudan was signed bringing to end the massive violence directed at the South by the North. In January of 2011, the people of South Sudan voted for independence despite the resistance of genocidaire Omar al-Bashir. July 9, 2011, stands as independence day for South Sudan—a new entry into the sovereign among nations.[14]

While violence in Sudan continues, the gradual reduction in violence is an important empirical lesson in success. Ultimately, the principal victims of genocide in the South prevailed in the domestic and international spheres to see the emergence of their own independent nation. This independence reduced the practical reach and impact of genocidaire Omar al-Bashir. Public activism played an important role in focusing and encouraging action on this matter. Important positive lessons learned from Sudan in reducing genocide are:

1. The ambivalence and reduced awareness about Sudan contributed to the highest levels of violence in the state during the 1990s.
2. Massive immigration flows are a strong indication of internal human rights violations that precede genocidal results.
3. Solutions to genocide can involve military force without necessarily relying on American soldiers.
4. Diplomacy can work in concert with broader conducts of war such as those that were pursued by the United States.
5. Sudan is much more peaceful today than it was in the 1990s.
6. The African Union is a credible military alternative against genocidal violence compared to NATO, the EU, the United States, and even UN forces.

IRAQ

A tremendous amount of intellectual capital was expending between 2002 and 2008 to stigmatize the American led effort to remove Saddam Hussein from power and build a democracy in his place. The consequence of these lengthy indictments is widespread misunderstanding about the successes sur-rounding the war in Iraq that began in 2003. Most importantly, the ethnic groups of Shiites and Kurds live at a much-reduced risk of genocide than they did prior to 2003.[15] Most evidently, the Shiites are now the dominant political power brokers with Kurds and Sunnis sharing subordinate roles in the new government shaped by elections in 2005. To understand this progression and reduction of genocide risk, it is important to detail an accurate chronology of how we arrived at this safer point for these two ethnic communities.

Saddam Hussein established himself as a genocidaire in the 1980s when his government dropped chemical weapons on Kurds in places such as Ha-labja.[16] Hussein's defense minister referred to those weapons as "human insecticides" and the secular Baathist government of Saddam Hussein viewed the weapon use against civilians as a practical internal tool of poli-tics. Hussein was the first sovereign to use chemical weapons in this manner since the gassing of Jews and other ethnic groups by Adolf Hitler. Hussein's pan-Arab vision led him to invade Kuwait and threaten Saudi Arabia in 1991. The U.S. lead allied invasion and repulsion of Iraqi forces nearly lead to the overthrow of Saddam Hussein in that first gulf war. In the aftermath of this first American war with Saddam, Iraqi minorities such as the Shiites and the Kurds rose up against the Iraqi government. The United States and the inter-national coalition did not feel comfortable pursuing the full removal of Sad-dam Hussein that would require an invasion of the central Bagdad region of the country. The decision was made to withdraw with an agreement that Saddam would rid his government of weapons of mass destruction and con-tain his aggression.

The immediate intensity of military force used against domestic civilians such as the Shiites in the aftermath of American withdrawal created a return to genocidal conditions in Iraq. Saddam Hussein now used conventional weapons such as assault helicopters to kill these ethnic groups.[17] To prevent wider and more steadfast genocidal policies, the United States and allies such as Britain established no-fly zones over northern and southern Iraq. These zones protected the largely Kurdish and Shiite populations respectively. While observation of this no-fly zone prohibiting flying Iraqi aircraft over these areas was spotty and erratic, it did reduce mortality and genocidal practices in the two regions.[18] The Iraqi no-fly zones are the inceptional model for recent calls to replicate such policies in Sudan and Syria. This is an important solution step in reducing genocide.

The requirement to rid his military arsenal of weapons of mass destruc-tion became the sticking point that ultimately led to another war between Iraq and an American coalition. By 1999 President Clinton and the Congress passed legislation establishing a U.S. policy seeking removal of Saddam Hussein.[19] This was in addition to strong sanctions already held against Iraq by the United States and other sympathetic nations. United Nations weapons inspectors provided varying degrees of confirmation that the Iraqi government was cooperating in destroying weapons of mass destruction (WMD). By the fall of 2002, the Bush administration was making broad public arguments at home and abroad that leaving Saddam Hussein with WMD was dangerous to the United States and the world, particularly with regard to the possibility of passing such weapons to terrorists. In March of 2003, the United States invaded Iraq. U.S. forces were greeted as liberators— especially in Southern and Northern Iraq where Kurdish and Shiite communities lived.[20] Provocative images of celebration emerged from Bagdad as Iraqi residents tore down statues of the genocidaire and pounded his sculpted face with their sandals and shoes. Ultimately, internal violence escalated in Iraq— lead especially by Sunnis and other Islamic radicals held in check by Saddam. Five years of American troops in Iraq lead to considerable fighting with local groups willing to fight the emergence of democracy. Northern Iraq was the most elated and pacified region of Iraq. Surveys of Iraqis consistently showed the Kurds to be highly appreciative of the invasion while the Sunnis and Shias were shown to be less supportive.[21] The Sunnis displaced from power were consistently the most displeased by the invasion.

For the U.S. government, the failure to find large chemical weapon stockpiles was a profound disappointment. Though dozens of old chemical weapons were found in Iraq, the large contemporary stockpiles were not in evidence.[22] Considerable sources argue that the weapons were transported to the Baathist government of Syria.[23] That concern arose fresh in the most recent crisis in Syria. Despite this setback for the United States, the five years of internal violence did turn the Iraqi public universally against Al Qaeda. Al Qaeda affiliated terrorists killed thousands of Iraqis in suicide bombings often targeting schools, businesses, and marketplaces. The savagery of their actions created one of the most hostile public views of Al Qaeda in the Muslim world.[24] The unrest and violence in Iraq after the invasion lead many to believe elections would be impossible. Ultimately, the Iraqis voted for a constitution and conducted a total of three national elections in 2005. All elections had higher participation than any American election. Elections ultimately confirmed the reversal of Shia marginalization toward political dominance. Despite the extravagant international debates about Iraq, today the Shiites and Kurds stand further away from the prospects and practices of genocide than ever before. Christian minorities face considerable violence and risk in Iraq and their numbers are greatly diminished. This remains one of the more ominous side effects of securing the public space of Kurds and Shias.

A number of important positive lessons can be derived from the U.S. war in Iraq:

1. America has considerable military power that can persist past conventional public sphere breaking points. America withdrew from Mogadishu and Somalia ten years prior to the Iraqi invasion with a relatively small set of losses. The withdrawal signified for Osama Bin Laden, America's status as a "paper tiger."[25] The thousands of American casualties that seared the international news could not galvanize the withdrawal common in cases such as Vietnam and Somalia.

2. Occupation resolves in the most unequivocal manner, the status of weapons of mass destruction. Despite the disappointment at not finding large stockpiles the United States could leave Iraq with higher confidence than most parts of the world that a common ingredient for mixing up genocide was now gone.

3. The Kurds and the Shias reversed their positions as genocide targets and emerged in a relatively short amount of time as political managers. Current prospects for both groups are better than they have been in decades.

LIBERIA

Less well known, but every bit as profound, is the interesting case of Liberia. One of the rhetorical hallmarks of this genocidal scene was a despicable leader of genocidal activity by the name of General Butt Naked. He worked for genocidaire Charles Taylor. In 2008, General Butt Naked confessed to killing more than twenty thousand of his fellow citizens. His outrageous battlefield alias was drawn from his common habit of marching into civilian annihilations wearing nothing but a pair of boots. According to the general and other observers, these slaughters began with the ritualistic killing of a young child, cutting out the heart, and feeding it to his loyal troops.[26] While not in combat, his soldiers would kick around human skulls in soccer matches. In all, the savage killings decimated more than two hundred and fifty thousand in this nation of three million people. Killings like these took place from 1979 until 2003 when the military leaders were forced from power.

These gruesome details from the continent of Africa, reported by CNN in January 2012, left out one important detail: how was the man in charge of these terrible atrocities forced from power?[27] The United Nations and other organizations had, for years, strongly condemned Charles Taylor for his terrible crimes against the people of Liberia and his involvement in the atrocities in neighboring Sierra Leone. It took more than UN condemnation to remove this strong man from power. In the summer of 2003, against the harsh backdrop of a spring invasion of Iraq, President Bush deployed thousands of troops off the coast of Liberia to support troops already sent to the capital.[28] Those troops had been sent to secure U.S. property and the embassy in Monrovia. The United States declared that the thousands of U.S. troops would enter Liberia if Charles Taylor would leave the country. A multinational force of largely African forces helped remove Taylor from Liberia and secured the entry of U.S. troops to begin the transition from dictatorial savagery to humanitarian democracy.

Today, Liberia boasts the first female president on the continent of Africa—who received her education in the United States at Harvard.[29] A nation founded by former American slaves won a new birth of freedom thanks to the coordinated military intervention of the United States and cooperative African states such as Nigeria. Charles Taylor and his military minions now face trials for war crimes committed over twenty years of illegitimate rule.

The violation of Liberia's sovereignty by military force did not attract the same attention as Iraq. The strategic silence of peace ideologues speaks volumes about global violence in this world and should challenge us to rethink the conventional dynamics of war and peace. Despite these conspicuous silences, it is important to celebrate the hard won triumphs of human life. Congratulations should be given to the soldiers of the many nations who risked their lives to remove Charles Taylor, and to the people of Liberia who no longer must provide the demoralizing deaths as text, written by Charles Taylor and his deranged henchmen.

The success of American and African military forces in ending eliminationist practices of Charles Taylor provide several important positive lessons about reducing genocide:

1. Almost any amount of military force can make a positive difference in the worlds of genocide. The world had for years lectured and hectored Charles Taylor with complaints about gross human rights misconduct. The African Union considered taking action as well. America's willingness to provide just six hundred troops on the ground provided the critical catalyst to a much larger force composed mostly of Nigerian troops to end the savage nightmare of Charles Taylor. This expenditure took place while tens of thousands of U.S. troops were stretched thinly across Afghanistan, Iraq, and other theaters of terrorism in 2003.

2. Profound immediate positive changes are possible with military action. In an instant, one of the worst leaders in the world was replaced by a positive example for the continent. The new leader was a woman and educated at Harvard. The expectations that change can only be gradual is shattered in the example of Liberia.

3. We are not told by general media the incredibly positive accomplishments of American military. We remain entranced with the myth that military force cannot accomplish anything. We must each take an

active interest in global news to overcome this profound limitation. We must tell the individual stories of soldier heroes fighting against aspirant genocidaires.

CONCLUSION

These are three examples of genocide being reduced in the last ten years. A broader more comprehensive set of examples can and should be embraced. This discussion does not include the growing and established international norm of R2P (Responsibility to Protect). This doctrine has arguably prevented further global atrocities.[30] These three examples noted in this chapter suffice to break the mysterious notion that genocide is inevitable and intractable. Had each of these three sovereign locations continued with the death rates they were experiencing during the genocide era, approximately four million additional people would have died in the nations of Liberia, Sudan, and Iraq. The consolidation and removal of genocidaires with aggressive diplomacy and smart military invasions brought to an end eras of death as a text written in geographic spaces controlled by the genocidaires of Bashir, Hussein, and Taylor.

NOTES

1. Rucyahana, John. 2007. *The Bishop of Rwanda: Finding Forgiveness Amidst a Pile of Bones*. W Publishing Group.

2. Goldhagen, Daniel. 2009. *Worse Than War: Genocide, Eliminationism, and the Ongoing Assault on Humanity*. New York: Public Affairs.

3. Goldhagen, Daniel. 2009. *Worse Than War: Genocide, Eliminationism, and the Ongoing Assault on Humanity*. New York: Public Affairs.

4. Hitchens, Christopher. 2005. "Realism in Darfur." *Slate*. Accessed September 15, 2013. http://www.slate.com/articles/news_and_politics/fighting_words/2005/11/realism_in_darfur.html.

5. Totten, Samuel. 2013. "Genocide in Darfur, Sudan" in Samuel Totten, and William Parsons, (Eds). *Century of Genocide: Critical Essays and Eyewitness Accounts*, 4th edition. New York & London: Routledge.

6. Power, Samantha. 2002. *A problem from Hell: America and the age of genocide*. New York: Harper Perennial.

7. *CNN*. 1998. "US missiles pound targets Afghanistan, Sudan." Accessed September 15, 2013. http://www.cnn.com/US/9808/20/us.strikes.02/.

8. *NPR*. 2012. "US Command fights terrorists on African soil." March 9. Accessed September 15, 2013. http://www.npr.org/2012/03/09/148278069/u-s-command-fights-terrorists-on-african-soil.

9. Weisman, Steven. 2004. *New York Times*. September 9. Accessed September 23, 2013. http://www.nytimes.com/2004/09/09/international/africa/09CND-SUDA.html.

10. Mamdani, Mahmood. 2007. "The Politics of Naming: Genocide, Civil War, Insurgency." *London Review of Books* 29 no. 5: 5–8. March 8. Accessed September 12, 2013. http://www.lrb.co.uk/v29/n05/mahmood-mamdani/the-politics-of-naming-genocide-civil-war-insurgency.

11. Pleming, Sue. 2007. "U.S. urges Sudan to agree fully to Darfur plan." *The Washington Post*. January 24. Accessed September 23, 2013. http://www.washingtonpost.com/wp-dyn/content/article/2007/01/24/AR2007012401600.html.

12. Mamdani, Mahmood. 2007. "The Politics of Naming: Genocide, Civil War, Insurgency." *London Review of Books* 29 no. 5: 5–8. March 8. Accessed September 12, 2013. http://www.lrb.co.uk/v29/n05/mahmood-mamdani/the-politics-of-naming-genocide-civil-war-insurgency.

13. Mamdani, Mahmood. 2007. "The Politics of Naming: Genocide, Civil War, Insurgency." *London Review of Books* 29 no. 5: 5–8. March 8. Accessed September 12, 2013. http://www.lrb.co.uk/v29/n05/mahmood-mamdani/the-politics-of-naming-genocide-civil-war-insurgency.

14. *BBC*. 2013. "South Sudan Profile." July 24. Accessed September 10, 2013. http://www.bbc.co.uk/news/world-africa-14019202.

15. *Wall Street Journal*. 2013. "Iraq in Retrospect." March 19. Accessed September 15, 2013. http://online.wsj.com/article/SB10001424127887323393304578358691247678454.html.

16. Leezenberg, Michiel. 2013. "The Anfal Operations in Iraqi Kurdistan" in Samuel Totten and William Parsons (Eds). *Century of Genocide: Critical Essays and Eyewitness Accounts*, 4th edition. New York & London: Routledge.

17. *Human Rights Watch*. 1992. "Endless Torment: The 1991 Uprising in Iraq and Its Aftermath." June. Accessed September 16, 2013. http://www.hrw.org/reports/1992/Iraq926.htm.

18. *Human Rights Watch*. 1992. "Endless Torment: The 1991 Uprising in Iraq and Its Aftermath." June. Accessed September 16, 2013. http://www.hrw.org/reports/1992/Iraq926.htm.

19. *The American Presidency Project*. 1998. Statement on Signing the Iraq Liberation Act of 1998. October 31, 1998. Accessed September 16, 2013. http://www.presidency.ucsb.edu/ws/index.php?pid=55205.

20. Rubin, Michael. 2013. "Remembering Iraq's liberation without revisionism." *Commentary*. April 10. Accessed September 16, 2013. http://www.commentarymagazine.com/2013/04/10/remembering-iraqs-liberation-without-revisionism/#more-822276.

21. Soriano, Cesar G. and Steven Komarow. 2004. "Poll: Iraqis out of patience," *USA Today* Accessed September 16, 2013. http://usatoday30.usatoday.com/news/world/iraq/2004-04-28-poll-cover_x.htm.

22. *Duelfer Report*. 2005. April 25. Accessed September 16, 2013. http://www.gpo.gov/fdsys/pkg/GPO-DUELFERREPORT/content-detail.html.

23. Stoll, Ira. 2006. "Iraq's WMD Secreted in Syria, Sada says." *New York Sun*. January 26. Accesed December 29, 2013. http://www.nysun.com/foreign/iraqs-wmd-secreted-in-syria-sada-says/26514/.

24. *World Public Opinion*. 2006. "All Iraqi Ethnic Groups Overwhelmingly Reject al Qaeda." September 27. Accessed September 16, 2013. http://www.worldpublicopinion.org/pipa/articles/brmiddleeastnafricara/248.php.

25. Voth, Ben. 2013. "Restoring the image of George W. Bush." *American Thinker*. Accessed September 16, 2013. http://www.americanthinker.com/2013/04/m-restoring_the_image_of_
president_george_w_bush.html.

26. Fernandes, Edna. 2010. "Face to face with General Butt Naked—'the most evil man in the world.'" *Daily Mail*. November 27. Accessed September 16, 2013. http://www.dailymail.co.uk/news/article-1333465/Liberias-General-Butt-Naked-The-evil-man-world.html.

27. Brumfield, Ben. 2012. "Charles Taylor sentenced to 50 years for War crimes." *CNN*. May 31. Accessed September 5, 2013. http://www.cnn.com/2012/05/30/world/africa/netherlands-taylor-sentencing/index.html.

28. *CNN*. 2003. "Bush orders troops to positions off Liberia." Accessed September 16, 2013. http://www.cnn.com/2003/US/07/25/us.liberia/.

29. Hayes, Stephen. 2013. "How Africa's First Female President Led Her Country Back from the Brink" *US News and World Report*. May 20. Accessed September 16, 2013. http://

www.usnews.com/opinion/blogs/world-report/2013/05/20/president-ellen-sirleaf-and-liberia
-comeback.
    30. Abramowitz, Michael. 2013. "Does the United States have a responsibility to protect."
The Washington Post. September 6. http://www.washingtonpost.com/opinions/does-the-united
-states-have-a-responsibility-to-protect-the-syrian-people/2013/09/06/5decf4c0-167d-11e3
-be6e-dc6ae8a5b3a8_story.html

Chapter Thirteen

Conclusion

A World without Genocide

Fairy tales are more than true—not because they tell us dragons exist, but because they tell us dragons can be beaten.—G.K. Chesterton[1]

Genocide can be abolished and ended by the conclusion of the twenty-first century. The primary obstacle to this incredible reality is our own cynicism and certitude that such a task cannot be done. Because idealism and optimism are the key ingredients leading to success on all important problems, this chapter establishes examples of how humanity is already making progress toward this ideal goal. These demonstrations are not intended to suggest that no further effort is needed but to make realistic the end of genocide. The staggering toll of genocide, democide and eliminationism suggests that more than 150 million people were killed by such despicable and cruel plans designed and argued for by men during the twentieth century.[2] This number is four times larger than the population killed by war—forty million.

POSITIVE HUMAN TRENDS

In the past 100 years, the trends for humanity are so positive, that it is difficult to imagine how the ideal goal cannot be realized. Think for a moment what the average global life expectancy was one hundred years ago in 1915. In the United States life expectancy was forty-five years. That is nearly half what it is today. Globally, life expectancy was likely much lower than forty-five. Global life expectancy has nearly doubled in the past one hundred years. This is a consequence of a broad array of factors that allow shared information and communication to improve the human condition—whether disseminating medical knowledge or the implementation of clean sanitation. The particular aspects of these positive changes are important to grasp in order to understand why the year 2100 will likely be a celebration of even greater successes toward improving the human condition.

GLOBAL POVERTY

One of the most important limitations to human living and cooperation is the scarcity of resources. The condition of poverty increases the probability of many undesirable outcomes including increased illness and reduced education. The changes in the most recent decades suggest powerful positive results. Poverty for global humanity has plummeted at rates never seen in human history. A recent Yale study describes the progress this way:

> We are in the midst of the fastest period of poverty reduction the world has ever seen. The global poverty rate, which stood at 25 percent in 2005, is ticking downwards at one to two percentage points a year, lifting around 70 million people—the population of Turkey or Thailand—out of destitution annually. Advances in human progress on such a scale are unprecedented, yet remain almost universally unacknowledged.[3]

This information is important for at least two reasons: 1) we are making incredible positive progress on one of the most important causes of human suffering and 2) we collectively ignore this progress. Most of us are surprised to find out in a course about genocide that the human condition is actually improving rapidly. We can reasonably expect that these trends will continue for the foreseeable future. More importantly, we are capable of ignoring and even actively hiding from ourselves the success against human suffering. This lack of awareness and appreciation for improving human condition raises ethical alarms for the silence we have now pierced. Why does our intellectual culture withhold and suppress the rapid progress humanity is making? What role does that suppression play in preventing further improvements? Many people may be inspired to make greater effort on all relevant fronts if they knew there were many examples of success.

One rhetorical cover offered to suppress or dispel this progress is the notion of "the Gap." The "gap between the poorest and the richest" is often used as an index for describing and reasserting the misery of global humanity. The gap between the richest and the poorest is growing more severe every day. That sounds rather ominous. How might we remedy that? Could we make everyone rich? To some extent, we have moved almost all of humanity beyond basic thresholds of poverty, but this logic of the gap persists. It does seem that the only empirical way to bring all of humanity to the same level economically is to begin a sustained loss of wealth until all people are impoverished. At that point, there would be no gap. If a rising gap coincides with the reduction of poverty, we should accept the gap as an apparent motive for lifting individuals out of poverty.

Only thirty years ago, nearly two billion people were in poverty. Today less than eight hundred million people are in poverty. Poverty has been cut more than half in thirty years. The other important aspect of this development is that in the past ten years, this trend has been accelerating rather than slowing. From 2005 to 2011, the global poverty rate was reduced by half a billion people.[4] Globalization, capitalism, and the decline of war are the primary drivers of this process and have elevated growth rates beyond levels of 1 and 2 percent and closer to 5 percent. When individuals have these increased resources, they can pursue options that make outcomes like genocide and eliminationism more difficult and less likely. There are several reasons why increased individual resources reduce the risk of genocide: 1) freedom of movement, 2) freedom of information, and 3) freedom of communication.

Freedom of movement is often contingent upon the resources an individual has to move. Do they have transportation means? Such means require resources. Once relocated, can they acquire property or housing? Movement is contingent upon resources. The ability to leave a location where genocide is being implemented remains a fundamental characteristic of genocides ranging from the Armenian genocide to the Rwandan genocide. Individuals want to have freedom of movement to escape these dire designs. Reductions of poverty make this more likely.

Freedom of information arises as income allows the purchase of communication technologies like cell phones. This has broader social practice as individuals can send children to school rather than keeping them for desperate short-term labor in impoverished agricultural settings. Money for school supplies and teaching all add up to individuals with more information and an ability to make choices, which elude the propaganda and simplicity, designed by the genocidaire.

Freedom to communicate suggests that individuals can lodge complaints, inform their neighbors, and seek assistance. The conditions of silence are inherently, to some extent, self-imposed. We choose silence because we do not want to jeopardize what we have. When individuals have more, they can jeopardize at a greater margin and seek more dramatic changes for the better. The technological means noted previously exponentially affect this development. All of these factors work together to make genocide less likely as poverty is reduced.

GLOBAL LIFE EXPECTANCY AND HEALTH

Over the past forty years, life expectancy has risen by more than a decade.[5] This is a strong indication of health care improving to broadly serve the global public. Almost 90 percent of the world now has access to cleaner water supplies—ahead of goals set by international leaders in 2000. That means six billion people now have clean water access.[6] Sanitation services are also important, and roughly 69 percent of the global population has access to improved sanitation services. In 1990, only 49 percent had access to these better sanitation services.[7] AIDS was one of the world's most pervasive killers at the turn of the century. Today its deadly reach is rapidly receding as documented by a recent UN report:

- New HIV infections have declined by 73 percent in Malawi, 71 percent in Botswana, 68 percent in Namibia, 58 percent in Zambia, 50 percent in Zimbabwe and 41 percent each in South Africa and Swaziland since 2001
- The number of people receiving powerful antiretroviral therapy to suppress HIV has increased by about 60 percent in just the last two years
- A drop of one-third in AIDS-related deaths in the last six years
- 24 percent decline in new HIV infections among children
- Five hundred thousand fewer people dying worldwide from AIDS in 2011 than died from the disease in 2005[8]

The reduction of this problem is interconnected to problems of global violence. AIDS orphans were ideal recruits for child soldiering. Intact families can raise and care for children in ways that defeat the cycles of war and genocide. The stress and strain of disease can lead to more desperate choices that increase societal conflict. This good news of disease reduction becomes compound to a process of stopping genocide in this century as grievances decline and the means to satisfy grievances increase. Undergirding all of these successes is a root of better communication blossoming with public advocacy and argument for the best solutions. When good arguments win in society, people win with more abundant life.

DEATH BY WAR

Part of why genocide has killed more than war is that the human behavior of war has been successfully reduced. In many respects, war may be considered the most spectacular case of public killing. Here again, the precipitous decline of war deaths is relatively recent—primarily since the end of World War II. American wars like those in Korea and Vietnam are dramatic—killing more than one hundred thousand Americans. That number is significantly surpassed by the four years of World War II that killed more than four hundred thousand American men and tens of millions of men outside America. More recently, wars in Iraq killed less than ten thousand American soldiers. The past decade has been the least deadly for the entire world in the past one hundred years.[9] Stephen Pinker offers the following summation for recent history:

> On the scale of decades, comprehensive data again paint a shockingly happy picture: Global violence has fallen steadily since the middle of the twentieth century. According to the Human Security Brief 2006, the number of battle deaths in interstate wars has declined from more than 65,000 per year in the 1950s to less than 2,000 per year in this decade. In Western Europe and the Americas, the second half of the century saw a steep decline in the number of wars, military coups, and deadly ethnic riots.[10]

War is not the reliable sweeping form of politics that flows so inevitably across years and continents. It is an action that immediately draws a larger public impatient with violence and steeped with greater vocal tools to object to the march of tyrants. The inevitability of war is fading from global practice.

WHAT CAN I DO?

One of the most common questions I hear as a professor in courses covering this subject matter is: What can I do? There are many things that students, teachers and general genocide opponents can do to reduce this problem globally:

1. Become aware. The information step of activism has become almost cliche. It remains vital to the reductions of genocide. What do we know about the world? There are almost two hundred sovereign nations in the world. What do we really know about the vast majority of them? Where do the more than six billion people in the world live? How do they live? How does human life vary in its experiences across these spaces? An exercise I often ask my students to consider is to imagine a button on their desk, which if pressed, would magically transport them to some populated part of the world. What would they typically find if they pressed that button? If we want the world to change, we must begin with an unquenchable hunger and desire to know more about the world. That attitude is not temporary and it does not solve itself. We do not become completely aware of the world. We become addicted to being a student of the world rather than its teacher. It is the notion of certitude about how things really are that seduces us

toward misjudgment. In most classes I teach, I ask five questions each class period about world events. I am not interested in creating mobile encyclopedias or World Factbooks. I am interested in creating a habit of wanting more information. As the community of interested individuals grows, the capacity of genocidaires to use the simple formulas of propaganda are reduced. Consequently, this first and easiest step is also the most important.

2. End your silence and communicate. One of our principal fears in communicating is that we will say or write something wrong. Indeed you will. But keeping silent will not make the world safer, and it will not increase your willingness to change the world. Telling others that you see a problem—even if it is more complex than you initially understand—is an important part of a human network developing to stop a larger systemic issue. Here we see how cynicism is such a practical barrier to the solution. We know that we can point out problems and limitations to the speech and writing of others, but we have a harder time explaining a solution for the problem being raised. Individuals, groups, and societies can become mired in cynicism to where communication is reduced primarily to picking apart what anyone else says. That spiral of cynicism[11] will damage us, those we care about, our community, and ultimately the entire world. It took a young, relatively uninitiated journalist to break the story of child abuse at Penn State. Senior journalists urged her to drop the story. Her persistence and conviction that more needed to be communicated about the matter ultimately broke the story and ended the pattern of abuse. We have to maintain courage in our communication processes. That is why communication practices like debate are so important.

Classrooms from elementary through college need to integrate actively public speaking curricula. In every subject, students need to be taught and offered an opportunity to express their point of view in public. The tradition and norm of having a voice builds the communal ethic that is resilient to genocidal processes like propaganda. We often fear the disruptive effects of hearing all these individual voices, but in these various educational settings the foundations are laid for a society that cannot only stop genocide but be fully resistant because of all of its members learn the respect for other voices and the ability to express their own. As noted in the introduction, a student I taught took her public speaking instructional skills into a rape survivor group and began a program of public speaking. The same instruction used with holocaust survivors in Washington DC began to change how rape victims saw themselves and even the limits of what that crime could mean for their future. Individual speaking is an intimate part of preventing, diminishing, and overcoming the scourge of genocide.

3. Debate and argue. Discursive complexity as an ethical principal and mode of action begins with each of us as individuals. Are we willing to listen to and read the opinions of those we disagree with? If the answer is "no" then we need to take active steps to solve that problem in our own lives. Practice with debate and civil argument is an essential pedagogy to moving forward on this problem. Our individual steps to be more active in civil argument will make us more aware of the world around us and gradually make us more sturdy in the pursuit of truth. Take time to volunteer for local college or high school debate programs in the role of judging. [12] Judging debates is a great way to gain appreciation for difference. In educational settings, seek out opportunities formally or informally to create debates in work projects for classes. Use debates as a way to encourage better decision-making within groups you affiliate.

   Debate has four basic elements: 1) a resolution of controversy, 2) two equal sides to advocate for and against the resolution, 3) equal time for each side to develop and present arguments in public and 4) a means to render a decision about the debate. These four elements can be adapted to many different age groups and settings. Debate is the central pedagogy of discursive complexity. It is the educational crucible where individuals recognize the need for society to center its convictions in forums analogous to debate. James Farmer Jr. realized as a young debater in Marshall, Texas, that his debate coach and professor was teaching him something more than how to win for his own self-interests. Coach Tolson was arming Farmer with an insight about how real social change is made in the face of systemic violence like that found in America's segregated societies of the 1930s and 1940s. Today, Wiley College models an important pedagogical tool for the world that can help prevent genocide—debate across the curriculum. Professor Chris Medina, the current director of debate at Wiley College is implementing a debate across the curriculum model that schools around the world could employ to bolster all parts of their curriculum and instill the vital ethic of discursive complexity that can turn any young mind into one of a "great debater." [13] Educators need to pursue and enact the curriculums like those now being taught at Wiley.

4. Use the internet to find and create more discursive complexity. For several years, I required my students to produce five minute YouTube videos about world problems. YouTube videos have considerable argumentative force. [14] Within months, several of the many dozen videos went viral. YouTube is increasingly a frontline to global conversation and consideration of genocide. The U.S. government used YouTube to build a case against the government of Syria for dropping chemical

weapons on civilians. Contributing to the larger internet conversation that tips the communication scales away from the AK-47 and in favor of the cell phone increases discursive complexity and reduces global violence. The spotlight created on problems such as human sex trafficking, other forms of human slavery, violent drug cartels, radical forms of political supremacism, the failure to stop preventable diseases, are all worthy efforts that begin to connect individuals to a larger chain of resistance to seemingly entrenched problems. In many instances, these projects can take an ironic turn toward heroism. Interview and preserve the voice of a hero. Students sometimes interview a grandparent who fought in World War II. Interviewing and preserving the words of those who inspire our present idealism is as important and reciprocal to solving world problems as isolating and focusing on the problems themselves. The world needs heroes, and taking time to record and remember the good is important. On the walls of the Holocaust museum in Washington DC are the words of the prophet Isaiah: "You are my witnesses." The fact that we can all be a witness to things that matter toward improving the human condition has never been more clear than in this interconnected world of technology. Be sure you include the internet in Aristotle's classic compendium of rhetoric that is aware of "all means of persuasion."

5. Visit and support genocide causes in your local area. Holocaust museums exist all around the world. They often host survivors and provide exhibits relevant to increasing community awareness on these topics. Immigrant communities are untapped groups in many locales. Fleeing the location of human rights abuses remains a common motive for migration. Contacting immigrant communities and finding out about underlying stories for immigration can be eye-opening. Finding their communities of worship and joining them for conversation about how they immigrated illuminates the dreadful disparities still evident in the world today. Most colleges and universities have activities and groups that also support the discovery of important human rights and genocide causes. Meeting with military personnel who have served in international locations can reveal cultural details and profound moral challenges that inspire us. Understanding how soldiers adapt, help and protect vulnerable populations is an important part of encouraging structural protections for potential victims of genocide. Remember that in all of these instances that having a conversation with someone who has suffered in any of these various settings is an important act in itself. For those who suffer, being heard is a powerful medicine and a stepping place toward a more secure sense of self, less haunted by a darker past.

FINAL CHALLENGE

Rhetoric is the process of changing the world from what is to what it should be. There is no more compelling and unique set of possibilities for doing that than you. Humanity has proven itself in the act of genocide, capable of utter depravity. Idealism, hope, perseverance, and gritty belief are always greater than that depravity. When I left the Holocaust museum in the summer of 2007 and I noticed those survivors sitting at their desk in the center of the museum under the beaming sunlight of the atrium, I did not see victims. I saw heroes. I saw people who volunteered to relive on a regular basis an analogy of the environment of systemic annihilation found at Auschwitz. Seeing those survivors there reminded me that humanity is not defined by its killers, mass murderers, or genocidaires. It is defined by people like you, reading this book, imagining a better world, and taking that first step—ending the silence that hurts the victim most.

NOTES

1. Chesterton, G. K. as quoted in *Coraline* (2004) by Neil Gaiman, epigraph.
2. Bassiouni, M. Cherif. 1998. "The Normative Framework of International Humanitarian Law: Overlaps, Gaps and Ambiguities," *Transnational Law & Contemporary Problems*, 8; Scharf, Michael. 2000. "Post-cold war international security threats: terrorism, drugs, and organized crime symposium." *Michigan Journal of International Law*, 21. Spring; Ratliff, Suellen. October 1999. "UN Representation Disputes: A Case Study of Cambodia and a New Accreditation Proposal for the Twenty-First Century." *California Law Review*, 87. Accessed September 16, 2013. http://scholarship.law.berkeley.edu/cgi/viewcontent.cgi?article=1545& context=californialawreview; Kelly, J. Michael. 2002. "Can sovereigns be brought to justice? The crime of genocide's evolution and the meaning of the Milosevic trial." *St. Johns Law Review*, 76, 257–332; and Gordon, Joy. 2002. "When Intent Makes All the Difference in the World: Economic Sanctions on Iraq and the Accusation of Genocide." *Yale Human Rights & Development Law Journal*, 5.
3. Chandy, Laurence. 2011. "With little notice, globalization reduced poverty." *Yale Global Online*. July 5. Accessed August 15, 2013. See also Mark Perry's "The greatest achievement in human history, and you never hear about it." http://www.allenskillicorn.com/2653/ greatest-achievement-human-history-never-hear/ accessed January 5, 2014.
4. Chandy, Laurence. 2011. "With little notice, globalization reduced poverty." *Yale Global Online*. July 5. Accessed August 15, 2013.
5. Boseley, Sarah. 2012. "Life expectancy around the world shows dramatic rise." *The Guardian*. Accessed September 16, 2013. http://www.theguardian.com/society/2012/dec/13/ life-expectancy-world-rise.
6. *WHO*. 2012. "Drinking Water, Sanitation & Hygiene." Accessed September 16, 2013. http://www.unwater.org/statistics_san.html.
7. *WHO*. 2012. "Drinking Water, Sanitation & Hygiene." Accessed September 16, 2013. http://www.unwater.org/statistics_san.html.
8. Gardner, Amanda. 2012. "AIDS Deaths, New HIV Infections Continue to Drop Worldwide." *US News and World Report*. Accessed September 16, 2013. http://health.usnews.com/ health-news/news/articles/2012/11/20/aids-deaths-new-hiv-infections-continue-to-drop -worldwide.
9. Goldstein, Josh. 2011. "Think again: War." *Foreign policy*. Accessed August 15, 2013. http://www.foreignpolicy.com/articles/2011/08/15/think_again_war.

10. Pinker, Stephen. 2007. "A history of violence." *Edge: The Third Culture.* Accessed August 15, 2013. http://www.edge.org/3rd_culture/pinker07/pinker07_index.html.

11. Jamieson, Kathleen Hall. 1996. *Spiral of Cynicism: The Press and the Public Good.* Oxford University Press.

12. Chemerinsky, Erwin. n.d. "Inner-city schools suffer when 'debaters' go silent." *USA Today*, n.d. Academic Search Complete, EBSCOhost (accessed September 15, 2013).

13. "Communicate through Debate: The Wiley College Quality Enhancement Plan." Accessed January 5, 2014. http://www.wileyc.edu/docs/2012QEPReport.pdf

14. Hess, Aaron. 2010. "Democracy Through the Polarized Lens of the Camcorder: Argumentation and Vernacular Spectacle on Youtube in the 2008 Election." *Argumentation & Advocacy* 47, no. 2: 106–22. Communication & Mass Media Complete, EBSCOhost (accessed September 15, 2013).

Appendix: Student Essay: Shia Islam

The Wave of Sectarian Warfare in the Muslim World

By Basma Raza, undergraduate communication student and debater

The contemporary conflict between Shiites and Sunnis was not born recently. It actually began with the death of Prophet Muhammad (Peace Be Upon Him). What people are not aware of is that even though the problems and differences are centuries old, or to be precise fourteen hundred years old, the recent wave of hatred and violence is a new low for the Muslim community. The two communities have lived side by side, intermarried, respected each other's faith, visited each other's homes and their children played together without anyone having to point a finger and call someone an "infidel." In this short essay, I would like to take you through history and discuss some of the earlier differences that began with the death of the Prophet and how they have gotten us to this point in our history today.

As long as the Prophet was alive, there were no divisions in the Muslim community, there were no sects, and everyone was united as one under the name of Allah. But after the Prophet passed away the question as to who would serve as his successor arose and ended in the first division of Islam. If followed and understood adequately, the Quran, the holy book of Muslims serves as the best guide to all problems which can arise. But, throughout the history of the world, people have manipulated religion (not just Islam) to fit their own personal agenda. In chapter three, verse 103, the Quran says, "And hold firmly to the rope of Allah all together and do not become divided. And remember the favor of Allah upon you—when you were enemies and He brought your hearts together and you became, by His favor, brothers." According to Islam, Muslims were never meant to break up in sects as they pleased; they were to stay united as one.

As the debate of successorship continued, Shiites believed that Hazrat Ali, cousin of Prophet Muhammadd (PBUH) would best serve as his successor. The rest chose Abu Bakr, the leader of one the most powerful tribes, as the first caliph. The word "Sunni" comes from the word *sunnah* as in followers of the life of the Prophet. And the word "Shiite" in Arabic was used to describe "those who love" and so the followers of Ali or those who believed Hazrat Ali to be the legitimate successor of the Prophet came to be called Shiites of Ali. Ali was also married to the Prophet's daughter, Fatima. The great divide in essence boiled down to one fact: should the successor be from the Prophet's family, Shiites, or should he be one of the loyal companions of the Prophet, Sunnis. The two caliphs that followed Abu Bakr as the second and third caliphs did not belong to the Prophet's family and Ali served as the fourth.

For the Shiites, Ali was the chosen leader of the Muslim community, also known as Imam Ali, and they refused to agree with the first three caliphs of the time. The Sunni believe in the four caliphates and the ones that came after them; Shiites believed that the reigns of Islam only belonged to the family of the Prophet. After the assassination of Ali, his son Hassan became the second Imam and leader of the Muslim world. Shiites believe in twelve Imams starting with Ali and his two sons. They believe the twelfth Imam is in occultation or in hiding and he is still alive. They believe he will return one day along with Jesus and restore peace and justice in the world. Sunnis, however, do not believe in the twelve Imams or that the twelfth will return one day. The practices of the two sects remain the same; they both follow the five pillars of Islam, that there is one God, Prophet Muhammad to be his prophet, praying five times daily, giving alms to the needy, fasting in the month of Ramadan and making a pilgrimage to Mecca if they are able to do so for Hajj.

The majority of the Muslim population in the world follows the Sunni faith and makes up 87–90 percent according to Pew Research. [1] Shiites, on the other hand account for only 10–13 percent of the Muslim community Research. [2] Most Shiites live in four major countries: India, Pakistan, Iran, and Iraq. Iran and Iraq are the only two countries that are majority Shiite Muslim. Even though these two groups had come into existence, there were no strict principle labels for the two groups. But as time passed, these differences took a deeper root, which affects much of the ideological differences perceived today.

An important cause of this sudden hatred and violence today may singlehandedly be explained by Wahhabism which was born out of Saudi Arabia. In order to rid the Arabian Peninsula of the Ottoman Empire, the British made a deal with the Ibn Saud family resulting in the formation of Saudi

Arabia. With the influence of the British and to further oppose the Ottoman Turks, the Saud family accepted Wahhabism as the state religion. Muhammad bin Abd al Wahhab, whose name serve the basis of this new term, sought to reverse the moral decline of his society and "return" to the pure and orthodox practice of the "fundamentals" of Islam, as embodied in the Quran and in the life of the Prophet Muhammad. "Wahhabism opposes most popular Islamic religious practices such as saint veneration, the celebration of the Prophet's birthday, most core Shiite traditions, and some practices associated with the mystical teachings of Sufism." [3] These radical ideologies bought Wahhabis in confrontation with other sects including, Sunni Muslims, Shiite Muslims, and non-Muslims in neighboring areas.

Wahhabism, which is a branch of Sunni Islam, is a rather radical and conservative school of thought. They believe in the literal interpretation of the Quran and anyone that differs from their beliefs is labeled as "infidels." Infidel according to the dictionary can be simply defined as "a person who does not believe in a religion that someone regards as the true religion," also known as non-believers or *kafir* which is the Arabic term. They also believe in the concept of *takfir*, which can be defined as "pronouncement of unbelief against someone," and can be translated as "excommunication." This concept has been rejected by most clerics and fundamentalist organizations within the Muslim community. Organizations such as Al-Qaeda and other militant groups use this concept to legitimize their killing of innocent people whether Muslim or non-Muslim.

After the revolution in Iran, Saudi Arabia was afraid of the growing influence the revolution could have on the neighboring countries of the Shiite sects and, in turn, began the dissemination of Wahhabism worldwide, especially in Pakistan. The person, responsible for bringing Wahhabism to Pakistan was General Zia-ul-Haq, the dictator of Pakistan during the invasion of Afghanistan by the Soviet Union.

In 1988, Zia ul-Haq dispatched a huge army of eighty thousand extremists to Shiites-populated Gilgit region to exterminate the Shiites completely. The villages in the vicinity such as Jalalabad, Bonji, Darot, Jaglot, Pari, and Manawar were demolished to the ground and over seven hundred Shiites Muslims were massacred. According to a Herald report,

> In May 1988, low-intensity political rivalry and sectarian tension ignited into full-scale carnage as thousands of armed tribesmen from outside Gilgit district invaded Gilgit along the Karakoram Highway. Nobody stopped them. They destroyed crops and houses, lynched and burnt people to death in the villages around Gilgit town. The number of dead and injured was put in the hundreds. But numbers alone tell nothing of the savagery of the invading hordes and the chilling impact it has left on these peaceful valleys. [4]

Zia ul-Haq also arranged for the Pakistan intelligence agency ISI to monitor the activities of Shiites organizations all over the country. This was done to prevent the Shiites Muslims from empowering themselves in the wake of the Iranian Revolution of 1979.

These atrocious beginnings of an extremist facet of the Islamic religion which was manipulated and distorted to further the political gains of those in need became known as Wahhabism. If the differences between the two groups are not vast as some might imagined then why the sudden need for an all out bloody warfare which calls for annihilating anyone that does not believe the same beliefs as the Wahhabi extremists? These extremists are not only killing Shiites on a daily basis in places such as Pakistan, but their targets also include Sunni Sufi (Barelvis), Ahmadis and Christians as well.[5]

The news of an explosion in some part of Pakistan can be heard of on a daily basis while the Pakistani government and the rest of the world sit idly by with little concern for the lives of the innocent. Especially as Shiites mourn for the death of the Prophet's grandson Hussein, in the Islamic month of Muharram, their gatherings are targeted for suicide bombings. Pakistan has been the catalyst in fueling this hatred, with mosques and madrasas (religious learning centers) operating on Saudi Arabia's funding; their sole purpose is to spark the hatred in the minds of the young and misunderstood.[6] The Shiites in Pakistan are not just randomly targeted as acts of terrorism, but they are also specifically targeted, based on their professions such as doctors, lawyers, and religious scholars.

The average people are also targeted on a daily basis; they receive slips of paper under their doors with a name of a family member that is being threatened by the neighborhood militant group. Not everyone in Pakistan possesses the resources to send their loved ones who are being threatened outside the country, and if they are unable to do so eventually death awaits them. The UK Parliament's Human Rights Group in February 2013 believed that the massacre of Shiites in Pakistan is genocide.[7] Sunni Muslims also stood in favor of these measures requesting that something should be done in Pakistan and Dr. Tahir-ul-Qadri, a Sunni scholar offered his services to combat the violence. Human Rights Watch says hundreds of Shiites were killed in Pakistan in 2012, which was the deadliest year on record for the Shiite Muslim community.[8] Even though human rights organizations continue to speak out against the atrocities, it has not affected the federal government of Pakistan which refuses to step up against this violence.

As a communication student, it has always surprised me how powerful words can be when they are used to serve a single purpose. The kind of distorted ideas and values these extremists must use in order to convince their delegates to kill innocents in the name of God for paradise and how easily they fall prey to these false teachings. The famous Quranic verse from chapter five, verse 32, which says to kill an innocent human being, is like killing all of humanity, and to save a life is like saving all of humanity. With such peaceful teachings laid out in the Quran, the amount of expertise it takes to distort them into negative statements requires a very skillful communication specialist.

The stories are abundant, whether it is in Pakistan, Iraq, Bahrain, or Syria. In Iraq, the Shiites suffered terribly under the oppressive regime of Saddam Hussein even though they made up the majority of the population. During the Iraq War, elections were held and Shiites were able to find their place in the political system. But as Shiites gained control of Iraq, dispute between Shiites, Sunnis, and Kurds have resulted in the deaths of thousands in the midst of a power struggle.

In Bahrain, the movement began in February of 2011, as the Arab Springs were sweeping the Middle East but this was also twisted into sectarian warfare and led to a divide. Bahrain, the country where Sunni and Shiites were living together peacefully and harmoniously had now become the breeding ground for hatred between the two groups leading to violence.

Syria, the most recent and captivating headline of the world which began with a goal of overthrowing of the dictator Bashar al-Assad, has now become the heart of this sectarian warfare. The minority sect of the Muslim religion known as Alawites in Syria and Shiites have gotten along well, perhaps because they are in the same boat when it comes to facing violence from the extremist group. Assad also belongs to the Alawite sect. The growing tension which has now become a full fledge sectarian war which can engulf the entire Middle East in its grasp began with Iran's influence on Syria and then the call to arms by Sunni clerics. Many Sunni scholars have mentioned the conflict in Syria as a war against the "infidels" mainly on the part of Shiites.

A prominent Sunni scholar, Yusuf al-Qaradawi, called on Sunnis to join the rebels in their fight in Syria. He referred to the Alawite sect, which is a branch of Shiite Islam "as more infidel than Christian and Jews."[9] He believed any able bodied Sunni from around the world should travel to Syria to annihilate the Alawite and Shiite minorities and if they are not able to do so, they are weak. This demonizing by such an influential figure of the Muslim community fueled the conflict much further. Such provocative statements when made public only call for more hatred and violence.

The gradual rise in sectarian tensions, which began in the early 1970s and escalated following the Iranian Revolution and the Afghan War, had to do with politics and competition for influence and power, notably between Iran and the countries based on Wahhabi ideology, especially Saudi Arabia, Qatar and UAE. This competition contributed to a sharp rise in sectarian tensions, especially in Pakistan and Afghanistan, as both sides tried to use religion as an instrument of policy. Non-Muslims no longer need to fear these extremist terrorists attacking them because these extremists are too busy killing their own by labeling them as "infidels." Where Sunni and Shiites lived side by side with not an ounce of hatred has now turned into one of the bloodiest battlegrounds the world has seen. Even when the Sunnis speak out against the atrocities, they themselves become the target of these hateful organizations and become victims.

Students studying this conflict should keep a few things in mind as we look toward the future. Certain measures need to be taken for the world to finally realize the seriousness of these crimes and take action. As American citizens, there have been certain times in our history, as in the case of the Rwanda genocide, when we have been too late in intervening. Further wait, will only result in more bloodshed. This message of hatred needs to be put to a halt. We as American citizens should petition the U.S. government to label these killings as genocide. The Pakistani government, which has been ignoring these problems with tremendous ease, would not be able to do so if pressured by the outside world. If we wait too long, the hatred will only spread further and the lives of not just Shiites or other minority Muslim sects, but also the lives of citizens around the world will be targeted by these extremists.

About this writer:
Basma Raza is an undergraduate student at Southern Methodist University. She completed numerous courses in communication and was president of the SMU debate team. She won numerous speaking awards as a debater and was part of the national championship team in the novice division of the Mid-America Debate Tournament in Kansas City in March of 2013. She and her Jewish debate partner were among the two of the top teams—both from SMU—that claimed first and second place in 2013.

Student's personal statement:
I am a Muslim American whose family immigrated to the United States when I was twelve years old due to political persecutions in Pakistan. I am an undergraduate student at Southern Methodist University, majoring in Communication Studies and minoring in Political Science. Upon completion of a Bachelor's degree from SMU, I plan on attending law school. As a successful debater with the SMU Speech and Debate team I had various discussions with Dr. Voth. The inspiration from a humanities discourse course, which I took in the spring of 2013, really opened my eyes to the topic of genocide. While working as Dr. Voth's research assistant during the summer, I read various books related to the topic of genocide and decided to take matters in my own hand. With my parent's background from Pakistan, and the wave of disputes at a new height in 2012 between Sunni and Shiites, I decided to bring some awareness of this issue to the world.

NOTES

1. "Pew muslim survey on sunnis and shias reveals worries about religious conflict." 2013. *Huffington Post.* November 9. Accessed on December 5, 2013. http://www.huffingtonpost.com/2013/11/09/pew-muslim-survey_n_4243243.html.

2. "Pew muslim survey on sunnis and shias reveals worries about religious conflict." 2013. *Huffington Post.* November 9. Accessed on December 5, 2013. http://www.huffingtonpost.com/2013/11/09/pew-muslim-survey_n_4243243.html.

3. Blanchard, Christopher M. 2008. *The islamic traditions of wahhabism and salafiyya* (RS21695). U.S. Congress. Accessed on December 5, 2013. http://www.fas.org/sgp/crs/misc/RS21695.pdf.

4. Salami, Ismail. 2012. *Target killing, mass murder of shia minority in pakistan* . Global Research. September 5. Accessed on December 5, 2013. http://www.globalresearch.ca/target-killing-mass-murder-of-shia-minority-in-pakistan

5. Pinault, David. 2002. "Pakistan's Christians Face Sectarian Violence." *America* 187.4 18. *Academic Search Complete.* Accessed December 5, 2013. http://americamagazine.org/issue/398/article/pakistans-christians-face-sectarian-violence.

6. Billquist, Daniel L., and Jason M. Colbert, 2012. *Pakistan, Madrassas, and Militancy.* Naval Postgraduate School. http://www.dtic.mil/dtic/tr/fulltext/u2/a460444.pdf.

7. Shah, Murtaza. 2013. "UN approached over targeted killings of pakistani shias." *The News* . June 1. Accessed on December 5, 2013. http://www.thenews.com.pk/Todays-News-2-181249-UN-approached-over-targeted-killings-of-Pakistani-Shias.

8. *Pakistan: Deter escalating attacks on shia muslims* . 2013. November 12. Accessed on December 5, 2013. http://www.hrw.org/news/2013/11/11/pakistan-deter-escalating-attacks-shia-muslims.

9. Bergen, Peter, and Jennifer Rowland. 2013. "Syria plunging mideast into sectarian war?" *CNN* . September 4. Accessed on December 5, 2013. http://www.cnn.com/2013/09/04/opinion/bergen-sectarian-war-syria/.

Bibliography

Bassiouni, M. Cherif. "The Normative Framework of International Humanitarian Law: Overlaps, Gaps and Ambiguities." *Transnational Law & Contemporary Problems* 8. 1998.

Boseley, Sarah. "Life Expectancy Around the World Shows Dramatic Rise." *The Guardian.* December 13, 2012. Accessed September 16, 2013. http://www.theguardian.com/society/2012/dec/13/life-expectancy-world-rise.

Boustany, Nora. "Iran Cited Over Execution of Minors 71 Child Offenders Are on Death Row, According to Rights Group." *Washington Post.* June 27, 2007. Accessed May 15, 2010. http://washingtonpost.com.

Brinkley, Joel. "Why the Taliban is Killing Unarmed Muslims." *San Francisco Gate.* November 7, 2010. Accessed September 15, 2013. http://www.sfgate.com/opinion/article/Why-the-Taliban-is-killing-unarmed-Muslims-3167043.php.

Britt, R. R. "Women More Religious Than Men." *LiveScience.* February 28, 2009. Accessed on August 25, 2013. http://www.livescience.com/7689-women-religious-men.html.

Broadwell, Paula. "The Doctrine of Power." *Prospect Magazine.* July 17, 2013. Accessed September 24, 2013. http://www.prospectmagazine.co.uk/magazine/the-doctrine-of-power-paula-broadwell-samantha-power/#.UkH4oRY9roM.

Bronner, Ethan, and Taghreed El-Khodary. "No Early End Seen to 'All-Out War' on Hamas in Gaza." *International Herald Tribune.* December 29, 2008. Accessed September 10, 2013. http://www.iht.com/articles/2008/12/29/mideast/gaza.php.

Brumfield, Ben. "Charles Taylor Sentenced to 50 years for War crimes." *CNN.* May 31, 2012. Accessed September 5, 2013. http://www.cnn.com/2012/05/30/world/africa/netherlands-taylor-sentencing/index.html.

Bruschke, Jon. "Argument and Evidence Evaluation: A Call for Scholars to Engage Contemporary Public Debates." *Argumentation & Advocacy* 49 (1) (2012): 59–75.

Burke, K. "The Rhetoric of Hitler's 'Battle.' *The Philosophy of Literary Form: Studies in Symbolic Action.* New York: Vintage, 1941: 191–220.

Burke, Kenneth. *A Grammar of Motives.* Berkeley: University of California Press, 1969.

Burkhalter, Holly J. "The Question of Genocide: The Clinton Administration and Rwanda," *World Policy Journal* 11 (4) (Winter 1994/1995): 44–54.

Campbell, Karlyn, Kohrs, and Huxman, Susan. *The Rhetorical Act,* 3rd Edition. Belmont, CA: Wadsworth, 2003.

Campos, Paul. "Striking Syria is Completely Illegal." *Time,* September 5, 2013. Accessed September 25, 2013. http://ideas.time.com/2013/09/05/obamas-plan-for-intervention-in-syria-is-illegal/.

Case, C. "Germans Reconsider Religion: Pope Benedict XVI's Challenge to Secularism Meets with Receptivity During His German Visit." *Christian Science Monitor,* September 15,

2006. Accessed September 4, 2013. http://www.csmonitor.com/2006/0915/p01s01 -woeu.html.

Castells, Manuell. "Communication, Power and Counter-power in the Network Society." *International Journal of Communication* 1 (2007): 238–66. Accessed September 14, 2013. http://ijoc.org/index.php/ijoc/article/viewFile/46/35.

Chandy, Laurence. "With Little Notice, Globalization Reduced Poverty." *Yale Global Online*, July 5, 2011. Accessed August 15, 2013. http://yaleglobal.yale.edu/content/little-notice -globalization-reduced-poverty.

Chemerinsky, Erwin. n.d. "Inner-city schools Suffer When 'Debaters' Go Silent." *USA Today*, January 31, 2008.

Chesterton, G. K. As quoted in *Coraline* (2004) by Neil Gaiman, epigraph.

Chivers, Chris. *The Gun*. New York: Simon & Schuster, 2010.

Chomsky, Noam. *9-11*. New York: Seven Stories Press, 2001.

CNN. "Bush Orders Troops to Positions Off Liberia." July 25, 2003. Accessed September 16, 2013. http://www.cnn.com/2003/US/07/25/us.liberia/.

CNN. "Taliban Shoot Woman 9 Times in Public Execution as Men Cheer." July 8, 2012. Accessed August 15, 2013. http://www.cnn.com/2012/07/08/world/asia/afghanistan-public -execution.

CNN. "US Missiles Pound Targets Afghanistan, Sudan." August 21, 1998. Accessed September 15, 2013. http://www.cnn.com/US/9808/20/us.strikes.02/.

CNN. "Former Klansman Found Guilty of Manslaughter." June 21, 2005. Accessed September 21, 2013. http://www.cnn.com/2005/LAW/06/21/mississippi.killings/.

Comas, James. "The Question of Defining Rhetoric." January 1, 2012. Accessed September 22, 2013. http://capone.mtsu.edu/jcomas/rhetoric/defining.html.

Convention on the Prevention and Punishment of the Crime of Genocide (1948). Article II

CPJ. "73 Journalists Killed in 2012." Committee to Protect Journalists. 2013. Accessed September 1, 2013.

Crilly, Rob. "Chinese Seek Resources, Profits in Africa." *USA TODAY*, June 22, 2005. p. 4B.

Crompton, Paul. "Mideast Task Force Needed to Fight Somali Piracy, Says Expert." *Al Arabiya*, September 13, 2013. Accessed September 23, 2013. http://english.alarabiya.net/en/ News/middle-east/2013/09/17/Mideast-task-force-needed-to-fight-Somali-piracy-says -expert.html.

Danby, Herbert. *The Mishnah*. London: Oxford University Press, 1933: 745–57.

Dearin, Robert. "Perelman's 'Quasi-logical Argument': A Critical Elaboration," in J. Robert Cox and Charles Arthur Willard, *Advances in Argumentation Theory*. Carbondale, IL: Southern Illinois Press, 1982: 78–94.

Deen, Thalif. "Politics: Annan Asks More Funds for Darfur-bound African Force." *IPS-Inter Press Service*, September 2, 2004.

DeLuca, Matthew. "Reporter Sara Ganim, Who Won a Pulitzer Prize for Breaking Sandusky Story." *The Daily Beast*, April 17, 2012. Accessed September 22, 2013. http:// www.thedailybeast.com/articles/2012/04/17/reporter-sara-ganim-who-won-a-pulitzer -for-breaking-sandusky-story.html.

Der Derian, James. *Virtuous War: Mapping the Military-industrial-media-entertainment Network*. Boulder, CO: Westview Press, 2001.

Dershowitz, Alan. *The Case for Israel*. Hoboken, NJ: Wiley, 2004.

Devine, Daniel. "The Female Holocaust." *World,* September 11, 2013.

Dixon, Maria. "With Faith in the Works of Words: The Beginnings of Reconciliation in South Africa, 1985-1995 (review)" *Rhetoric & Public Affairs* 14 (3) (2011): 562–65.

Dobie, Alex. "North Korea Unveils Android Smartphone." *Androidcentral*. August 12, 2013. Accessed August 20, 2013. http://www.androidcentral.com/north-korea-unveils-android -smartphone.

Drye, Willie. "Pirate Coast Campaign Was U.S.'s First War on Terror, Authors Say." *National Geographic*, December 2, 2005. Accessed September 1, 2013. http:// news.nationalgeographic.com/news/2005/12/1202_051202_pirate_coast_2.html.

Duelfer Report. April 25, 2005. Accessed September 16, 2013. http://www.gpo.gov/fdsys/pkg/ GPO-DUELFERREPORT/content-detail.html.

Duffy, Matt. "Smartphones in the Arab Spring." *IPI*. 2011. Accessed September 14, 2013. http://www.academia.edu/1911044/Smartphones_in_the_Arab_Spring.

Dwyer, John. "No Subsitute for Victory." *American Thinker*, November 24, 2005. Accessed September 1, 2013. http://www.americanthinker.com/2005/11/no_substitute_for_victory.html.

Eberstadt, Nicholas. "The Global War on Baby Girls," *The New Atlantis; A Journal of Technology and Society* Fall (2011). Accessed January 25, 2012. http://www.thenewatlantis.com/publications/the-global-war-against-baby-girls.

English, Cynthia, and Lee Becker. "Majorities in Most Countries Perceive Their Media as Free." *Gallup*, May 3, 2013. Accessed August 15, 2013. http://www.gallup.com/poll/162179/majorities-countries-perceive-media-free.aspx.

Falk, Tyler. "There are (Almost) as Many Cell Phone Subscriptions as People." *Smartplanet*, July 2, 2013. Accessed August 20, 2013. http://www.smartplanet.com/blog/bulletin/there-are-almost-as-many-cell-phone-subscriptions-as-people/23353.

Farmer, J. *Freedom When*. New York: Random House, 1965.

Farmer, J. *Lay Bare the Heart: An Autobiography of the Civil Rights Movement*. Fort Worth: Texas Christian University Press, 1985.

Fernandes, Edna. "Face to Face with General Butt Naked—'The Most Evil Man in the World.'" *Daily Mail*, November 27, 2010. Accessed September 16, 2013. http://www.dailymail.co.uk/news/article-1333465/Liberias-General-Butt-Naked-The-evil-man-world.html.

First Amendment to the United States Constitution. 1791.

Fisher, Max. "The Emperor's Speech: 67 Years Ago, Hirohito Transformed Japan Forever." *The Atlantic*, August 15, 2012. Accessed September 23, 2013. http://www.theatlantic.com/international/archive/2012/08/the-emperors-speech-67-years-ago-hirohito-transformed-japan-forever/261166/.

Fisk, Robert. "We British Go Out of Our Way to Avoid Using the Word 'Muslim.'" *The Independent*, July 7, 2013. Accessed September 15, 2013. http://www.independent.co.uk/voices/comment/we-british-go-out-of-our-way-to-avoid-using-the-word-muslim-8693702.html.

Foucault, Michel. "Politics and Reason," in *Michel Foucault: Politics, Philosophy, Culture: Interviews and Other Writings: 1977-1984*, trans. Alan Sheridan et al., ed. Lawrence D. Kritzman, New York: Routledge, 1988.

Foucault, Michel. *Discipline and Punish: the Birth of the Prison*, trans. A. Sheridan. New York: Pantheon Books, 1977.

Fox, Zoe. "Kony 2012 One year later: Success or Failure?" *Mashable*, March 5, 2013. Accessed September 17, 2013. http://mashable.com/2013/03/05/kony-2012-retrospective/.

Freedom House report. "Middle East Volatility Amid Global Decline." 2013. Accessed August 15, 2013. http://www.freedomhouse.org/report/freedom-press/freedom-press-2013.

Freire, Paulo. *Pedagogy of the Oppressed*. New York: Continuum Publishing Company, 1970.

Gardner, Amanda. "AIDS Deaths, New HIV Infections Continue to Drop Worldwide." *US News and World Report*, November 20, 2012. Accessed September 16, 2013. http://health.usnews.com/health-news/news/articles/2012/11/20/aids-deaths-new-hiv-infections-continue-to-drop-worldwide.

Gee, Harvey. "Book Review: The Refugee Burden: A Closer Look at the Refugee Act of 1980," *N.C.J. Int'l L. & Com. Reg* 26 Spring (2001): 559–608.

Gettelman, Jeffrey, and Nicholas Kulish. "Gunmen Kill Dozens in Terror Attack at Kenyan Mall." *New York Times*, September 21, 2013. Accessed September 23, 2013. http://www.nytimes.com/2013/09/22/world/africa/nairobi-mall-shooting.html?pagewanted=all&_r=1&.

Gold, David. "Nothing Educates Us Like a Shock: The Integrated Rhetoric of Melvin B. Tolson" *CCC* 55:2 December (2003): 226–53.

Goldhagen, Daniel. *Worse Than War: Genocide, Eliminationism, and the Ongoing Assault on Humanity*. New York: Public Affairs, 2009.

Goldstein, Josh. "Think again: War." *Foreign Policy*, August 15, 2011. Accessed August 15, 2013. http://www.foreignpolicy.com/articles/2011/08/15/think_again_war.

Gordon, Joy. "When Intent Makes All the Difference in the World: Economic Sanctions on Iraq and the Accusation of Genocide." *Yale Human Rights & Development Law Journal* 5 (2002): 57–84.

Gross, Terry. "Get on the Bus: Freedom Riders of 1961." *NPR*, January 12, 2006. Accessed September 25, 2013. http://www.npr.org/2006/01/12/5149667/get-on-the-bus-the-freedom-riders-of-1961.

Gubert, Betty. "James Farmer." *African American Lives*. Editors: Henry Louis Gates and Brooks Higginbotham. London, Oxford University Press: 2004. 287.

Habermas, Jürgen. *Communication and the Evolution of Society*. Boston: Beacon Press, 1979.

Habermas, Jürgen. "A Post-Secular Society: What Does that Mean?" Dialogues on Civilizations RESETDOC. 2008. Accessed September 5, 2013. http://www.resetdoc.org/story/00000000926.

Hanscom, Aaron. "Confronting a Worldwide Jew-Hatred." *Frontpage*, April 24, 2007.

"Hate Crime Statistics 2005," *U.S. Department of Justice—Federal Bureau of Investigation*, Release Date: October 2006.

"Hate Crime Statistics 2011," *U.S. Department of Justice—Federal Bureau of Investigation*, Release Date: October 2012. Acccessed September 24, 2013. http://www.fbi.gov/about-us/cjis/ucr/hate-crime/2011/narratives/victims.

Hayes, Stephen. "How Africa's First Female President Led Her Country Back from the Brink." *US News and World Report*, May 20, 2013. Accessed September 16, 2013. http://www.usnews.com/opinion/blogs/world-report/2013/05/20/president-ellen-sirleaf-and-liberia-comeback.

Hentoff, Nat. "The World's Oldest Hatred Hasn't Gone Away." *Aspen Daily News*, August 20, 2006.

Hess, Aaron. "Democracy Through the Polarized Lens of the Camcorder: Argumentation and Vernacular Spectacle on Youtube in the 2008 Election." *Argumentation & Advocacy* 47 (2) (2010): 106–22.

Hitchens, Christopher. "Realism in Darfur." *Slate*, November 7, 2005 Accessed September 15, 2013. http://www.slate.com/articles/news_and_politics/fighting_words/2005/11/realism_in_darfur.html.

Huie, William Bradford. *Three Lives for Mississippi*. New York: WCC books, 1965.

Human Rights Watch. "Endless Torment: The 1991 Uprising in Iraq And Its Aftermath." June 1992. Accessed September 16, 2013. http://www.hrw.org/reports/1992/Iraq926.htm.

Inscription on the tombstone of James Earl Chaney in Meridian, Mississippi.

International Herald Tribune. "EU says U.N. Human Rights Watchdog Can Do Job Despite Flaws." 2007.

Internet Encyclopedia of Philosophy. "The Frankfurt School and Critical Theory." Accessed September 23, 2013. http://www.iep.utm.edu/frankfur/.

"Iran 'Public Hanging' Video Emerges." *Telegraph*, July 22, 2011. Accessed September 5, 2013. http://www.telegraph.co.uk/news/worldnews/middleeast/iran/8653780/Iran-public-hanging-video-emerges.html.

"Iranian Protesters Back Gaza and Burn Obama Pictures." *Reuters*, January 13, 2009. Accessed September 15, 2013. http://uk.reuters.com/article/UKNews1/idUKTRE50C4IQ20090113.

Iskandar, Abdallah. "Al-Bashir and Sudan's Sovereignty." *Al Arabiya*, March 26, 2009. Accessed May 15, 2010. http://www.alarabiya.net/.

Issa, Darrell. "Arab Americans Must Reject Tyranny." *Los Angeles Times*, March 21, 2003. p. 15.

James Meredith and the Integration of Ole Miss. With James Meredith, Burke Marshall, and John Doar; Moderated by Juan Williams. John F. Kennedy Library and Foundation. September 30, 2002. Accessed June 2, 2009. http://www.jfklibrary.org.

Jamieson, Kathleen Hall. *Spiral of Cynicism: The Press and the Public Good*. Oxford University Press, 1996.

John 18:10. Scripture taken from the New American Standard Bible®, Copyright © 1960, 1962, 1963, 1968, 1971, 1972, 1973, 1975, 1977, 1995 by The Lockman Foundation. Used by permission.

John 19:26–27. Scripture taken from the New American Standard Bible®, Copyright © 1960, 1962, 1963, 1968, 1971, 1972, 1973, 1975, 1977, 1995 by The Lockman Foundation. Used by permission.

Jones, Melanie. "Joseph Kony 2012 Campaign Now Most Successful Viral Video In History." *International Business Times*, March 12, 2012. Accessed September 17, 2013. http://www.ibtimes.com/joseph-kony-2012-campaign-now-most-successful-viral-video-history-423988.

Junhong, Chu. "Prenatal Sex Determination and Sex-Selective Abortion in Rural Central China." *Population and Development Review* 27 (2001): 259–81. doi: 10.1111/j.1728-4457.2001.00259.x.

Kanuma, Shyaka. "Rwanda: My Proudest Achievement Will be to Hand Over Power." *AllAfrica*, January 20, 2009. Accessed January 23, 2009. http://allafrica.com/stories/200901210722.html.

Kavoori, Anandam. "The Word and the World: Rethinking International Communication." Conference Papers. *International Communication Association*, 2007.

Keating, Joshua. "Blaming the Jews for the Honduras Coup." *Foreign Policy*. October 5, 2009. Accessed September 19, 2013. http://blog.foreignpolicy.com/posts/2009/10/05/blaming_the_jews_for_the_honduras_coup.

Keener, Craig. *A Commentary on the Gospel of Matthew*. Cambridge U.K.: William B. Eerdmans Publishing, 1999.

Kelly, J. Michael. "Can Sovereigns be Brought to Justice? The Crime of Genocide's Evolution and the Meaning of the Milosevic Trial." *St. Johns Law Review* 76 (2002): 257–332.

Kennedy, David. "The Horror: Should the Japanese Atrocities in Nanking be Equated with the Nazi Holocaust?" *The Atlantic*, April 1, 1998. Accessed September 23, 2013. http://www.theatlantic.com/magazine/archive/1998/04/the-horror/306532/.

Khan, Ismail, and Salman Masood. "Scores Are Killed by Suicide Bomb Attack at Historic Church in Pakistan." *New York Times*, September 22, 2013. Accessed September 23, 2013. http://www.nytimes.com/2013/09/23/world/asia/pakistan-church-bombing.html.

Khazan, Olga, and Rama Lakshmi. "10 Reasons Why India has a Sexual Violence Problem." *Washington Post*, December 29, 2012. Accessed September 23, 2013. http://www.washingtonpost.com/blogs/worldviews/wp/2012/12/29/india-rape-victim-dies-sexual-violence-proble/.

Kidd, Nancy, and Trevor Parry-Giles. "Another View on Communication Scholarship." *Inside Higher Ed*, August 13, 2013. Accessed August 15, 2013. http://www.insidehighered.com/views/2013/08/13/essay-defends-state-communications-scholarship#ixzz2eLqUIrBE.

King, Martin Luther, Jr. *Stride Toward Freedom: the Montgomery Story*. New York: Harper Collins, 1958.

Kohm, Lynne Marie. "Sex Selection Abortion and the Boomerang Effect of a Woman's Right to Choose: A Paradox of the Skeptics." *William. & Mary Journal of Women & the Law* 91 (1997): 91–128. Accessed September 16. 2013. http://scholarship.law.wm.edu/wmjowl/vol4/iss1/3.

Kortschak, Irfan. "Defining Waria." *Inside Indonesia*, October–December, 2007. Accessed September 16, 2013. http://www.insideindonesia.org/weekly-articles/defining-waria

Krieger, Hilary. "Jewish World Marks Rise in Antisemitism." *Jerusalem Post online edition*, August 1, 2006. Accessed September 5, 2013. http://www.jpost.com/Jewish-World/Jewish-News/Jews-note-rise-in-anti-Semitism.

Kucera, Joshua. "The World's Worst Spies." *Slate*, May 22, 2008. Accessed August 15, 2013. http://www.slate.com/id/2197134/entry/2191673/.

Kulish, Nicholas. "Kenya Presses Assault Against Militants in Mall Siege." *New York Times,* September 22, 2013. Accessed September 23, 2013.

Kuypers, Jim. *Partisan Journalism: A History of Media Bias in the United States*. Lanham, Maryland: Rowman & Littlefield, 2014.

Leezenberg, Michiel. "The Anfal Operations in Iraqi Kurdistan." in Samuel Totten and William Parsons (Eds). *Century of Genocide: Critical Essays and Eyewitness Accounts*, 4th edition. New York & London: Routledge, 2013.

Leopold, Evelyn. "UN Envoy Says Deaths in Darfur Underestimated." *Reuters*, February 1, 2005.

Ling, Chai. *A Heart for Freedom*. Carol Stream, Illinois: Tyndale, 2011.

Luke 24:1-12. Scripture taken from the New American Standard Bible®, Copyright © 1960, 1962, 1963, 1968, 1971, 1972, 1973, 1975, 1977, 1995 by The Lockman Foundation. Used by permission.

MacFarquhar, Neil. "Peacekeepers Sex Scandals Linger, On Screen and Off." *New York Times*, September 7, 2011. Accessed September 25, 2013. http://www.nytimes.com/2011/09/08/world/08nations.html?pagewanted=all.

Mamdani, Mahmood. "The Politics of Naming: Genocide, Civil War, Insurgency." *London Review of Books* 29 no. 5: 5–8. March 8, 2007. Accessed September 12, 2013. http://www.lrb.co.uk/v29/n05/mahmood-mamdani/the-politics-of-naming-genocide-civil-war-insurgency."

Mason, Rowena. "The Abortion of Unwanted Girls Taking Place in the UK." *The Telegraph*, January 10, 2013. Accessed September 16, 2013. http://www.telegraph.co.uk/news/uknews/crime/9794577/The-abortion-of-unwanted-girls-taking-place-in-the-UK.html.

Matthew 14:28–30. Scripture taken from the New American Standard Bible®, Copyright © 1960, 1962, 1963, 1968, 1971, 1972, 1973, 1975, 1977, 1995 by The Lockman Foundation. Used by permission.

Matthew 26:74–75. Scripture taken from the New American Standard Bible®, Copyright © 1960, 1962, 1963, 1968, 1971, 1972, 1973, 1975, 1977, 1995 by The Lockman Foundation. Used by permission.

McPhail, Mark. "The Price of an Apology: Richard Molpus: Rhetoric of Reconciliation." *Paper presented at the annual meeting of the NCA 94th Annual Convention*, San Diego, CA. Accessed May 6, 2013. http://citation.allacademic.com/meta/p256357_index.html.

MDAH Digital Collections. "Sovereignty Commission Online Agency History." 2009. Accessed June 2, 2009. http://mdah.state.ms.us/bugle/sovcom/scagencycasehistory.php.

Memmot, Mark. "Rev. Wright: Them Jews Ain't Going to Let Him Talk to Obama." *NPR*, June 11, 2009. Accessed September 24, 2013. http://www.npr.org/blogs/thetwo-way/2009/06/rev_wright_jews_aint_going_to.html.

Metaxas, Eric. *Bonhoeffer: Pastor, Martyr, Prophet, Spy*. Nashville: Thomas Nelson, 2011.

Mitchell, Andrea. "Sudanese Scuffle Symbolic of Disregard for Own U.S.-Sudanese Disagreement Over Darfur Region Expected to Continue." *MSNBC*, July 21, 2005. Accessed August 1, 2005. http://www.msnbc.msn.com/id/8655411/.

Molpus, Richard. "Remarks By Secretary of State Dick Molpus Ecumenical Memorial Service Mount Zion Church." *The Philadelphia Coalition*, June 21, 1989. Accessed June 1, 2009. http://www.neshobajustice.com/pages/molpus89.htm.

Myers, Christine. "Sex Selective Abortion in India." *Global Tides* 6:3. April 1, 2012. Accessed August 10, 2013. http://digitalcommons.pepperdine.edu/cgi/viewcontent.cgi?article=1049&context=globaltides.

Nanda, Ved P. "Global Response to Darfur Pitiful U.N., Superpowers Not Doing Enough After Sudan Genocide." *Denver Post*, June 26, 2005. p. B-07. Accessed August 15, 2005. http://www.denverpost.com/opinion/ci_2804617.

NBC News. "Professor Fired After 9-11, Nazi Comparison." July 24, 2007. Accessed September 24, 2013. http://www.nbcnews.com/id/19940243/ns/us_news-education/t/professor-fired-after--nazi-comparison/#.UkJL8RY9roM.

NBC News. "India Hangs Only Surviving Gunman of 2008 Mumbai Attacks." November 12, 2012. Accessed August 15, 2013. http://worldnews.nbcnews.com/_news/2012/11/21/15328783-india-hangs-only-surviving-gunman-of-2008-mumbai-attacks?lite.

New York Post. "Fort Hood: Diversity Rules." October 29, 2012. Accessed September 15, 2013. http://nypost.com/2012/10/29/fort-hood-diversity-rules/.

Newton, M. A., and Michael P. Sharf. *Enemy of the State: The Trial and Execution of Saddam Hussein*. New York: St. Martin's Press, 2008.

NPR. "US Command Fights Terrorists on African Soil." March 9, 2012. Accessed September 15, 2013. http://www.npr.org/2012/03/09/148278069/u-s-command-fights-terrorists-on

-african-soil.

Odokonyero, Moses. "Joseph Kony Losing Control Over the LRA." *Sudan Tribune*, July 31, 2013. Accessed September 10, 2013. http://www.sudantribune.com/spip.php?article47495.

Orwell, George. "Notes on Nationalism (1945)." *Fifty Essays*. Project Gutenberg of Australia, 2010. http://gutenberg.net.au/ebooks03/0300011h.html#part30.

Özdemir, Cemeren. "Controversy Over Turkish Movie: Beyond the Valley of the Wolves." *Speigel Online*. February 22, 2006. Accessed August 1, 2007. http://www.spiegel.de/inter national/0,1518,401565,00.html.

Palczewski, Catherine Helen, and John Fritch. "Introduction." *Argumentation & Advocacy* 49, no. 3: (2013): 228.

Palmer, Ewan. "20,000 Prisoners 'Disappear' from North Korean Camp." *International Business Times*, September 6, 2013. Accessed September 10, 2013. http://www.ibtimes.co.uk/articles/504258/20130906/20000-prisoners-disappear-north-korean-camp-22.htm.

PBS. "Mumbai Massacre: Background Information." November 24, 2009. Accessed August 15, 2013. http://www.pbs.org/wnet/secrets/features/mumbai-massacre-background-in formation/502/.

Perry, Mark. "The Greatest Achievement in Human History, and You Never Hear About It." *Taxpayers for Skillicorn*, 2014. Accessed January 5, 2014. http://www.allenskillicorn.com/2653/greatest-achievement-human-history-never-hear/.

Pew Research Global Attitudes Project. "Unfavorable Views of Jews and Muslims on the Increase in Europe." September 17, 2008. Accessed September 24, 2013. http://www.pewglobal.org/2008/09/17/chapter-1-views-of-religious-groups/.

Pinker, Stephen. "A History of Violence." *Edge: The Third Culture*, 2007. Accessed August 15, 2013. http://www.edge.org/3rd_culture/pinker07/pinker07_index.html.

Platt, Carrie Anne, and Zoltan P. Majdik. "The Place of Religion in Habermas's Transformed Public Sphere." *Argumentation & Advocacy* 49 (2) (2012): 138–141.

Pleming, Sue. "U.S. Urges Sudan to Agree Fully to Darfur Plan." *Washington Post*, January 24, 2007. Accessed September 23, 2013. http://www.washingtonpost.com/wp-dyn/content/arti cle/2007/01/24/AR2007012401600.html.

Power, Samantha. *A Problem from Hell: America and the Age of Genocide.* New York: Harper Perennial, 2002.

Putin, Vladimir. "A Plea for Caution from Russia." *New York Times*, September 11, 2013. Accessed September 17, 2013. http://www.nytimes.com/2013/09/12/opinion/putin-plea-for -caution-from-russia-on-syria.html?_r=0.

Quartz, Leo Mirani. "Mobile Phones Are Booming In North Korea, Of All Places;" *Business Insider*, April 26, 2013. Accessed August 15, 2013. http://www.businessinsider.com/mobile-phones-are-booming-in-north-korea-of-all-places-2013-4.

Raines, H. *My Soul Is Rested: Movement Days in the Deep South Remembered.* New York: Penguin Books, 1977.

Ratliff, Suellen. "UN Representation Disputes: A Case Study of Cambodia and a New Accredi-tation Proposal for the Twenty-First Century." *California Law Review* 87 (October 1999): 1207–1274. Accessed September 16, 2013. http://scholarship.law.berkeley.edu/cgi/view content.cgi?article=1545&context=californialawreview.

Religion Clauses of the First Amendment to the United States Constitution. 1791.

Ricoeur, Paul. *The Rule of Metaphor: Multi-disciplinary Studies of the Meaning in Language.* Buffalo: University of Toronto Press, 1975.

Rizvi, Ali. "An Atheist Muslim's Perspective on the 'Root Causes' of Islamist Jihadism and the Politics of Islamophobia." *Huffington Post*, May 3, 2013. Accessed August 25, 2013.

Rubin, Michael. "Remembering Iraq's Liberation Without Revisionism." *Commentary*, April 10, 2013. Accessed September 16, 2013. http://www.commentarymagazine.com/2013/04/10/remembering-iraqs-liberation-without-revisionism/#more-822276.

Rucyahana, John. *The Bishop of Rwanda: Finding Forgiveness Amidst a Pile of Bones.* Nash-ville, TN: Nelson Publishing, 2007.

Rudoren, Jodi. "Collaboration in Gaza Leads to Grisly Fate." *New York Times*, December 2, 2012. Accessed September 24, 2013. http://www.nytimes.com/2012/12/03/world/middle

east/preyed-on-by-both-sides-gaza-collaborators-have-grim-plight.html?pagewanted=all&
   _r=0.

Rummel, Rudolph. *Death by Government*. London: Transaction Publishers, 2004.

Said, Edward. *Orientalism: Western Conceptions of the Orient*. London, UK: Penguin Books, 2003.

Satloff, Robert. *Among the Righteous: Lost Stories from the Holocaust's Long Reach into Arab Lands*. New York: Public Affairs, 2006.

Scharf, Michael. "Post-Cold War International Security Threats: Terrorism, Drugs, and Organized Crime Symposium." *Michigan Journal of International Law* 21. Spring 2000.

Scherman, Tony. "The Great Debaters," *American Legacy*, Spring 1997.

Semino, Matt. "Jerry Sandusky and the Pain of Silence." *Huffingston Post*, June 13, 2012. Accessed September 22, 2013. http://www.huffingtonpost.com/matt-semino/jerry-sandusky -trial_b_1594397.html.

Severo, Richard. "James Farmer, Civil Rights Giant In the 50's and 60's, Is Dead at 79." *New York Times*, July 10, 1999. Archives. Accessed August 2, 2013. http://www.nytimes.com/ 1999/07/10/us/james-farmer-civil-rights-giant-in-the-50-s-and-60-s -is-dead-at-79.html?pagewanted=all&src=pm.

Sharansky, Natan. *The Case for Democracy*. New York: New Leaf, 2006.

Shetterly, Robert. "John Lewis." *Americans Who Tell the Truth*. Accessed September 21, 2013. http://www.americanswhotellthetruth.org/portraits/john-lewis.

Shuter, Robert. "Part II. Chapter Ten: Ethical Issues in Global Communication." In *Communication & Global Society* 181–90. N.p.: Peter Lang Publishing, Inc., 2000.

Sidhu, Jasmeet. "Gender Selection Has Become A Multimillion-Dollar Industry." *Slate*, September 7, 2012.

Simon, Natalie. "Rwandan Genocidaire Convicted, Sentenced in the US." *SA News*, July 16, 2013. Accessed September 23, 2013. http://za.news.yahoo.com/rwandan-genocidaire -convicted-sentenced-us-085715475.html.

Slevin, Peter. "Outside the Cockpit Door, a Fight to Save the Plane." *Washington Post*, July 24, 2004. p. A10. Accessed September 24, 2013. http://www.washingtonpost.com/wp-dyn/articles/A10206-2004Jul23_2.html.

Smith, Craig S. "Ruling Seen as Victory, but not for a Free Press." *International Herald Tribune*, June 28, 2005. p. 7. Accessed September 16, 2013. http://www.nytimes.com/2005/ 06/27/world/europe/27iht-france.html.

Smith, Chris, and Ben Voth. "The Role of Humor in Political Argument: How 'Strategery' and 'Lockboxes' Changed a Political Campaign," *Argumentation & Advocacy* 39 (2) (2002): 110–30.

Solzhenitsyn, Aleksandr I. *The Gulag Archipelago*. New York: Harper Collins, 1978, 174.

Soriano, Cesar G., and Steven Komarow. "Poll: Iraqis Out of Patience." *USA Today*, April 28, 2004. Accessed September 16, 2013. http://usatoday30.usatoday.com/news/world/iraq/ 2004-04-28-poll-cover_x.htm.

Spain, David. "Mississippi Autopsy." *Mississippi Eyewitness. Ramparts Magazine Special Issue*, 1964. Accessed June 1, 2009. http://mdah.state.ms.us/arrec/digital_archives/sovcom/ result.php?image=/data/sov_commission/images/png/cd09/068354.png&otherstuff=10|60|0| 30|49|1|1|67477|.

Spitzer, Kirk. "Japan is Still not Sorry Enough." *Time*, December 12, 2012. Accessed September 15, 2013. http://nation.time.com/2012/12/11/why-japan-is-still-not-sorry-enough/.

Stolberg, Sheryl. "A New US Player, Put on the World Stage by Syria." September 23, 2013. *New York Times*, Accessed September 25, 2013. http://www.nytimes.com/2013/09/23/ world/a-new-us-player-put-on-world-stage-by-syria.html?pagewanted=all&_r=0.

Stoll, Ira. "Iraq's WMD Secreted in Syria, Sada Says." *New York Sun*, January 26, 2006. Accesed December 29, 2013. http://www.nysun.com/foreign/iraqs-wmd-secreted-in-syria -sada-says/26514/.

"Sudan Bombs Darfur Rebels." *Agency France Press*, January 14, 2009. Accessed March 10, 2009.   http://www.google.com/hostednews/afparticleALeqM5jiSwZhWIQAzCfAKG GGi4GK2RUH0g.

"Sudan: Darfur Suffers 'Worst Violence in a Year.'" *AllAfrica*, January 28, 2009. Accessed November 5, 2013. http://allafrica.com/stories/200901290570.html.

The American Presidency Project. "Statement on Signing the Iraq Liberation Act of 1998." 1998.

Thomas, Erika M. "The Rhetoric of the Modern American Menstrual Taboo." Electronic Thesis or Dissertation Miami University. https://etd.ohiolink.edu/. 2008.

Tisdall, Susan. "Sudan Fears US Military Action Over Darfur: Clinton Warns of 'Need to Sound Alarm' Over Crisis: Obama Urged to Keep Pledge to End Genocide." *The Guardian,* January 16, 2009. p. 24.

Totten, Samuel, and William Parsons. *Century of Genocide: Critical Essays and Eyewitness Accounts*, 4th edition. New York & London: Routledge, 2012.

UNFPA. "Reproductive Health: Ensuring Every Pregnancy is Wanted." 2013. Accessed September 23, 2013. http://www.unfpa.org/rh/planning.htm.

Vogel, Lauren. "Sex-selective Abortions: No Simple Solutions." *CMAJ* 184 3 (February 21, 2012): 286–88. Accessed September 23, 2013. http://www.ncbi.nlm.nih.gov/pmc/articles/PMC3281151/.

Voth, Ben. "Making the Best Argument for Unborn Life: Understanding the Racist and Sexist Assumptions of Abortion," *Life and Learning XIII: Proceedings of the Thirteenth University Faculty for Life Conference*, ed. Joseph W. Koterski, S.J. 2004.

Voth, Ben, and Aaron Noland. "Vietnam as Paradigmatic Metaphor," *Controversia: An International Journal of Debate and Democratic Renewal* 5(1). Fall (2006): 57–84.

Voth, Ben, and Aaron Noland. "Argumentation and the International Problem of Genocide." *Contemporary Argumentation and Debate* 28 (2007): 38–46.

Voth, Ben. "Toward a Critical Christian Rhetoric." *Paper presented at the annual meeting of the NCA 93rd Annual Convention*, TBA, Chicago, IL, Nov 15, 2007. Accessed September 12, 2013. http://citation.allacademic.com/meta/p191658_index.html.

Voth, Ben. "Death as a Text: State Killings as Public Argument," in Dennis Gouran, *The Functions of Argument and Social Context*, Washington: 16th Biennial Conference, National Communication Association and the American Forensic Association, (2010): 543–49.

Voth, Ben. "Top Ten Things America has Done for Muslims." *American Thinker*, August 27, 2010. Accessed September 15, 2013. http://www.americanthinker.com/2010/08/top_ten_things_america_has_don.html.

Voth, Ben. "Restoring the Image of George W. Bush." *American Thinker*, April 23, 2013. Accessed September 16, 2013. http://www.americanthinker.com/2013/04/m-restoring_the_image_
of_president_george_w_bush.html.

Wall Street Journal. "Iraq in Retrospect." March 19, 2013. Accessed September 15, 2013. http://online.wsj.com/article/SB10001424127887323393304578358691247678454.html.

Weisman, Steven. "Powell Declares Genocide in Sudan in Bid to Raise Pressure." *New York Times*, September 9, 2004. Accessed September 23, 2013. http://www.nytimes.com/2004/09/09/international/africa/09CND-SUDA.html.

Whillock, Rita Kirk, and David Slayden (eds.) *Hate Speech*. Newbury Park, CA: Sage, 1995.

WHO. "Drinking Water, Sanitation & Hygiene." 2012. Accessed September 16, 2013. http://www.unwater.org/statistics_san.html.

Wiesel, Elie. "Foreword." *The Courage to Care*. Eds. Carol Rittmer, and Sondra Myers. New York: New York University Press, 1986.

Wikipedia. "The New Anti Semitism." Accessed May 15, 2007. http://en.wikipedia.org/wiki/New_antisemitism.

Wilkinson, Ian. "Taliban Militants in Northwest Pakistan Kidnapped about 400 Students from a Military-run College on Monday Along with Their Teachers and Relatives." June 1, 2009. *The Telegraph*, Accessed June 1, 2009. http://www.telegraph.co.uk/news/worldnews/asia/pakistan/5423750/Taliban-kidnap-400-Pakistani-students.html.

Williams, Ian. "Death to America." *NBC News*, March 17, 2007. Accessed September 15, 2013. http://dailynightly.nbcnews.com/_news/2007/03/17/6536180-death-to-america?lite

Wilson, E. O. *The Social Conquest of the Earth*. New York: Liveright, 2013.

Wilson, Ernest J. "Communication Scholars Need to Communicate." *Inside Higher Ed*, July 29, 2013. Accessed August 15. Ernest J. Wilson III, http://www.insidehighered.com/views/2013/07/29/essay-state-communications-scholarship#ixzz2eLqcyeyp.

World Public Opinion. "All Iraqi Ethnic Groups Overwhelmingly Reject al Qaeda." September 27, 2006. Accessed September 16, 2013. http://www.worldpublicopinion.org/pipa/articles/brmiddleeastnafricara/248.php.

Yehoshua, Y. "The Image Of The Jew In The Ramadan TV Show 'Khaybar'–Treacherous, Hateful Of The Other, Scheming, And Corrupt." *MEMRI*, July 10, 2013. Accessed September 24, 2013. http://www.memri.org/report/en/0/0/0/0/0/51/7279.htm.

Zoga, Diana. "Man Says He's the Victim of a Hate Crime." *KMOV*, September 27, 2011. Accessed September 21, 2013. http://www.kmov.com/news/local/St-Louis-man-says-hes-the
-victim-of-a-hate-crime-130680978.html.

Index

About the Author

Ben Voth is an associate professor of communication at Southern Methodist University. His teaching and scholarship are dedicated to a principle of equipping individuals to have their voice. His teaching and scholarship have equipped a diverse range of individuals including dozens of Holocaust survivors at the *United States Holocaust Memorial Museum* in Washington DC, several national collegiate champions of speech, elimination round qualifiers to the prestigious *National Debate Tournament*, major professional business clients, undergraduate and graduate students of Communication Study. He is on the editorial board of *Argumentation and Advocacy* and he has served as editor for the academic journal *Contemporary Argumentation and Debate*. His expertise is published in a variety of major media outlets including *NPR* affiliates in Ohio and Texas, the *Dallas Morning News*, *Fox Business National*, and *USA Today*. He is an advisor for the *Bush Institute* in Dallas. He recently served as the Chair of the Communication Studies division in the Meadows School of the Arts at SMU and presently serves as the Director of Speech and Debate programs. He previously worked as director of forensics for 14 years at Miami University in Ohio.